^{THE}
SUSPECT CULTURE
BOOK

Acknowledgements

A book like this incurs many debts. We are very grateful to Robert Dallas Gray for his design; to Patrick Macklin and Louisa MacIver for contributing images and ideas; to Brian Daly for his generosity in supporting this last phase of the company's life; Joana Craveiro for translation work; to Andrew Walby at Oberon Books for overseeing a complicated process of assembly, design and production; finally, to Creative Scotland, for supporting this publication.

The impossible ambition of this book is to capture twenty years of one company's work and to reflect and recognise the countless contributions that together made up that history. Of course, some of the key players can have their say: the writers, directors and artists who were instrumental in the company's development. We would like to thank everyone who has contributed images, writing, memories and thoughts to this volume.

It would take another book to do justice to the contributions of those maybe not in the spotlight here but who were vital to what Suspect Culture became: the producers and general managers who nurtured the work and brought it to the stage; people like David Smith who was key to the company's formative identity and those who followed him in overseeing the company's development, Julie Ellen, Purni Morell and David Morgan. Pamela Carter developed the company's Strange Behaviour programme and contributed so much creatively and organisationally. The administrative staff who supported us over the years, Colin Morrison, Fran Crumley, Simon Girdler, Devina Kumar and Judith Riddell, as well as the freelance staff, project managers, and finance officers without whom the company would not have been able to function. We were lucky to be steered through all the challenges of running a touring theatre company by a supportive and wise Board of Directors, successively chaired by Brian Gorman, Neil Murray and Hugh Hodgart.

We were particularly fortunate at Suspect Culture to build strong and loyal relationships with several actors. People like Louise Ludgate, Kate Dickie, Paul Thomas Hickey, Callum Cuthbertson, Paul Blair, Selina Boyack and Sergio Romano were decisively involved in the development of many shows, including the three whose texts are reproduced here. The openness of these and all the actors we worked with enabled Suspect Culture to experiment with our theatre-making process in ways that were fundamental to what we were. This creative process made similar demands of stage managers, technicians and design assistants including Shona Rattray, an essential member of the company, William Maxwell, Dave Shea, Claire Halleran and Vicky Wilson, who amongst many others demonstrated the flexibility, determination and skill to help us realise our ambitious staging ideas and tour them to often radically different venues. We owe them all more than we can say.

To everybody who worked with us, supported us, programmed us, came to see us, put up with us and thought about what we made, thank you.

Contents

Preface

GRAHAM EATOUGH & DAN REBELLATO

Suspect Culture always had a complicated relationship with books. We adapted Voltaire's *Candide* and Apuleius's *The Golden Ass*. One show was inspired by the diaries of Giacomo Casanova, another by *The Tempest*, a third by Adam Phillips's *Houdini's Box*. But we were wary of publishing ourselves. British theatre's tendency to see the written text as the central component of the theatrical matrix is so ingrained that we resisted publishing the scripts, in case this normalized a company for whom music, gesture, text, design always mingled and clashed as equals. We relaxed a bit about this in our second decade but we continued to try finding ways of publishing that captured the horizontal creativity of the company.

We find the company regularly talked about as people survey the astonishing vitality of Scotland's theatre in the 1990s and 2000s, and the company has – intermittently and imperfectly – made its way into the emerging cultural archive of British theatre. All archives have their gaps, their secrets, their accidents, and the company is also archived in the minds of those who made the work and those who came to see it. Theatre vanishes and archives degrade, but Suspect Culture wouldn't be Suspect Culture if we didn't want to send a signal out across the spaces, to touch fingers in the darkness, to seize smoke. Anyone exploring the last twenty years of theatre should have a fighting chance to see the particular contribution our company made to it.

So, this book is our latest attempt to square the circle of theatre's liveness and writing's permanence. Everyone who works in theatre has to get used to the cruelty of continual disappearance; the last night, floor painted over, sets broken up, costumes back in the van. But Suspect Culture is currently in a state of suspension and it has felt to all of us that we wanted to find a way to reflect on the last twenty years of work, to mark what we achieved and what we didn't, what happened and what we like to believe happened.

Suspect Culture always wanted the various elements of theatrical production to bleed into one another, for the inside and outside of performance to be hard to separate. It was a company whose shows could be led by the music, or led by the choreography, or led by its performers. The show would be a continuous creative process from the poster to the curtain call. We're not sure if we're exaggerating. What for some people looked like elegantly restrained aesthetic minimalism could feel, from the inside, like wonderful chaos.

But the book you're holding in your hands is also our attempt to find some continuity with our theatre shows. It is, for now anyway, the last Suspect Culture production. This book wants to give you music and graphic design, ground plans and scripts, memory and interpretation. Recollections tumble past photographs and the scripts sit alongside theatre designs and we like it that way.

That Harlequin on the cover is Paul Thomas Hickey and it's from Graham's large-scale visual art installation piece, created with Graham Fagen, *Killing Time*. In the work, it's only on a digital projection that we see Harlequin. We chose the image because it's theatre and it's not theatre. As visitors explored the installation they found a series of apparent stage sets, sometimes inhabited, sometimes abandoned, but through it there were signs that Harlequin had been here. Was it visual art filled with the traces and remnants of theatre? Or theatre framed and intensified by visual art? It's a set of questions we could ask about all Suspect Culture's work.

Suspect Culture was a deeply collaborative company and this book is the result of another collaboration. Graham Eatough has been at the centre of the company from its inception, directing most of the shows, and acting as artistic director for its second decade. Dan Rebellato's journey with the company began as supporter, mutated into academic commentator, and finally artistic associate of the company. We bring complementary insights into the shape of the company's history and this book is both an archive of the company and an embodiment of it: in it we've tried to bring the company alive as we lay it to rest.

The book begins with a collage of memories and testimonials from those involved in the work, both as makers and audiences. Graham Eatough's detailed interview offers his own overview of the work across two decades, reflecting on the ideas at play in the company's foundation, the evolution of its style, the constant battles over working conditions, and the dynamics of each show. This is followed by reflections on the company by administrators and associate artists, critics and academics. Three of the performance texts – *Timeless*, *Mainstream*, and *Lament* – follow, published here for the first time. Finally, Dan Rebellato wraps up the book with a substantial scholarly overview, finding his own paths through the work of the company that sought to take its audience seriously, by pushing ourselves to make the most daring work we could find it in our hearts to make, seeking out new theatrical geometries to give us new shapes for new times.

An Interview with Graham Eatough

Graham Eatough and David Greig co-founded Suspect Culture in the early 1990s, after they met and worked together at the University of Bristol, where they both studied Drama and English. Graham directed almost all of Suspect Culture's shows and acted as Artistic Director for most of its history. In this extended interview with Dan Rebellato, Graham reflects on the key moments, productions and ideas that shaped Suspect Culture.

BRISTOL

It's interesting to think that in the space of only a few years that drama department at Bristol produced Mark Ravenhill, Tim Crouch, Sarah Kane, David Walliams, Simon Pegg, David Young, Myfanwy Moore, Suspect Culture, us... I think it's a strange alchemy that leads to those moments. It was a good department, the teaching was great and so on. But there was something else: it was a very politicised student body on the whole, especially around gender politics. That meant if you were making work you were forced to constantly interrogate it and have it interrogated in a pretty rigorous way – I say rigorous, we were still kids really, but we would ask questions about the politics of the work and take it seriously. And second, the department was good but it was possibly a bit conservative too, traditional. And so there was a reaction against that which meant we were very motivated. What links all of those people you mention is being very driven. An odd mixture of artistic aspiration with a kind of Eighties Thatcherite drive! We all knew what we wanted to do from very early on.

In my first term at Bristol, I acted in a production of Howard Barker's *Victory* alongside Sarah Kane, with David Greig, Simon Pegg and others. It was a very important moment for David and me in different ways. In some of the early Suspect Culture shows I think you could definitely see the influence of Barker, not just on the writing but on what the shows were setting out to achieve, politically and intellectually. What Barker does, whether or not the plays are successful, he scouts out the possibilities for alternative theatres. He neither points towards a mainstream theatre style but nor is he swept up in current avant-garde movements. At that time there was a slightly ludicrous division between the 'text-based theatre' people and the 'physical theatre' people. And for those who didn't want to leave playwriting behind, Barker was a model for something that could still be radical, which I think was important for David. And it was important for me too, because it mapped out a place that a theatre company could potentially exist. We wanted to create a text-rich

Graham Eatough and Sarah Kane in Howard Barker's *Victory* at Bristol University.

theatre which was also aesthetically rich; that was interested in bodies and so on and complex stage imagery but was also about great writing.

A SAVAGE REMINISCENCE

A Savage Reminiscence was the first thing we did together. We did it in the Students' Union and then at the Hen and Chickens pub theatre in a double bill with Sarah Kane's *Comic Monologue*. At that point I don't think we thought we were forming a company, just putting on a show really – and working with a friend. And that was the ambition, 'can we do a show that is physical in interesting ways and at the same time textually rich?' Obviously, they're broad aspirations but even then it was about trying to draw out things from different production elements that we weren't seeing in mainstream or even avant-garde theatre at the time. I guess we were exploring that space between those areas.

Reno Pelakanou and Graham Eatough in *… and the opera house remained unbuilt.*

Nick Powell was studying at Bristol as well and wrote the music for all of our early shows. So he, and music as a production area, became a very important part of what we were doing from the start.

I saw myself as an actor in that show. It was a collaboration but that's really where I saw myself at that point. David was always very open; he was writer/director but the directing was partly shared. Later, when we made *One Way Street* it was a reaction to just having done a big show (*Europe*) and then trying to get back to the working methods we'd used in *A Savage Reminiscence*, but by that stage I had a more developed sense of what I wanted the production to do visually and physically. And I suppose by then I was beginning to be focused on things like gesture and different styles of physicality on stage. With *Airport*, because it was a larger ensemble, even though I was in it, I think I was more conventionally the director. Then with *Timeless*, because of the nature of the ideas we were working with, I wanted to step out completely and concentrate on directing.

That was a pretty quick follow-up to *A Savage Reminiscence*. We'd been at the [Edinburgh] Festival with *A Savage Reminiscence* in 1991 and we took *Opera House* there in 1992, along with a whole bunch of other stuff. I was concentrating on acting but David, in collaboration with Andy Thompson, another Bristol graduate, wanted to run a venue, Theatre Zoo. And in a manic burst of energy that has never stopped *(laughs)*, he managed to put on four shows: *Opera House*, *The Garden*, *Stalinland*, *Life after Life*, Sarah Kane did *Dreams, Screams and Silence* with Vince O'Connell, plus David and his partner Lucie ran the café. Lots of it went really well, *Stalinland* for example, got a Fringe First I think. But I suppose the undertaking of a major enterprise like running a venue sort of prepared us for thinking about running a theatre company.

PHYSICAL LANGUAGE

And the other thing that happened was one of those epiphanies you can only have when you're in your early twenties: at that second Edinburgh Festival, I saw Pina Bausch's *Café Müller* which was there that year. It didn't just blow me away as a piece of theatre, it suddenly opened up different possibilities about what bodies on stage could be and how powerful very simple gestural performance can be. Work of that kind was probably as big an influence for me as Barker was for David at that stage.

And you can definitely see that influence in those early shows; *One Way Street*, *Airport* and *Timeless* all contain gestural motifs of reaching out, longing and so on. But because we were making narrative theatre (albeit experimentally) rather than dance theatre, our gestural work was more associated with character and had more impact on the story-telling. Also there was a theoretical framework to that physical work from people like Benjamin and Adorno (via Brecht) who talked about gesture as a kind of memory of something lost – an interruption to an idea of a continuous, homogenous present. I think that was as important to me as its aesthetic or choreographic qualities.

We were asking, how do you get the most out of each production area and – if you can see the body as a production area – we thought there was so much potential there for communicating with the audience that it seemed almost neglectful not to make full use of it. In the same way that the script wouldn't be naturalistic, we thought the bodies don't have to be either. We started with some fairly obvious things where, say, the speech is saying one thing and the body another, so the gestures become a form of subtext. So in *Timeless*, for example, people are saying things very confidently but there are these interruptions that allow the body to give away a different frame of mind, an anxiety.

We wanted to acknowledge the presence of the performer on stage, not just the character (Brecht was a big influence in this respect). And the body is a really clear means of introducing that complexity through non-naturalistic movement. Because immediately it's about form and representation rather than just playing the game of pretending.

ONE-WAY STREET

After the '92 festival, David moved from Edinburgh to Glasgow and I moved up to Glasgow too. And that's when we started putting together funding applications and a publicity package and that led to *Europe*, the double-bill at The Arches of David's play *Petra's Explanation* and *Stations on the Border* which was a wholly devised show. Two very important shows for us but with quite a difficult rehearsal process.

I tend to romanticise that period but it was pretty fucking miserable at the time. I got lucky with a flat that was one of those beautiful Glasgow bedsits you some-times get, but it was winter and it was fucking cold and I had no money. I know it's a cliché, but I remember not having 50p to put in the meter for heating. But you could just about do it then: you'd do a bar job on the sly, live on the dole, and try to start a theatre company. I'm not sure that's possible now. But that was four years. It was only with *Airport* that we were able to pay ourselves something. So that period was quite a slog and after *Europe* we decided to take a break.

I'd always been interested in woodwork and guitars and I'd had this long-held ambition to learn how to make guitars so I went off and did that. I did a course and worked with some experienced luthiers in Glasgow. It was utterly fantastic. It crops up as one of the fantasy scenes in *Lament* actually. But then *One Way Street* was the end of that break and that was a really wonderful process. Natural, rich, all the Benjamin ideas about psycho-geography, it was just so creative. We were con-sciously going back to basics by creating a one-man show as we'd done with our first, *A Savage Reminiscence*.

One Way Street got us some recognition from the funding bodies so we were now on the ladder, but it's the international side of that show that was so important. Set in Berlin, it was very inspired by Walter Benjamin's writings *One Way Street* and *A Berlin Chronicle*. It was a time when the British Council were active in promot-ing young companies abroad, and they helped get us out to Germany. We did this tour of the former East – places like Magdeburg, Chemnitz and Dresden – not that long after the reunification which was a central theme of the show. So it was kind of perfect really. And that really established the internationalist agenda of the company, because it gave us the ambition to have some kind of international dimension for much of the work; co-producers, international casts, and so on. We'd always felt more in common with work coming out of mainland Europe, and North America to a certain extent, than with British theatre so it felt like a very natural progression.

AIRPORT

When Ian Scott got involved with the company for *Airport*, this became the core creative team along with David, Nick and me. Ian really helped to establish the visual look of the work, and those non-naturalistic, saturated colours that we had in pretty much every show as well as the music became central to what the company was about. The physicality too was very important in *Airport* which came from me trying to apply what I'd discovered doing the solo work in *One Way Street* to an ensemble.

We managed to persuade the British Council to let us go to Madrid and this incredible guy, David Codling, who ran the arts section of the British Council in Spain, arranged for us to do a workshop in this wonderful arts foundation in an olive grove in Madrid where Lorca used to live. We stayed there, worked there, met lots of Spanish actors, three of whom ended up being in the show. Nick still works with one of them, Andrés Lima who, apart from being a great actor, is now one of the most important directors in Spain. It was a very exciting time, meeting artists from different cultural backgrounds and working out what we had in common.

NON-PLACES

The previous show [*Europe*] was set around train stations and even then we thought maybe this is a bit old-fashioned. We started working on *Airport* around the time air travel was becoming much cheaper, Easyjet and so on, so it caught a bit of a moment. It was also about where we were in our career; we'd started to get some recognition, working in different places, having different travel experiences, and so on.

We were very drawn to these kinds of location – styled wine bars, airports, boutique hotels, shopping malls. In some ways they'd become emblematic of what has happened to public space, the ways in which it's been privatised. They're homogenous spaces that you're supposed to feel comfortable in no matter who you are or what culture you're from. Places that want you to feel at home but in which you rarely do.

I don't know if people talked about globalisation at that point so much but we were drawn to the spaces that you'd associate with global economics: retail spaces, entertainment spaces, travel spaces. These spaces are built for particular economic, political reasons and what the theatre does well is to explore what happens to people when they're placed in situations they're not sure how to negotiate. We were very interested in the juxtaposition of the surface of modern life and modern environments with the humanity inside them: what people want to achieve, what they are able to achieve, what isn't permitted in these environments. Whether it's the kids hanging around the shopping mall in *Candide 2000* or the euro-travellers in *Airport*, we were asking what happens to people, how they're affected by these processes and pressures, what gets edited out, the lack felt as a result.

These shows are filled with very sincere, earnest, but ultimately failed attempts at communication and human contact – '*contacto personal*' as Andrés says more than once in *Airport*. So what these environments give you dramatically is the antagonist, in a sense; they're environments in which it's very difficult to achieve a meaningful human exchange, or maybe you do but in unexpected, slightly perverse (as in *Mainstream*) or comic ways (as in *Airport*). So it was our encounter with those spaces at a particular point in our development and at a particular point in their development that produced the feel of a lot of those shows.

GEOGRAPHY

There's been an ongoing concern with geography in our work – from the Berlin Wall coming down when we were starting out and fed directly into the work, through Benjamin's version of psycho-geography, ideas of the city as an imaginative space, to these globalized spaces. They're all ideas of geography which are inherently theatrical. So spaces like homogenised shopping malls are ready-made sets, already often representations of other places they are not – city squares, parks, high streets. Like theatre. And the restricted methods of presentation they employ become theatrically interesting to explore. An airport similarly has its own rather extraordinary kind of constructed geography and for us the theatre was a way of exploring that.

THEATRE FOR WEST END YUPPIES

That was a quote about us in the press around the time we received our first revenue funding. In an unfortunate bit of timing we gained our funding at the same time as Wildcat (which was a kind of successor to 7:84) lost theirs. And ironically I work a lot now with David McLennan who ran Wildcat, in a theatre he now runs in

Glasgow's West End. That was about a change-over in politics really. It was about trying to establish a different kind of politics in the theatre, doing something other than agitprop which was amazing in the 1970s but didn't feel particularly relevant in the 1990s. We felt a lack of confidence about making seemingly straightforward political statements in theatre and simple political statements in general at that time. They didn't seem to ring true anymore. It wasn't something we were particularly happy about. In fact much of our work was about the anxieties caused by this lack of confidence. It felt more appropriate to us to use theatre to explore political issues in a different way and I think what is frustrating to the agitproppers is that it is a bit ambivalent. It's about complexity rather than certainty and I can see why that would annoy people but at that time it seemed harder to rely on those political certainties that had been around in the Seventies.

TIMELESS

That was about form for me. I'd wanted to work with a string quartet on stage for a while and the basic idea was to structure three acts around three movements in a piece of music and to integrate the action with the music rather than just have it as a kind of accompaniment. And that relationship with music has remained really central for me. I'd had the idea that the three acts might represent past, present and future and David very cleverly ordered them as present, past and future, which worked so well dramatically in terms of story. And we had the idea of four characters that mirrored the four musicians in the quartet.

We worked on that for quite a while; I worked on some physical ideas for the show with a Canadian choreographer and dancer called Nisha Kumar working on different physical motifs. David and I threw around story ideas. Nick had a very good relationship with some strings players and worked on ideas for the quartet so it all felt very doable. And Nick got to push himself and move his work to the centre of the piece. Brian McMaster who was running the Edinburgh International Festival at the time had seen or heard about *Airport* I think and he decided to commission us. They wanted to showcase some emerging theatre companies and there was a season in this smaller venue, the Gateway Theatre on the Leith Walk, alongside work by Tamasha and Zhang Yuan.

Then we re-staged it at the Tramway, which for me was the best version. It was my first time working in Tramway 1, which is where I'd first seen shows by The Wooster Group and Robert Lepage. Physically, it's a great space, but for me it was also one of the most important spaces in Britain in terms of the work it was

Top: Kate Dickie, Molly Innes, Paul Thomas Hickey and Keith Macpherson in *Timeless*; **right:** Callum Cuthbertson, Louise Ludgate and Pamela Carter; seated, Phil Collins and Kate Dickie, in Tobermory during workshops for *Mainstream*; **below:** participants in the *Strange Behaviour* event 'Theatre and the World of Money'.

programming so having the opportunity to direct there with *Timeless* was very exciting and the start of an important relationship with that space.

We did some fairly involved reworking of *Timeless*, particularly of the third act. That act was always a struggle. How do you stage the future? If you stage it, it becomes present. The way we addressed that was through abstraction and focusing on the characters' aspirations, so it's about their imagined futures. The first two acts are more story-driven but involved a lot of work with mirrors and gesture – characters checking themselves and so on.

People talk very kindly about *Timeless* at the Festival now and in hindsight people remember it being a very successful show. Some critics got it; but some really didn't. We were quite uncertain about it whilst we were making it. But by the time we got to Tramway we were more confident and knew it was an important work for the company.

And it went down to the Donmar Warehouse in a season with the unfortunate title 'Four Corners: Work from the Celtic Fringe'. Lucy Davies, who was at the Donmar then, came up to see it and liked it and seemed to champion it. It was quite a difficult space for the show and it really made us aware of what it means to present work in London, how difficult that is. There was a mood in Scottish theatre of looking beyond London at that time. Scottish visual artists, for example, were beginning to dominate the British art scene by establishing themselves internationally and people were making creative connections with Europe and North America and there was money for that and so on. There was a sense of nationhood that was moving towards devolution, and people were thinking about how the arts might be in the vanguard of that: there was a Quebecois season at the Traverse and 7:84 were collaborating in Catalonia. And we kind of ignored London to a certain extent, which was more appropriate than we realised. We found when we eventually went there that there weren't the kinds of spaces in London that we were used to working in; there wasn't a Tramway in London for example. So we went to the Donmar with *Timeless* and The Bush with *Mainstream* and they're obviously both fantastic theatres but maybe not quite the right fit for us.

STRANGE BEHAVIOUR

We had this idea that we wanted to look outside theatre and at other disciplines, other spheres of knowledge, which was already there in our creative process but we wanted to formalise it. So David Greig and Pamela Carter began to curate a series of symposia we called Strange Behaviour. We did quite a few of those: Theatre and ... Sciences of the Mind, The World of Money, Mathematics, Divinity, Geography, Italy, and Futurology. The format was always the same, a symposium day which would bring together theatre practitioners and 'experts' from another field for lectures, discussions and workshops. As well as being fascinating days in and of themselves they also provided a lot of inspiration for the creation of new shows. Two shows came directly out of the first one: Theatre and Sciences of the Mind. There was a workshop with a psychologist who we paired up with Katie Mitchell. He had this theory about the different parts of the brain and how they function in communication, and in a fairly literal way we kind of dramatised that in the workshop through two characters played by four actors. And the form of *Mainstream* pretty directly came out of that. And another speaker was talking about the psychology of *Casanova* as part of the same day which sowed the seed for our contemporary version.

MAINSTREAM

Timeless didn't really take off in London and didn't get any international touring because it was too big, really. Even though the British Council were actively promoting our work, they wanted two- or three-handers not a show with eight people on stage, which that was. But then came *Mainstream*, which probably toured more than anything else we did internationally, which was very satisfying because it went to some really interesting places and was a very good fit in those places. We toured to Croatia, Bulgaria, Greece and the Czech Republic and we made some very strong connections there.

We'd settled into a process for making work which involved a development workshop of a week or two weeks when we'd take a group of actors and the core creative team and work fairly loosely around a set of ideas. Sometimes that would be quite unrepresentative of the final show because it would be about providing lots of ideas so that we could then go away and produce something more considered. So the first workshop for *Mainstream* was much more consciously experimental: much more like the Wooster Group or Forced Entertainment than the final show. And then there would be a second workshop and finally as long a rehearsal period as we could get. But that would be a year-long process in total and by the time we got to rehearsal we already had clear first drafts in each area, of the text, the music, the physical work. And rehearsal would be about putting those drafts together and integrating and reworking them.

Mainstream was interesting because the script that David produced was a very open text that had no specific settings for the scenes and no characters either. One of the enjoyable devising jobs was playing around with which performers would play the two characters in each scene, what location they'd be set in, and how to

Top: Kate Dickie, Callum Cuthbertson and Louise Ludgate, *Mainstream* workshop; **right:** young cast members of *Candide 2000*; below: cast of *Local*.

represent these locations. These questions led to the physical language of the show: how do you show through someone's physicality that they're in a bar, say, and at a certain point in their relationship?

We got very interested in repetition – of which there's quite a lot in *Mainstream*! – and how you can fundamentally shift the meaning of things within repetition, so we have the same scenes played by different genders, or the same scene is played out with different outcomes, or scenes that seem to be the same but are part of a different story.

It was a very developed design. Because we had four actors playing two characters, we needed an onstage offstage space; the conceit was that the actors would seem to be negotiating who would go on to play the next scenario. And we thought we wanted the offstage space to visibly mirror the onstage space with variations, which is again about the play of repetition and difference in the show.

By this stage we'd started to identify a core group of actors who we would work with again and again on shows. People like Louise Ludgate, Callum Cuthbertson, Kate Dickie, Paul Thomas Hickey (who were all in *Mainstream*) and later Paul Blair. These actors were really instrumental in the devising of shows like *Mainstream* and became an essential part of the company. Their knowledge and understanding of what we were trying to do allowed us to really push things technically and emotionally in ways you maybe couldn't with other actors.

LOCAL

Local was our first attempt to work with non-professional performers, mainly young people. It was devised – we used the techniques we'd normally use – but with a group identified through the Tramway and some sixth-form colleges. It was about them and the city of Glasgow and their experiences of the city told through fragments of stories. We used a lot of their writing and it was very gestural. We also used the long depth of Tramway 4 to play with projection and images moving in and out of focus. We were influenced working on that show by les ballets C de la B, and in particular a show called *La Tristeza Complice*, which we saw when we were making *Airport*. Alain Platel who directed and choreographed that show (and worked with Ghent company Victoria), worked with non-professional performers, and made this remarkable choreography, danced to Purcell played by a live accordion orchestra. And that way of creating a distinctive performance style with non-professionals that made a virtue of their different experience was in my mind when we were making it. And these ideas then developed on a larger scale with *Candide 2000*.

This was our attempt at developing a new and artistically exciting approach to doing what was then called outreach work. There was often a requirement, tied up with your funding, that you'd do work with young people, maybe in schools or with communities, and there was a set of expectations and conventions associated with that. Groups like Victoria and Alain Platel just blew all that out of the water: these shows weren't apologetic or second best ('this isn't quite as polished as we would normally do, but…') – no, it was some of the best theatre you'd ever seen. So it challenged you to do work that was *better* because it had involvement of these young, non-professional actors. That was the aspiration with *Candide 2000* which integrated different casts of young people from the towns the show played with a touring cast of professional actors.

So there was that inspiration from Platel; then there was the Voltaire novel, which I'd always been interested in as a theatrical challenge: how might you stage that kind of picaresque journey around the world? That connected with these ideas about geography and globalisation we'd been playing around with in previous shows. And then how might you bring all that together in some kind of relevant context? And the setting – a shopping mall – was a natural follow-on from the hotel of *Mainstream* and *Airport*, a really interesting place to explore. The mall, as a kind of homogenised, commercialised representation of the whole world seemed perfect for *Candide*, which also connected with the central character's naivety. Just as Candide buys into Pangloss's philosophy, our Candide (Colin) buys into the philosophy and exciting possibilities represented in the sheen of the shopping mall, both for worker and consumer – 'the best of all possible worlds'.

Graham Eatough, Louise Ludgate, Callum Cuthbertson and Kate Dickie in *Lament*.

And then the idea that this place might be populated by youth was kind of obvious. When I was growing up in Blackburn, we would sometimes get the train into Manchester and hang out in the Arndale Centre. And those kids, spitting down on the passers-by from these Eighties glass balconies comes directly from that kind of experience. That combination of sanctioned space – in which, like an airport, everyone is processed and everything points towards defined economic procedures – and youthful activity which is, by its nature, transgressive and illicit, created a really interesting set of tensions to explore.

It was also another show with onstage musicians. We were keen to extend the collaboration with Nick and the musicians. *Mainstream* had a really interesting soundscape – it had musical motifs but also these other sounds, buzzing, static, and so on – but with this we wanted to bring the use of music more to the fore as it had been in *Timeless*. We wanted this environment to be larger than life in a slightly cartoonish way and the music really helped with that.

The cartoonish aspect was about trying to reflect the relationship between the reality of the shopping mall and what it was trying to represent – so for example between the shopping mall's food court and the actual food cultures it was representing. A Mexican restaurant in a shopping mall is only going to bear a cartoonish resemblance to a restaurant in Mexico. And we followed that through the whole show, so the violence, for example, was very cartoon-like; we had these time jumps where we skip forward a few hours or days, which the music helped with. They were very satisfying techniques to develop. I think it was one of the more artistically successful things we made.

Suspect Culture artistic associates, 2000: Pamela Carter, David Greig, Patrick Macklin, Andrés Lima, Lucy Wilkins, Nick Powell, David Smith, Mauricio Paroni de Castro, Ian Scott and Graham Eatough.

And it was done at the Lyceum Theatre in Edinburgh, which is part of an ongoing story for the company of trying to find the right spaces for our work. It was a co-production with the Tramway though I think the Tramway was being rebuilt then so we actually performed in the Old Fruitmarket in Glasgow. The Lyceum is this gilded Italianate theatre which felt like an interesting fit for the scale and aesthetic of this show as it was later for *Casanova*.

It was very ambitious; we worked with different groups of young people across the country, Glasgow, Edinburgh, Aberdeen, Dundee, Inverness and Newcastle. All these groups would be learning the material as it was generated and when we got to each city, we spent the first half of the week working with the new young actors integrating them into the show and the second half of the week performing. So it was pretty tough on the professional actors as well.

THE GOLDEN ASS

We first started talking about that in Prague when we were touring *Mainstream*. We did a workshop about *Casanova* with Mauricio [Paroni de Castro], who is a director that I'd met in Milan through *Airport*. The British Council had sent him the script of *Airport* and he wanted to do a version of it there with an international cast; we met, worked on it together and started collaborating and talking about various projects. He was about to do an adaptation of Apuleius's *The Golden Ass* at CRT in Milan and we came up with the idea of doing a version of it, again with a mixture of professional and non-professional performers, in Glasgow. We worked with a group of young people most of whom were in transitional housing from the Gorbals in Glasgow, and a lot of the show was devised with them. That went on at the Tron at the end of 2000.

Of the core creative team, only Nick and I worked on that. David and Ian weren't involved, which was part of the evolution of how the company was working. I'd been Artistic Director from the beginnings of Suspect Culture as a formal company. We'd played around with that – David and I were co-Artistic Directors at one point, then he was Company Dramaturg. David was pursuing his independent playwriting career, so it made sense to develop separate projects where not all of the core creative team had to be involved. By 2000 we were looking to work in different ways, particularly with the international artistic associates. Mauricio wrote the script and co-directed and a collaborator of his from Italy, Sergio Romano, was the main actor. The design was by Italian artists Laura Trevisan and Giampaolo Kohler.

CASANOVA

This felt more like putting on a play than anything we'd done up to that point. I guess I felt more involved in the story of *Casanova* than I did with a lot of the others, but that's also testament to the fact that it wasn't really devised. We did a development workshop in Prague and maybe another one in Glasgow and then I think David and I started to talk about story ideas. What if he's an art collector? What if he travels the world looking for exhibits? So it was a different process. More like a conventional New Writing process I guess after those initial discussions. With all of the shows he worked on, David went away and took ownership of the text but what was important to us was that the process started with input from all our collaborators: Nick, Ian, the actors through the workshops.

LAMENT

The idea was to devise a show in a self-contained process: not to come to the first day of rehearsal with anything. There were lots of reasons for that: partly it was a reaction to *Casanova* having been more 'play-like', and artistically we had this idea of trying to represent a thought process. I remember doing a workshop at the RSAMD with students trying to dramatise people's thought processes, getting people lying on the floor and letting their minds wander, and then trying to stage what they'd just been thinking. Of course, it's impossible, but we were interested in exploring that; the attempt, seeing how it might affect staging, design, imagery, language. We wanted somehow to embody that in the show – not that *Lament* is one person's thought process, but that early section, which we rather clumsily called the 'maelstrom', was about that: the seemingly random, media-determined, connections between different things happening in your head and the different things happening in the world. It's not that long a section but it was quite manic, with lots of flashing lights and music and tiny scenes that range from buying a house to some crass representation of the intifada through to someone having a nervous breakdown. And that was trying to capture a thought process: a feeling of being overwhelmed by a certain kind of knowledge of the world and the anxiety of not knowing your place within it. Yeah, that's all! *(laughs)* But that's what that show is; it's all that show is.

It was a very personal show. For everyone involved, it was a much more personal show than anything else we'd done I think. The video bit at the beginning was about trying to create characters out of ourselves, to create emblems, types of ourselves. We were thinking, what sort of character would we be on stage? This connects to *Mainstream*: the idea that the performers who stepped onto the stage would be in themselves characters. In *Lament* we used our own names, but we were versions of ourselves, necessarily because we were performing.

The other thing about *Lament* was a desire to do a political show. We wanted to try and create a show that was in a certain sense unironic, irony being the prevalent tone of the day. Something that addressed serious, difficult issues with honesty and integrity. And of course there's inevitably lots of irony in it, but also, and what connects it with all the other Suspect Culture shows, there's a longing in it. It may sound rather romantic but there's a yearning in it, which is political: it's about wanting to be sincere, wanting to communicate, wanting to have meaningful interactions with others, but also wanting to connect with important world events – and the feeling that that's not possible. The show is riddled with holes and gaps and absences. You might have that desire but it's inarticulate and failed. These gaps and breakdowns are actually in the fabric of David's writing for this show and the ways in which it was staged.

For a lot of people on that show it was a very difficult time personally, and on a broader political level it was very difficult too, post 9/11, the 'War on Terror' and so on. So the inarticulacy and sense of loss in the show came from a personal as well as political perspective and how those two interact. Along with some of David's funniest writing I think, it has a deep level of melancholy. It's called *Lament* and the main set piece is a big chain-link fence where people hang up mementos of loss. And the choreography of the show is about physical rituals of loss.

ONE TWO

Lament was a pretty draining experience for everybody. We took a year break after that. We'd had the idea for *8000m* which was going to be an ambitious show, and we didn't feel that it was achievable in the rhythm we'd established of a show every year. David, in particular, felt he needed longer to write that, so we decided to make a show centred on Nick's music. It was an attempt to play with form. We wanted to put a band on stage and rather than have them accompanying a performance, we'd weave a performance in and around them.

For me it was a chance to continue the interest in choreographing to live music and a chance to work with different kinds of performers – Nick and the musicians and also the performer Sharon Smith who'd been involved with groups like Gob Squad and her group Max Factory. I wrote some text for the show inspired by the music but it was pretty non-narrative and more about the atmospheres and pictures that sprang from the music than anything resembling a play. I think there was an issue with where we put the show on that clashed with this a bit. We did a run at the Traverse during the festival which I think possibly set up expectations about the show that it wasn't ever going to meet. But that's always an issue with devising work that needs to be sold to venues and marketed before you even know what it is and one that never really went away for us.

8000M

Quite a lot of people think of this as being a rather anomalous show, the least 'Suspect Culture' show that we've done. It's also probably our most successful! *(laughs)* That may be significant. I agree in lots of ways; I was very proud of it and it was a lovely process developing that show, but it does feel very different from most Suspect Culture shows. There are thematic links with other shows and some visual similarities but I think the nature of the narrative marks it out as different. That was built into the show from the beginning of course; David had a longstanding interest in mountaineering and the idea of a kind of linear narrative – quite literally, rising to a peak – was maybe a response to the complexity of *Lament* and other shows.

But for me it was also about Tramway 1 and the 'Peter Brook Wall' as it's called and how brilliant it would be to see people climbing up and down that. And that that would be a really interesting way of building up a physical language to represent the world of the play. And in a way it's another show that starts with obvious questions about representation: how do you represent something as huge as climbing a mountain on stage? Like, how do you represent the whole world on stage (in *Candide 2000*) or how do you represent a thought process on stage (in *Lament*)?

It was quite site-specific in the end; we couldn't tour it. But at the Tramway it did very well. Critics who'd struggled with other shows really liked it. I was attracted to the subject matter because it implied a ready-made choreography and it was another chance to work in my favourite theatre space. And to use that theatre in a way that really did it justice, because it's quite a difficult theatre to put work into, to fill, and that show really did I think.

THE ESCAPOLOGIST

The idea for this show came from a book. David Harrower had recommended *Houdini's Box* by Adam Phillips and I loved it and thought it was very dramatic, very theatrical – not just Houdini's story but the way Phillips connects it to a psycho-analytic process. That felt like very appropriate subject matter for Suspect Culture because it had the combination of spectacle and physicality with an intellectually

Top: cast and band, *One Two…* rehearsals; **right:** Paul Blair, *8000m* workshop; **below:** Mary Anne Lynch Small and Kevin McMonagle in *The Escapologist*.

complex world. And Jack Bradley at the National Theatre hooked us up with writer Simon Bent and we found he had a really interesting relationship to the material.

It felt like a departure, working with a writer who wasn't David Greig. No two writers are the same, obviously, though in fact the process was very similar to working with David – we did workshops, we talked about it in the same way; it was scripted in the same way. That was part of the investigation, seeing how far new people could slot into that development process.

A DIFFERENT LANGUAGE

This was a very deliberate decision to make use of our international associates and to pursue the internationalism of the company. The idea that it would be a bilingual show was in there from the start, that it would have one Italian and one British actor in it as well. That all felt natural – perhaps more than *The Escapologist* actually – it felt very familiar to the experiences we'd had doing things like that in *Airport* and *The Golden Ass*. And Renato Gabrielli, who wrote it, was already associated with the company, liked the company, had things in common with us.

We met Renato also through working on *Airport* in Milan and through Mauricio. And we already knew Sergio from working on *The Golden Ass*. We developed the show with them and the British actress Selina Boyack, doing a workshop at the co-producing theatre in Trieste and then a workshop over here.

A Different Language definitely touches on themes common to much of Suspect Culture's work. The story is about a man and a woman from different countries who meet over the internet through a personality matching site and how they try and start a relationship. It's about alienation in the face of modern communications technologies – what happens to individuals emotionally when they try to represent themselves by those means. So in many ways it picks up on concerns raised in *Airport* and *Mainstream*. This show toured extensively in Italy and continued a very important relationship for me with that country and its theatre culture.

FUTUROLOGY

This was a very big project – not so much because it was a National Theatre of Scotland co-production – but because there was an ambition, probably driven by me, that we would involve all of the company's many artistic associates in it and we'd find a form that could involve them all. We were interested in globalisation and we thought this might be a set of ideas that could logically involve a global artistic team.

Left: Sergio Romano and Selina Boyack, publicity still for *A Different Language*; **right:** Victoria di Pace in *Futurology*.

More than most projects, that show went through some pretty radical changes of form during its development. There was an idea at one stage of it being a sort of cabaret environment, that there might be different rooms you go into, that it might be site-specific. And David had a very interesting idea of trying to make the show a closed economic system in itself, that the audience would be entering into payments and exchanges within the show. And finally it morphed into a show based around a climate change conference but still with some reference to all of those other ideas.

It being co-produced by the National Theatre of Scotland raised the stakes a bit in terms of production values and scale. I think there's a temptation for companies who get a National stage to perform on for the first time to drift away from the techniques and ideas that have served them well at a smaller scale. One of the main challenges for us was that as the form of the show changed the venues we thought. we might be working in changed, from some kind of warehouse where we'd put in a type of installation, to thinking maybe we should perform it in a theatre, and finally deciding to pick up on the conference theme and perform it in conference centres.

Scene from *Killing Time* video installation.

I think whatever the strengths and weaknesses of the show, venue was one of the main difficulties in the end.

The things that really succeeded for me were the tone of it, which I think was quintessentially Suspect Culture; Nick's music for it, which was great; and the way we incorporated physicality with the cabaret performance style, all of that was a really mature realisation of what Suspect Culture does well. Also, that overwhelming sense of political frustration that we'd looked at in other shows was maybe never better expressed. There's a song in the show which has lyrics listing a litany of global problems and then says 'When we think about the future / We haven't got a clue / So we pull ourselves together / And this is what we do' leading into a ridiculous music-hall-style nonsense chorus 'Whistle Bang Slap' in which the performers hit themselves and make silly noises. It's classic Suspect Culture but in a kind of Pythonesque cabaret mode.

There were some confusions in that show though. There was a confusion around the role of the audience, how involved they were going to be. And maybe we weren't fully clear about how far the central character's story would integrate with the cabaret style. But it was an extraordinary juxtaposition of form and subject matter, climate change and cabaret, those ideas colliding; and maybe that was bound to create some confusions, but I thought it was a really worthwhile experiment. And very funny, which is quite an achievement with climate change. It made me laugh anyway.

One of the things that I guess always happens when you do an interview like this is that you see threads through the work that maybe you hadn't seen at the time. And one of the things that has really been important for us – or any theatre company that wants to experiment with form – is the issue of finding the right venue to perform the work. How do we make the existing theatre spaces work for the kinds of things we want to do? Sometimes, as in *8ooom*, that really comes off and you get a real marriage of the show and the venue – and sometimes it doesn't, and in *Futurology* it didn't fully.

Theatre and climate change was a fascinating connection. There was a debate running through the project about our own environmental impact and you don't have to get very far into this debate to realise just how brilliant theatre is as the appropriate artform for the end of the world. Compared to film and television or almost any other art form, it's really resource-efficient and very cheap.

KILLING TIME

One of the things Suspect Culture did in the latter part of its life was to expand in two ways; one was to expand the artistic associates it worked with and the other was to expand into new art forms. We'd always had an outward-looking agenda – we worked with film and dance within the shows and through the *Strange Behaviour* events we drew on other, non-theatre disciplines – and eventually we started looking to other art forms as areas we actually wanted to work in.

I collaborated with the visual artist Graham Fagen on an installation at Dundee Contemporary Arts called *Killing Time*. There was a direct link between that and *Lament* in that the curator of *Killing Time*, Katrina Brown, came to see *Lament* in St Andrews and recognised a lot of similarities with visual artwork that she was presenting at that time, like video installations that were rather like the video work in the show, and the use of space, the look of the show. And that was the beginning of a conversation that led through residencies and workshops to *Killing Time*.

There was always a grand ambition in Suspect Culture that we might be creating a body of work that might have more affinities with the way a visual artist might think, that you don't start again with each show, that there's a story to be told across all Suspect Culture's work.

Barbara Rafferty in *Missing*.

MISSING

During *The Escapologist* the filmshoots and the editing were a major part of the creation of the show and around this time I became interested in working more with film. I was part of a scheme called Digicult, that commissioned short film in Scotland, and I wrote a screenplay for them. I was inspired by a book by Andrew O'Hagan, *The Missing*, and a particular chapter about people who'd lost loved ones without explanation: literally, they were there one day and gone the next and they didn't know where they were or why they'd left. What fascinated me is what people do with that absence, how you fill that gap, imagining, creating stories for those people. And that felt very resonant with work like *Lament*. And *Missing* was the result.

STATIC

Jenny Sealey, Artistic Director of Graeae Theatre Company, had liked *One Two* and Ian Scott had lit a lot of Graeae's work which we'd seen. Jenny had just done *Blasted*, which I really liked. I'd been interested in sign language for a while; we'd tried to get it into *Lament*, where it had morphed into a ritualistic gestural sequence. We

The Moment When by David Greig and *Automated Scene-changer* by Nick Powell and Jonny Dawe in *Stage Fright*, CCA, Glasgow.

had done workshops on signing prayers as well. I wasn't so interested theatrically in its real function, and its real importance, as a means of communication; I was fascinated by the aesthetics of it and the other things it communicates beyond its literal meanings. So I'd been keen to work with them for a while and whenever we met up we always talked about it.

Of course it is a real functioning language and I think there was a tension between how Jenny saw its use on stage and my way into it which I can completely understand. For a BSL user it must be a bit like an Italian being told that their language sounds so romantic. But I think the heed we paid to both these things, its communicative use and its choreographic presence on stage, hopefully stopped it being too superficial.

And there was real common ground between the two companies. Graeae are obviously interested in different forms of communication and the body's role in that and that's what I'm interested in. I think, in all the best ways, it's a very typical Suspect Culture show. It's tonally a bit different because of your writing and because of working with Graeae. Thematically, though, all those ideas of reaching out, things you've lost, that attempt to communicate in a pure way, it feels to me very connected to the work we'd done for over a decade.

STAGE FRIGHT

This was a very conscious attempt to examine Suspect Culture methods and concerns in a new presentational context, i.e. in an art gallery. And it was part of a much broader debate about theatre and theatricality in the visual arts, which goes back to Michael Fried in the late Sixties and is very live today. We wanted to bring together theatre-makers and visual artists to work at the interface between theatre and visual art in a way that wasn't live art, which has often been driven by a rejection of aspects of theatricality – pretending and artifice etc. I thought it was a successful show but, if anything, I would have liked to see more 'performance' in it – your own piece was really the only bit of real performance in there. But perhaps we were all a bit too keen to be visual artists, me included. It was a very important show for me though; it pushed me a lot towards some of the work I've been doing since, the research and other work in visual arts contexts.

Of course, like all the other shows, it's about asking questions about what theatre might be – what forms might it usefully take to communicate its ideas today. So the same old questions again about form. And also some of the same philosophical questions. What are we actually able to articulate to each other anyway about anything important, complicated? How do we fulfill that need? How do we deal with those frustrations? There's a quote from Wittgenstein that we used at the very start of *A Savage Reminiscence* all those years ago that goes 'in the end, when one is doing philosophy, one gets to the point when one would just like to emit an inarticulate sound'. I've only just thought of that actually: those are the very first words in the very first Suspect Culture show and they probably remained the defining idea throughout the work, across all those years.

That Moment

DAVID SMITH

There is a moment when working on something where the hairs stand up on the back of your arm. When you are almost giddy and dizzy with the excitement and something rises from inside you to form tears of happiness and a rush of emotion. It is the culmination of what you have accomplished with a creative group. You usually have it quietly sitting with the audience who are unaware of the van driving, the arguments, the logistical challenges, the bruised egos, the immature outbursts, the artistic decisions that have got you to that moment. It is when it all becomes worthwhile and you realise why you make art with other people. I had a number of those moments in my years with Suspect Culture. I have not had so many since.

- Our first performance of *Airport* in Tramway 4.
- A shady hot afternoon under the olive tree during a workshop at the Fundación Olivar de Castillejo in Madrid.
- The first performance of *Timeless* at the Edinburgh International Festival.
- *Airport* in the Basque Country.
- *Mainstream* in the Divadlo Archa in Prague.

David Smith was the Administrative Producer of Suspect Culture from 1996 to 2000.

Haunted By You

DAVID GREIG

Thinking about it now, Suspect Culture shows were always somehow ghostly – never quite there. Even now they only seem present to me by the sheer force of their absence – hovering in the background of everything thing I do. I sometimes catch glimpses of them just outside my eyeline: a thought, a line, or a feeling in something I'm doing which somehow conjures a Suspect Culture play flickering briefly back into existence. The moment I try to put any more solidity to the memory it slips away.

It isn't always this way for me with my previous work – most shows are born, they have their lives and ultimately they're laid to rest. Published perhaps? There always comes a point when a work seems finished and I can move on to other things. But the Suspect Culture shows linger, ungraspable, unsettled, never quite resolved.

It's possibly a factor of youth. Nick, Ian, Graham and I were in our twenties when we made these shows. We had not yet made for ourselves any kind of place in the world. So to make our work we had to set about making the space for our work as well. We formed a company. We developed a touring circuit that would take our work. We developed a process to make the work. We found a group of actors and musicians who were collaborators in creating it. By building our own workspace it's inevitable that we also formed ourselves as artists at the same time. No matter what work we do now it has the ghost of Suspect Culture in its bones.

The shows we made were created collaboratively, intensely, and in a spirit of exploration. We never knew where the work would end up when we set out. And we approached the work with a spirit of total and utter commitment to emotional honesty. All the self-consciousness, awkwardness, arrogance, self-hatred, sadness and silliness of us went into the process making each show a snapshot of a particular moment in our lives. Perhaps it would have been better if we had been more self-protected. As it was, we imprint ourselves in the shows with the result that now they have become a cast, a mask of our 'us-ness' at the time, captured in the transience of script, or video.

One Way Street, Airport, Timeless, Mainstream, Casanova, Candide, 8000m, Lament and *Futurology*: each show was built around a question, a nugget of emotional grit that all four of us shared. 'Are we all the same?' 'What will become of us?' 'What would happen if we let go?' These questions would hover until we found a formal question with which they could marry up – 'are characters and actors the same?' 'Is

Top: Paul Blair in *Lament*; **right:** Louise Ludgate in *Mainstream*; **below:** rehearsals for *Timeless*.

gesture possible within a text?' With a question and a form we would set off into the dark.

It was a corollary of youth that we were not concerned with pleasing the audience. We wanted to disrupt their ease, to shake them up and to communicate to them our disquiet in the hope that some would share it and find in that sharing some comfort. We didn't want the audience to 'like' us but we wanted them to find themselves in ourselves. I think we wanted connection. That's all – only to connect.

Our twenties are lived intensely and the colours of that intensity haunt us. So it could be that the presence of the Suspect Culture shows is simply a product of the natural process of artistic ageing. Maybe all artists are haunted by the work they did in their first few years? But, I think there is more to the ghostliness of Suspect Culture texts than just nostalgia. There's something else – I think the Suspect Culture texts are peculiarly disembodied works, uncontained, and inclined, therefore, to float.

We were always fascinated with the passing of time and the shows were full of the creation of rituals in order to somehow conquer the inexorable flow of moment. Past, present and future were never simple in a Suspect Culture show. The three texts in this volume in particular capture this.

Take *Timeless*. In the 'Present' four young people gather to remember a moment from the Past when they were spiritually together. When we see the past we witness them gather to create a moment which they will be able to remember in the future. In the final act of the play – they all project forwards – to an imagined future in which they will look back with understanding and contentment on the events of now. Caught up amongst these muddled projections forward and backwards is a moment of actual reality – always achingly just out of reach – a picnic on a beach when they ate pakora bought from a shop. That moment doesn't exist in the text nor was it performed in the show. Maybe it didn't even happen. But whatever its reality, the present/absent moment obsesses the characters – haunts them.

In *Mainstream*, the two characters, A&R and Personnel, are played by four different actors, two men and two women, during a sequence of 55 short scenes. This form forces the 'characters' to become ghosts temporarily inhabited and animated by different bodies. The narrative also contains ghosts. We were very influenced at the time by ideas of the 'possible worlds' theory. The central narrative follows an encounter between someone who works for a record company and a personnel manager. They meet for an official interview, their encounter breaks down, they go for a drink in the hotel bar then something happens between them and they go to one of their bedrooms. Do they sleep together? It's unclear. Then, the next morning they have breakfast together, awkwardly.

This basic narrative, however is fragmented: at some points events follow an expected path, at other moments a tiny event – for example, someone trying and failing to catch a peanut in their mouth – causes events to take a different turn. Each possible world – ghost world – hovers in and out of vision, never quite resolved. There is no way of saying they definitely spent the night together. All we can say is that the story contains that possibility. Further to that complication is added the fact that the narrative is fragmented in time as well. It's as if four slightly different pots, each decorated with a slightly different story, had been smashed on the floor together. Then a selection of the broken pieces is given to an archaeologist whose job is to reconstruct the object. In this analogy the audience is the archaeologist. There is a sense in which the show *Mainstream* doesn't actually exist in any concrete form. All that exists is the show that you think you see: a show that is contained within the imagination of each audience member.

Lament takes our journey into ghostliness even further. This time we created a show without a story. To make the show we discussed with the performers their fantasy selves – the selves they wanted to be. We explored their dreams, memories and delusions. At the beginning of *Lament* the performers revealed all this material to the audience in video extracts of interviews. Then we created a text in which the performers' fantasy selves can exist: one character in the middle of a *Seinfeld* episode, another learning how to tango in Argentina.

But no matter how hard the performers try, each fantasy proves ungraspable and as each world breaks down slowly the actors gather on the stage and begin to create a ritual – a wordless enactment in fire and music during which they attempt to somehow let go of the imaginary ghost self and find, instead, a reality with which they can be content.

In some ways the last act of *Lament* is the most emblematic Suspect Culture moment. I always felt that Suspect Culture shows were as much about the ritual of theatre as they were about anything else. A typical Suspect Culture show contained ghost characters engaged in ghost moments, haunting ghost worlds. Yet, every night, those ghosts had to be physically embodied by performers and every night a ritual of performance revealed the show in a temporary reality. In production we aimed for an aesthetic of uncertainty; we were not interested in realism but in etherealism.

Much of Suspect Culture's work concerned itself with embodiment and disembodiment but these three shows in particular seem to be the most forcefully realised on that journey which is why it makes sense that they should be collected here together and offered as a glimpse of our particular body of work. It took us a long time to publish the texts of our shows. Partly this was because we were worried that the prevailing theatre culture of authorship would subsume our collectivity and misrepresent it. But also, we genuinely felt the text of a Suspect Culture show was the show itself. These texts aren't plays, they're something else: a record of an event? A line drawing of a landscape? Ghosts?

At the centre of *Mainstream* is an image which in some sense speaks for all three plays and possibly also speaks for the entire Suspect Culture project. A&R and Personnel are in a hotel bedroom. After a long time together they have each broken down and been stripped to a kind of late night, half-drunk vulnerable core of their being. In the dark Personnel tells A&R:

Think of me
Imagine me
Conjure me up
Touch yourself.

It's a very elusive moment. In some possible worlds the moment didn't even happen. But in one world it did happen. It happens and we glimpse it. One person, by imagining another, embodies that other person in themselves, and the other person, watching, finds relief in the fact that they have been embodied. A ghost moment of connection between two people – so elusive it's almost impossible to describe – and yet somehow the fulfilment of a deep and terrible ache. Only to connect.

That's what Suspect Culture shows tried to do, connect ourselves to others in the dark. Which is as grand and impossible a task as trying to reach out and catch hold of a full moon.

David Greig was the co-founder, writer and dramaturg with Suspect Culture.

Graham Eatough in *One Way Street*.

One Way Street

JOYCE MCMILLAN

Cultural colonialism works in infinitely subtle ways; and when I was a child, I noticed at a very early age that there was a strange split in the world I inhabited. The places where I lived and moved in real life – a dozen miles or so from Glasgow – did not seem to have the romance, or the inherent magic, that clung to the places that I read about in books, or saw on television. London, Paris, New York, Rome, or the mythical English countryside where all the boarding schools were – these places had presence, glamour, potential; our places had none and on the one occasion when I saw a familiar local place-name mentioned in a girls' adventure story I was reading, I almost fainted with shock.

All this began to change, of course, as I grew up. In the early Sixties, barely into my teens, I heard the sound coming out of Liverpool, and knew that there was a place redefining itself – almost overnight – as one of the sexiest, most significant, and most magical locations on earth. And by the middle of the Seventies, the same thing was beginning to happen in Scotland, as a generation of artists – led, in a sense, by the great linguistic and visual maverick John Byrne, who deferred to no one in his invincible conviction that the view from Ferguslie Park mattered as much as (and was probably funnier and sharper than) the view from Hampstead or Bloomsbury. It was part of the postmodern impulse to redefine the periphery as the cutting-edge, and to see the great metropolitan centres of Western modernism as increasingly out of touch and behind the times. Through the Seventies and Eighties, in Scotland, that effort of cultural self-redefinition continued with terrific force, as writers, painters, musicians, and thinkers reimagined the nation in ways that defied the old provincial stereotypes, and created a multiple universe of brand-new Scotlands, each more interesting than the last.

So it might seem that by 1995 – when I walked into the Traverse and saw my first Suspect Culture show, *One Way Street* – there would have been little left to say about the changing psychogeography of Scotland, and its cities; but there was something in that short, intense piece of theatre – its poise, its sophistication, its sadness – that somehow took account of all that had gone before, and then moved on to a completely new phase. The central idea of the piece told the story of a young man pursuing his lost love through the streets of East Berlin; but it illustrated the story with haunting still images of the backstreets, council flats and canals of Edinburgh, as if to assert that for all the historic drama of Berlin as a setting, the romance of love and loss could strike just as powerfully in Tollcross or Slateford.

It wasn't that there had been no previous Scottish theatre with a strong European feel; Communicado, for example, had already been producing brilliantly stylised European-influenced classics for more than a decade. Not that previous work hadn't sought to assert Scotland's presence as a nation among others in Europe, rather than as a province of the UK; the programme of Glasgow's Year as European City of Culture, in 1990, had been largely built around that idea. But *One Way Street* was the first Scottish-made piece of theatre I had seen which simply and completely incorporated the new, post-Cold-War map of Europe into its sense of identity, and moved on, without pause or argument.

The show's style was flawlessly contemporary, a seamless synthesis of text, performance, music and visual imagery for which many companies strove at the time, but which few achieved so completely. The key to the show's success, though – and to Suspect Culture's future – was that the company had also found the intellectual and emotional content to match the style: the political geography of a new Europe that was unifying, converging, removing barriers to movement and communication; and – most importantly – the emerging emotional geography of a world where a new intensity of communication, and similarity of urban experience across the globe, did not seem to deliver love, fulfilment, or a true sense of connection with other people.

Because of its intelligence, and its less-is-more coolness of style, Suspect Culture's work has sometimes been described as cerebral or unemotional, at least by some observers. Yet one glance at that first show, and its basic elements – the images, the idea, the desperate love story – acts as a reminder that almost all of Suspect Culture's work was finally about the search for love, and for human connection, in a post-post-modern world that often seemed strangely hostile to those basic needs. And for me, the fact that that yearning was often expressed through clever and elegant theatrical forms never diminished its power. On the contrary, for me it always heightened the emotional impact of work created to reflect an age when our ingenuity in creating new technologies and systems has never been more dazzling; and yet when our sense of loneliness and unfulfillment has never been greater, whether we seek our lost loves in Berlin or Barcelona, Edinburgh or Glasgow.

Joyce McMillan is the theatre critic for The Scotsman.

Spinning Through Nothingness:
Suspect Culture Travelling

MARILENA ZAROULIA

'I have a very profound fear of falling out of the sky. [...] My fear is that I will die falling through the air and my last sensation will be of spinning, my arms and legs searching desperately for something solid to hold on to.'

Airport

In the opening scene of *Airport* (1996), Cecilia and Andrés share their fears of flying, suggesting ways of escaping them by bringing in mind 'some nice memory, some memory of being safe'. They are smoothly being moved forward as they walk on two conveyor belts. When they reach the belts' end, they abruptly stop; they are on the edge and there is only air around them. They reach out to hold on to something, while gradually being pulled back. Their heartbeats are rising and their hands, placed by their chests, follow the heartbeat until a poetic movement indicates their hearts 'flying away'. A childhood memory calms them down; a perfect place with 'a sunset and a tree' is projected on the background. The imaginative travelling to this memory of an ideal place, this return 'home' makes them escape their fear of flying and momentarily offers them the opportunity to form a bond with someone else, a stranger speaking in a different language. In this transitional space of travelling – the airplane – where relations are temporary, a shared feeling of moving to a better place emerges.

The poetics of travel, both as leisure activity and as a condition of displacement generating feelings of estrangement, is a key element in Suspect Culture's work and emerges via a number of dramaturgical strategies. Flannery's *flânerie* in East Berlin (*One Way Street*, 1995) is a critique of travel writing – an issue revisited with Colin's 'perfect' travel guides in *Airport* – recognising the inevitable mapping of one's autobiography on the places that they visit. *Candide 2000* situates Voltaire's philosophical treatise, the story of a traveller in exploration of the 'best of all possible worlds', in a contemporary setting. *Different Language* (2005) extends the company's work on how language barriers can be transgressed, recognising linguistic and social systems as bound up with spatial order. *Lament's* (2002) melancholic fragments happen in various places while the characters in *Mainstream* (1999) are travellers, seeking refuge in the anonymity and role-playing of the hotel.

Cast of *Airport*.

The company has consistently interrogated two key issues in contemporary theatre: place and displacement. Suspect Culture's frequent collaborations with artists from other countries and their touring beyond the British borders further support an analysis of their work, employing travel as interpretative framework. For Suspect Culture, travel is a thematic trope, determines aesthetics but also as a practice actually informed their ways of theatremaking. In this respect, the Scottish company is one of a number of British theatre companies and playwrights of the 1990s and 2000s – such as Complicité, Forced Entertainment, and David Greig's plays outside the company – who often focused on mobility and place.

Set in the paramount 'non-place' of Marc Augé's *Non-Places: Towards a Theory of Supermodernity* where time and space are 'in excess', *Airport* exemplifies two interrelated yet conflicting experiences that are central to Suspect Culture's work: in allegorical terms, the feeling of 'spinning through nothingness' and the quest for 'something solid to hold on to'. The first scene of this early piece engages with what Tim Creswell, in *On the Move: Mobility in the Modern Western World*, calls 'the metaphysics of fixity and flow', contesting perceptions of fixity as reactionary stasis and

Cast and company of *Airport* in the Basque Country.

questioning how mobility can signify progress, without ignoring difference. The use of the conveyor belt recognises that theatre is unable to fully articulate spatial distance and movement but this limitation of the medium, evident in the performance's scenography, allows for an accurate representation of mobility as inextricably linked to rootedness. The rapid succession of excessive movement and stillness in the performance suggests that people can still be firmly located in a sense of place even when they are moving.

Throughout *Airport*, images of the commodified anonymity of global tourism, of cultural stereotypes emerging in this 'non-place' of ephemeral interaction and of the actual conditions of border-crossing appear and fluidly change, whilst being juxtaposed with a shared longing for roots. The performance is underpinned by the dialectics of mobility and belonging in the contemporary, globalised world. It would be problematic to suggest that *Airport* is simply a celebration of fixed identities rooted in places, either actual ones or memories of them. Instead, the significance of *Airport* lies in the approach to certain travellers as neither consumers of a commodified travel lifestyle, nor as having a specific destination. Instead, they appear to be undecided whether to leave the airport: Gordon, for example, is always missing his flight to Glasgow, while Theresa does not show any intention of leaving the dying Alberto. These undecidable characters, like the conveyor belt, convey an illusion of movement but in fact remain 'stuck' in the same place. In Zygmunt Bauman's terms, from *Modernity and Ambivalence*, each of them is a stranger, 'an eternal wanderer, homeless always and everywhere, without hope of ever "arriving"'. These strangers challenge established, binary understandings of mobility and place, as their encounters – with Aire and Alberto, respectively – present us with the possibilities of a more truthful, yet brief, relation in the non-place.

Suspect Culture's engagement with travel contests Augé's proposition that 'the traveller's space is the archetype of the non-place'. Although the performance recognises the limitations of the non-place, the strangers in *Airport* articulate the complexities of a world on the move. The performance negotiates failed attempts to balance between fixity and flow, and approaches travelling as walking on a conveyor belt. The most memorable image of these failed yet persistent attempts to balance between mobility and belonging, though, is the tango at the start of *Airport*: a pair of characters suddenly meets, passionately embraces, tangos for four steps backwards, then breaks and returns to their solitary position. This desperate dance alludes to encounters at airport lounges, articulating the travellers' undecidability to move on and perhaps the ambivalence and paradoxes of this 'spinning' world, which is still 'desperately seeking something solid to hold on to.'

Marilena Zaroulia is Lecturer in the Department of Performing Arts, University of Winchester.

Still Timeless After All These Years

NEIL COOPER

I'd been waiting for Suspect Culture to happen for a very long time. By the time I walked down Leith Walk in Edinburgh on 27 August 1997 to spend my thirty-third birthday watching the company's Edinburgh International Festival contribution, *Timeless*, at the now derelict Gateway Theatre, it already felt like we shared the same world. By the time I walked back up the Walk, towards town and late night celebrations, that world had been rocked forever.

As inarticulate as I felt in my immediate responses to the play, it was clear from this treatise on friendship, loss and the pains of shared experience that the company weren't just talking about my generation, even though they were a few crucial years younger than me. Graham Eatough, David Greig, Nick Powell, Ian Scott, their cast of four and the quartet of musicians that soundtracked *Timeless* weren't even just in tune with contemporary mores. Rather, to a greater or lesser degree, they were attempting to navigate their way through – live through, if you like – those increasingly confusing times just as we all were.

But my God, how did we get here?

Anyone who came of age in Britain during the Thatcher years will understand how fucked up it was. The Tory iron lady may have walked to stubborn victory on the back of the Falklands War, the Miners Strike, the IRA hunger strikes, the Yuppie invasion and the denial of society, but there remained, against all odds, a cogently ideological sense of resistance. Sired on the intellectual if not actual barricades of 1968, that resistance understood its own history, and, for many a young shaver, provided a practical education that turned protest into spectacle by way of marches and, in Brixton, Toxteth and elsewhere in 1981, full-on riots that provoked the first ever use of CS gas in mainland Britain.

Culturally, while the post-punk music scene was righteously tense, alternative cabaret flourished on the cheap. The arrival of Channel 4 in 1982 opened up already crazy mixed-up kids to the avant-garde of Fassbinder and Godard, not to mention the puerile delight of nudity and swearing. On John Peel's late night Radio 1 show, serious young men exiled under the bed-clothes are listening to the Gramsci-inspired Scritti Politti's Green Gartside sing jaunty Country and gospel-tinged paeans to philosopher Jacques Derrida or else getting even more post-modern on our asses by deconstructing the love song in a honeyed concoction called 'The "Sweetest Girl"' – ironic inverted commas Gartside's – which concluded its opaquely bittersweet conspiracy with the didactic proclamation how 'politics is prior to the vagaries of science,' and how the presumed 'Girl' of the title 'left because she understood the value of defiance'. With gender studies high on the agenda, the personal had become political, and vice versa.

Essentially, all of this was about ideas. Which is where Suspect Culture came in. Although, to be honest, at that time, or certainly a few years later, they were probably hanging about the drama sections of sixth-form libraries. Probably among the Bs; Barker, Beckett, Bond, Brenton, poets all.

As the Berlin Wall came down, we found ourselves floating uncertainly in a state of ontological flux. Art became more scattershot, less focused. Theatre became physical, and sometimes liked to throw itself around the room to a techno soundtrack for no apparent reason. In England, something called the in-yer-face generation turned up, which actually turned out to be more poetic than the initial outrage that greeted Sarah Kane's *Blasted* and Mark Ravenhill's *Shopping and Fucking* suggested. In Scotland things were quieter. David Harrower's *Knives in Hens* and David Greig's *Europe* were just as fractured in their search for meaning and identity among the madness, but their ideas – them again – were more meditative in approach.

And now, as if by magic, here we were in 1997, a world of Brit-pop optimism in which friends had become the new family and in which a perma-smiling Tony Blair had convinced us by way of an electro-pop anthem that things could only get better. If the Nineties were just the Sixties turned upside down, as some wag – possibly Edwyn Collins – suggested, the glossy iconography looked naggingly familiar.

Left: Keith Macpherson in *Timeless*; **right:** Kate Dickie, *Timeless* rehearsals.

Suspect Culture had already made an impact in a small way with their first two professional shows since forming at Bristol University. *One Way Street* was a solo piece based on the life of German-Jewish intellectual Walter Benjamin. *Airport* was about arrivals and departures. Both, in different ways, were about lives criss-crossing in urban spaces.

Timeless was something else again. The fact that such a young company as Suspect Culture were in the Edinburgh International Festival spoke volumes about how much they'd come of age. Here was a late twentieth-century *fin-de-siècle* epic about friendship and all the littler epiphanies that bind people. Unlike other plays that looked at disaffected twentysomethings, it spoke eloquently and moved fluidly and, in a deceptively domestic scenario, didn't smash the furniture around. If it had been a novel, it would have been Gordon Legge's *The Shoe* or Geoff Dyer's *The Colour of Memory*, both of which looked at the unspoken ties that bind, love, estrange and sometimes, just sometimes, break hearts.

Best of all, *Timeless* was soundtracked by a live string quartet, who underscored the action with Nick Powell's poignant compositions. That's right. A string quartet. This wasn't some live-fast-die-young-leave-a-beautiful-corpse tale of rock'n'roll rebellion. Neither was it some nihilistic punk future fantasy. *Timeless* wore its heart on its sleeve with the most plaintively emotional musical instruments in a way that Estonian composer Arvo Pärt might. All these elements were knitted together to make a beautifully sad meditation on love and life, which, if it happened to be your thirty-third birthday, was bound to hit a nerve.

Of course, all of the above is culled from memory, and may or may not have happened.

Suspect Culture may not have been rock and roll, but they were honest-to-goodness indie-kids at heart, the geeks who, like Belle and Sebastian, would inherit at least some of the earth.

Nick had played with Strangelove and The Blue Aeroplanes, two very hip left-field troupes who will eventually be hailed as post-punk auteurs par excellence. Graham would go on to work with Stephen Pastel and Japanese toy-shop savants Maher Shalal Hash Baz and David, in *Midsummer*, got to work with Edinburgh's ultimate John Peel band, Ballboy.

Best of all was the string section, because in these increasingly baroque musical times, string sections are always in demand. Violinist Lucy Wilkins' name in particular was scattered about the credits of my CD collection. She played on *The Magical World of the Strands*, and toured with Tindersticks when they were at their full or-chestral glory. I saw them at the Royal Albert Hall, and one side of the stage was occupied by what appeared to be an army of stringed-instrument wielding blonde women dressed in black. Lucy would go on to play live with Bryan Ferry and Roxy Music, with Ferry even going so far as to rearrange his tour dates to accommodate Lucy playing in Suspect Culture's *Candide 2000*. And how cool was that?

On the Sunday after *Timeless* rocked my world, my gushing review of the show appeared. It suggested, in its suitably over-the-top way, that everyone who saw *Timeless* should immediately turn to the friend next to them and squeeze their hand in some silently undemonstrative display of emotional solidarity. If anyone did or not isn't on record, but it's doubtful. I certainly didn't. In retrospect, it's doubtful whether anyone even read the review. Because the same day's paper carried a hastily put together supplement following breaking news in the middle of the night, when I and most Edinburgh Festival-philes were probably just making it home, dead-drunk and dead to the world. Princess Diana and her lover Dodi Fayed had been killed in a high-speed car crash on the run from the paparazzi. Things would never be the same again, public displays of emotion in particular.

So what happened next?

Suspect Culture followed *Timeless* with *Mainstream*, which was about two strangers making connections in the limbo of a cheap hotel. Other shows followed, some of which were better than others, but all of which used a particularly personal aesthetic to engage with ideas great and small.

I wrote an essay for a booklet that accompanied Suspect Culture's tenth anniversary. I called it 'Ten Years In Open-Necked Shirts', after the John Cooper Clarke poem. In style and syntax it was wilfully idiosyncratic. In tone it was confessional, attempting to capture how Suspect Culture summed up my and their generation in a way that hoped to match the spirit of their work. It didn't and never could do, but it was then and remains the most honest thing I've ever written.

In 1997 I would never have described *Timeless* as political. Today, as we huddle together for comfort in the face of socio-economic adversity, it feels like the most personally political play in the world.

The core group behind Suspect Culture are ploughing other furrows, their part-debating-society, part-gang mentality having given way to more individual lines of creative inquiries. It's not that we might never see them work together again – all the best bands eventually reform, after all – it's more that they've grown up, moved on and have other things going on in their lives.

In this way, what were once new kids on the block have become elder statesmen. So what happened in-between? That would be telling. That would be *Timeless*.

Neil Cooper is an arts writer and theatre critic with the Herald.

A Different Language

RENATO GABRIELLI

I am grateful to Suspect Culture because, in the years we worked together, I felt young, or at least younger than I was. Actually, Suspect Culture's values and working methods were very similar to those of the group with whom I began my writing career in Milan towards the end of the Eighties. The director of this group, which included the actor Sergio Romano, was Mauricio Paroni de Castro; and it's no coincidence that around ten years after our group disolved, it was Mauricio and Sergio that put me in touch with Graham Eatough. From this initial contact came the project, *A Different Language*.

I remember the rehearsals for this show with affection. A big advantage of working in a bilingual company was that we were able to attribute any disagreements between the Italians (me, Sergio and set designer Luigi Mattiazzi) and the British (Graham, the actress Selina Boyack and sound designer Kenny MacLeod) to linguistic or cultural misunderstandings. In this way any tensions were quickly dissolved. We enjoyed ourselves, and in the end the audience enjoyed themselves as well, appreciating the show more than the critics perhaps. But it was a comedy. And annoying the critics is a good way of continuing to feel young.

Renato Gabrielli was an associate artist with Suspect Culture and is a playwright, dramaturg and teacher based in Milan.

Selina Boyack and Sergio Romano in *A Different Language*.

Theatre, Geography and Existence

MAURICIO PARONI DE CASTRO

'Most of the people I know who are seriously interested in the theater don't really like it very much. There is the situation being played out on the stage (the play), and there is the situation of actually being in the theater – the relationship between the actors and the audience. It is this living situation that is unique to the theater, and the impulses of a new and more open theater want to manifest it.

When I go uptown and see a Broadway play, I go to see primarily the ushers, the box office, and the environment of the physical theater. This situation has become more present than the situation being played out on the stage.

The joy in theater comes through discovery and the capacity to discover. What limits the discoveries a person can make is the idea or image he may come to have of himself (...).'

Joseph Chaikin, The Presence of the Actor, 1972

In 1996, the British Council organised a festival of Scottish drama in Milan. I had been instructed by the theatre where I was director at the time (Centro di Ricerca per il Teatro) to direct one of the texts from a selection sent by the British Council according to their usual policy of promoting the work of young British dramatists abroad. David Greig, co-founder of Suspect Culture, was one of these dramatists at this point. There were many to choose from, but his text *Airport*, written in Spanish, English and Basque, caught my eye. It was not a simple simultaneous translation of an English text, but rather took a dramaturgical approach to the use of different languages in a style that seemed to me more European than British. I told the theatre my choice, and was informed the author would get in touch with me to discuss his ideas towards an Italian staging. In the end however, it was actor/director Graham Eatough, an Englishman based in Scotland and the other co-founder of Suspect Culture, who gave me a call instead.

I was slightly surprised by this, aware as I was of the lack of importance of the stage director in the hierarchy of British New Writing theatre relative to the writer. The mainland European system I was more used to, that sees the director as the author of the theatre show as a work of art, seems seldom applied in Britain. As

Graham reminded me throughout our artistic acquaintanceship, in their approach to making theatre 'the British do things *slightly differently*'. As I got to know the company I began to understand Suspect Culture's relationship to these issues as fundamental to their project and as an existential struggle in which I was delighted to share.

At Suspect Culture the text was written for the company by the author, but directly supported by the director, and based on exercises carried out with actors and other members of the creative team. I was happy to confirm that this was precisely the type of work I was interested in. I was also happy to come across a text written in several languages emerging from a British dramaturgy that seemed otherwise comparatively conventional: a dramaturgy embodied in the work of the Royal Court Theatre in London since its 'angry young men' of the 1950s. Graham outlined Suspect Culture's ongoing attempts to challenge this model in terms of its working methods and where it positioned itself in contemporary British theatre culture.

Increasingly eager to find out more, I boarded a plane to Glasgow and was introduced to Suspect Culture and its members. The company felt more like a family, such was the warmth of their relationships, quite different from the cliché one expects from theatre people in the UK. And it wasn't only due to the fact that we were in the supposedly more friendly city of Glasgow, since the majority of its members came from England.

We established some guidelines for the Italian staging of *Airport*. The text ended up being performed in English, Italian (instead of Spanish) and Portuguese (instead of Basque), because those were the languages spoken by the actors in my company. I could already feel this experience was not just about a specific staging. It was rather an artistic adventure, fuelled by everybody's tendency to regard the existential side of acting as paramount, inasmuch as being a 'successful' actor depends upon *personal* – and not merely professional – efforts. As that attitude has always guided me no matter where I work, a deep and ongoing relationship with the company was born.

This relationship has led to many collaborations including *The Golden Ass* with its participants from different nationalities and backgrounds including designer Laura Trevisan, translator Sylvia Soares, painter Giampaolo Kohler, dramaturges Renata Molinari and Michela Marelli, and all those forgotten citizens of the Gorbals – where Graham's partner, Sarah Ward, worked (again the important intersection between the personal and theatrical). As well as my own involvement with the company, new collaborations came into being between Suspect Culture and former members of my company in Italy, such as *A Different Language* with playwright Renato Gabrielli and actor Sergio Romano. Another result of these relationships was an Italian Theatre Festival with performances at the Royal Scottish Academy

Cast and company of *The Golden Ass*, Aviano, Italy.

of Music and Drama. Here I met Joana Craveiro and Tania Guerreiro from Teatro do Vestido in Portugal, with whom I still work. With *Candide* and *Casanova* we developed separate and distinct stagings in the UK and Italy but inspired by the same material and conversations. I also adapted the text of Spanish writer/director and Suspect Culture associate Andrés Lima, *Pornografia Barata* [*Cheap Pornography*] for performance with my company in a nightclub in Sao Paulo – a performance which eventually incorporated into its wake scene the ashes of the owner of the venue, who had been recently murdered by his lover; he used to attend the performances daily. These experiences made me let go of any reticence about bringing reality and theatre together. I still remember the day when we had to break into the nightclub to perform our show – before an astonished audience, Graham included – because the managers of the place were nowhere to be found, in the aftermath of a massive hangover caused by the previous night's excesses.

The Suspect Culture way of being theatre left well-behaved conventionality behind. Director, writer, and whoever took part in any performance worked together, played their roles to the full, maintaining their personal, professional and artistic characteristics all at the same time. This collaborative approach was extended to shared decision-making within the company, with the composer Nick Powell and

Nick Powell, Mauricio Paroni de Castro and Graham Eatough, São Paolo, Brazil.

stage designer Ian Scott both playing their part. True group theatre. Also of crucial importance were the voices of producer David Smith and dramaturge Pamela Carter. Graham made everybody decide, and that is rather uncommon. Suffice to say that at the end of one of our collaborations Graham and Sarah gave their first child Samuel an English version of Mauricio for his middle name.

In the end, what is it all about? Theatre or private life? It is existential theatre. In the UK it is suspicious. But it is possible. It is Suspect Culture.

Wherever I have worked (Italy, Brazil and even Norway), I have introduced a technique, invented by Suspect Culture, that was at the heart of the monologue performed by Graham in 1994, *One Way Street* (inspired by the philosophical essay of the same title by Walter Benjamin). The show addresses its audience as a group of tourists taking 'Ten Short Walks in the Former East' of the newly re-unified Berlin. The disheveled Lancastrian tour guide Graham played, instead of guiding them through the obvious tourist attractions found on any postcard, takes them instead to the places significant to his personal experiences of Berlin; the site of his first kiss, the place where he used to eat, the gutter where he once threw up. Places that

Cast and company of *Mainstream*, Croatia.

unveil memories so personal that they conjure up a unique sense of the city – an emotional geography.

The exercise deals with the concept of emotional cartography. Benjamin's book, *One Way Street* – and Suspect Culture's wanderings, mine included – presents a number of non-linear narratives, intimate recollections of personal memories triggered by the stimuli of little details of the places where Benjamin used to go as a child. Some narratives call to mind Baudelaire's delusional fragments in *Artificial Paradises*. Benjamin comments on the difficulty of getting lost – of losing our selves – even when we want to do so. Our efforts to be 'rational' mean being conditioned to follow traffic signs, road signs, traffic lights. In the same way, we follow fashion, aesthetic tendencies, collective delusion, mass tourism. We travel miles just to pose in front of a postcard.

This Suspect Culture exercise, or '*dérive*' as the Situationists called it, involves the participant going on a walk through the city following a route determined by some arbitrary set of rules – 'always turn right into the next available street after seeing red'. It creates a kind of drifting that generates real situations, in public places, in which the actor performs an act of displacement from previously fixed coordinates. This leads to a flow of actions, defined by the route that has been taken. At the end of the exercise, considerations and reflections are made to understand and put this emotional path into context.

I have been practising this technique, developing it in practical and theoretical terms, ever since Graham first tried it with actors in Milan on our first meeting. The axis is the actor, inasmuch as he supports the dramaturgy. In my opinion, this exercise is Suspect Culture's hallmark, inseparable from the life of its members and artistic partners.

I believe in a theatre where the dramaturgy is based upon the actors, and not the other way round. The benefits of such a reversal are manifold: they range through the conceptual, creative and interpretative.

Tadeusz Kantor used to tell us at drama school that the theatrical act should happen as art *in front of* the audience, and not just for the audience. Physically – geographically – locating the work in this way has led me to the conclusion that the notion of *subtext* – character-related – must be replaced by the notion of *context* – action-related – in order to provide the actor with a proper role along the way. A context that draws on the imaginings, experiences and conflicts of the performers' (and the audiences') daily lives.

This emotional geography – imaginary or real, taking in the actors' experiences of the city in which they live – becomes the frame of the show in the same way the proscenium frames traditional Italian drama and the black box experimental theatre. Such an approach fuels a dramaturgy that connects the actors' biography with the characters' biography through a relationship with the city's people and places. It is the main foundation of the shows I direct nowadays. And that is something I have learnt while in Suspect Culture's artistic and personal company.

Today's actor has the chance to take the kind of responsibility in his work that would turn him into a creator: author of not only the *play*text, but also the text of his own performance, the text lived on stage, made of words, gestures, sounds, rhythms, the shape of the story and of its articulation. Such an approach offers virtually in-finite theatrical creativity. It is up to the dramatist to open up to an actor offering this kind of input in order for them to carry out the writing of the show together. This method can orchestrate the interaction of conceptual and creative spheres, establishing the rules and parameters needed to open the way to new discoveries.

Such discoveries only come about if we create the right conditions. The epiph-any might even happen by chance, but when there is the will to find it, we will recognize it and never lose sight of it again. We can thus avoid the generic attitude of the actor who acts for himself. Any work I have done after dealing with Suspect Culture has involved exercises (exercises we have 'lived') that in themselves have the potential to become works – 'in process', but works nonetheless. Works that generate engagement and reflection in whoever watches them, works that are born out of, and have a direct bearing on the life of the actor who practises them. *Practises*, not merely performs.

The archaeology of the show that some pretend to practice in Western drama nowadays is a chimera. The essential tool for communication in the theatre is the creation of a relationship in time and space between actors and audience. I state here the formulation of the problem, based upon the theatrical practice of American director Joseph Chaikin. I assert that the theatrical act is the apex of an intersection of two performances. One is that of the actors, who study, rehearse, perform and leave the space where the performance took place. The other belongs to the audience, who chooses the date, companions and programme, and watches the show, leaves for dinner, and maybe will comment upon or remember it. There is a battle being fought in which most of today's directors seek, through any means possible, to dictate the experience of watching the show and its specific reading. As a kind of Don Quixote, the director will always lose: the audience will forever be much more influenced by their everyday lives than by the tools he has at his disposal through the show's meagre language and short duration.

Suspect Culture's answer to all of this has always been serene and casual, more in tune with the world around them and less with the isolationism sometimes at the root of British artistic activity. Theatre, existence and art concur in a precise geography: Glasgow. To be honest, I cannot understand how such a unique situation can have come to an end. But one must never be a pessimist. Graham, myself and other participants in this cultural adventure have taken inspiration from the Buddhist philosophy of teachers like Tsunesaburo Makiguchi (author of *The Geography of Human Life*) who emphasises the enduring value of creating and sharing knowledge through human experience.

And anyway the Suspect Culture company is still alive and kicking in Brazil with Manufactura Suspeita; in Aviano, Italy, with Laura Trevisan's land art; in Il Lumacuore and Manifattura dei Sogni in Portugal and Spain; and in all of those who have taken part in its journey. The fruits of these relationships will still surprise people. Its precious knowledge will continue its journey.

Mauricio Paroni de Castro was an associate artist with Suspect Culture and is a director and writer based in São Paulo, Brazil.

Special thanks to Tania Guerreiro and Joana Craveiro for the English version, Lisbon 2011.

Designing Suspect Culture: Memories

IAN SCOTT

AIRPORT (1996)

A Sunset, Moonlight, Ripples, Costa Coffee, Nebula, Graham in it, Grid, Holodeck, Lightbox, Trolleys, Miniveyors, Boutique, Gesture, Downlighter, Basque Country, Stevey B

TIMELESS (1997)

Smoked Lexan Polycarbonate, Projects, Moldova, Nick's score, Pepper's Ghost, Reflections we have, Reflections we really really want but can't have, Smoking, Being quoted by a character, Cream not beige, Polo shirts, Musician's chair, Musician's cardigan, Gateway, Couples, Pakora

LOCAL (1998)

Castlemilk, Tramway, Graham's sketches, Screens, Projection, Stories, People, True things

MAINSTREAM (1999)

Contra 'H', Starck chair, Static shock, Lightbox, Floating plates, Tomorrow People, Perforations, Shona, Gabe crying, David's words, Stirling, Arches, Prague

CANDIDE 2000 (2000)

Escalators, Money, Staircases, Lightbox steps, Dave wiring striplights, Nick & Lucy rocking, Foster pylon, Plastic plants, Dodgy moving lights

CASANOVA (2001)

Big lightbox, Elegant, Grid floor, Callum undressed, Flight map, Uplighters, Smoke, Rotation, Reflections, Vicki

Floor plans for *Timeless* and *Lament* by Ian Scott.

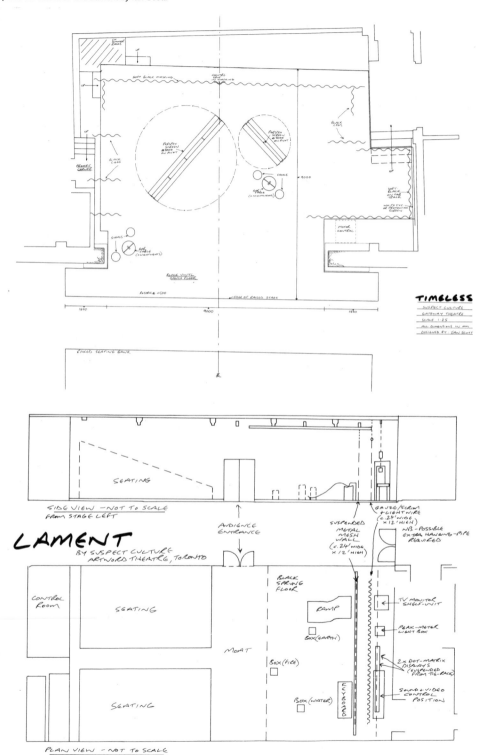

LAMENT (2002)

Roadside shrine, Guggenheim ramp, Lightwire, TVs, Graham & The Smiths, Angry Tron Man, Pammy, Sparkle strobes, Flight map, Oscilloscope, Louise & George Bush, Toronto

ONE-TWO ... (2003)

OSKAR, Hacienda, Hazard tape, Aeros, Beams, Sharon, Transistor radio, Graham's words, Fast fold screens, Road signs, Musician's chair, Platforms, Late night turnaround at the Traverse

8000M (2004)

Brook wall, Meetings about bolts, Glencoe, Sponsorship, Pat, Artex, Claire, Health & safety, Paul's daylight build, Lightbox tents

THE ESCAPOLOGIST (2006)

Mystical green, Loft insulation, ropelight, 59, Piano, Smoke & mirrors, Water tank, Mechanisms, Shattering glass chase

FUTUROLOGY (2007)

Sandwich Islands, Tri-wall, Grant, Ventriloquism, Patrick, Fluorescent lighting, Palettes, Song & Dance, Explosion

STATIC (2008)

Non-speaking Speakers, Signing, Mirror floor, Dark wood, Varnish, Not static, Cassette tapes, Rufus, Lightbox, Kenny

Ian Scott was an associate artist with Suspect Culture and created set and lighting for the company from 1996.

Casanova

TRISH REID

The eponymous hero of Suspect Culture's *Casanova* (2001) is a contemporary Scottish lothario, an ageing seducer who spends his working life crossing continental Europe collecting art on behalf of his wealthy benefactor, Mrs Tennant. Like his eighteenth-century predecessor, he beds countless women along the way. As the play opens he is still on the move, curating a retrospective exhibition of objects commemorating his own sexual conquests. He tells the audience of his quest for one last exhibit, a woman who will be his final chapter, who will perhaps allow him to retire from a career as an itinerant sexual adventurer. He dallies. He notches up four or five more conquests. He continues to search. Meanwhile, back in Scotland, a cabinet-maker, working on the cases that will hold the final exhibits, is planning his revenge. A cuckolded victim of the lothario, the cabinet-maker is a plaintive soul, caught between a desire to settle the score and a powerful need to idealise his wife. He hires Kate, a private detective. In the play's Pinteresque dénouement Kate succeeds in persuading a disillusioned Casanova to step into one of the cabinets, thus ending his life and becoming his own final exhibit.

David Greig's text for *Casanova* is elegiac in tone, filled with the sense of a journey's ending. It is also complex and opaque like much of the playwright's work for the company. It's not that his Casanova is repentant. On the contrary, he remains convinced that far from being exploitative, his numerous sexual encounters have been not only consensual but also liberating and transcendent. His insistence on the never-ending pursuit of pleasure for its own sake constitutes a kind of radical 'nowness' that is in obvious tension with traditional constructions of identity, not to mention history. There is no cause and effect in Casanova's philosophy, there is only the 'moment'. However, his progressive stance ultimately proves exhausting. Even at the outset he expresses a desire for closure, for one final lover, and although the exact circumstances of his death are never revealed, in the end he willingly enters the cabinet suggesting, however obliquely, that he may find his own death desirable. The sadness of this moment is as much in witnessing the fatigue of age overcoming the energy of youth, I think, than the failure of Casanova's utopian vision for sexual relations.

In one sense, then, Casanova's radical stance evidences Suspect Culture's utopian vision of the transcendence of borders, both national and personal, discussed more fully elsewhere in this volume. It also, I would argue, bears the mark of their

Vicki Liddell in *Casanova*.

Scottishness, which seems ever more pronounced in retrospect. The work so often features displaced characters whose continual wanderings suggest ambivalence about the homeland. In one sense this ambivalence connects them to a strain of cultural pessimism that runs deep among Scottish intellectuals, from Hugh MacDiarmid to Tom Nairn, and bemoans a perceived absence of a 'rounded' and authentic Scottish culture. We might also note that Casanova embodies aspects of Scotland's long mi-grant tradition and the melancholic experience of the diaspora, combining as he does a dread of returning with the impossibility of leaving, at least permanently. Until act 2, scene 14, he appears only in neutral or 'non' places – hotel rooms, air-ports, aeroplanes etc. However, Scotland exists in his narrative as an increasingly present absence. From hotel room to hotel room, from one conquest to another, he acts only to delay the inevitable return to his homeland and his final encounter with history, with the man who lives only in the 'past'.

Trish Reid is Deputy Head of School of Performance and Screen Studies at Kingston University London.

Something in its Place:
Misremembering Suspect Culture

NICK POWELL

I watched various sections of *Timeless* the other day for the first time in well over ten years and found myself taken aback by the flood of memories it released in me. I had thought that watching it would help me remember how it felt when the company was still fairly young, that it would help me recall what our motivations were at the time, but I was not prepared for feeling like I was being viscerally squeezed back into my twenty-seven-year-old body and made to relive all the excitement and anxiety of that time. If I had to put a word to the sensation I was revisiting, it would be 'yearning'. A sense of yearning that contained a desperate hunger for the future to unfold but which, by token of it being a form of emptiness, also contained the qualities of loss. A feeling of the imperative to express and create, even when you don't know what to say or make.

'Blah blah, blah blah blah blah.'
Timeless

And, of course, that sensation was exactly what *Timeless* was about. That sensation and what happens to that sensation with the passing of time.
This is the nature of those earlier shows in my memory. When they were working I had no mental separation between who we were and what we were doing. There were moments when what we were creating was who we were at the time. We were creating ourselves, and sometimes the work was creating us. For years the only theatre that I was involved with was Suspect Culture. This meant I could live in blissful ignorance of what it was to 'work' in theatre. This also meant I could do things that might appear like hubris: like when we decided I would write for a string quartet for the Edinburgh International Festival when I had absolutely no idea what I was doing really, simply because I didn't realise it was a big deal.

Some of these memories may be accurate:
One, arriving at a rehearsal for *Airport* in Glasgow directly from being on a ravaging European tour with Strangelove, the band I was in. I walk into the dark of Tramway 4 and am almost immediately assaulted by a dizzying, vertiginous feeling: I hardly know what country I'm in, and I feel like my life has spun out of control,

Left: Catherine Keating, Ian Scott and Nick Powell on Buachaille Etive Mòr during the development of *8000m*; **top:** Gabriel Quigley, *Mainstream* tour; **below:** David Greig, structure diagram for *Lament*.

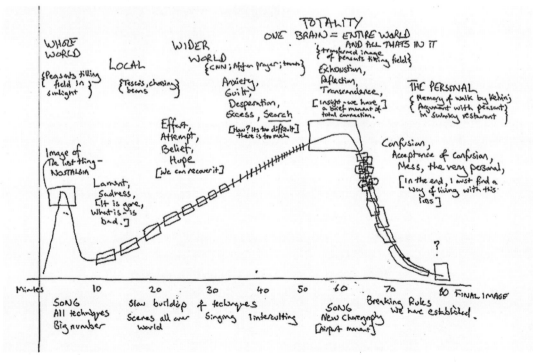

Nick Powell and Lucy Wilkins.

that nothing around me is real: basically a panic attack. I find myself being looked after by the slightly bemused company. The reassuring thing is that this is a very Suspect Culture moment. I am in the right place for this to be happening since we are doing a show about what happens to our concept of Home when our bodies are always in transit and our emotional ties so dispersed. And so I *am* Home.

Two, during the original *Timeless* rehearsals I live in a flat at the West End of Sauchiehall Street with the girls of the quartet. We don't have long to get the show together and so, after rehearsing all day with the actors, we rehearse again in the flat each evening up until just before last orders when we run round to the pub to see how much alcohol it's physically possible to consume in ten minutes. Before leaving the house, though, we develop a nightly ritual of shaking away the intensity of the work process through a group dance/mosh to the Prodigy's 'Smack My Bitch Up'.

Three, Tramway 1, the huge ex-tramshed gallery that has now been broken up to make way for the new bar area. We are re-rehearsing *Timeless* for the tour that will end up at the Donmar in London, and I am working with the string quartet away from the actors within the theatre. The quartet begin to play the overture to

Nick Powell; Molly Innes and Lucy Wilkins.

the first act and spontaneously Lucy and Ruth the violinists and then Becky the viola player begin to walk, tracing patterns around each other through the space while I sit on the floor near Jo, the seated cellist. The room has a long natural reverb and the music spirals around me and curls through the iron beams above me. For a happy moment it sounds better than anything I could have written. Which is actually true since Lucy Wilkins helped a lot…

Four, I write the music for *Mainstream* in a seventy-two hour marathon in my room at Fortress Studios in London. I have a load of recordings that I made with my friend Matt Silver at the BBC World Service. We sent random sound sources to a giant loop of half-inch tape fed through four reel-to-reel machines arrayed around one of the control rooms and, as the machines continually played and re-recorded what they played and re-recorded, the sound decayed and morphed and degraded and we put this down to DAT. I also have isolated lines from the text spoken by the cast, the sound of Shona, our Stage Manager's car windscreen wipers by way of a drum machine, various machines for generating radio static, a guitar amp turned up so loud it constantly feeds back, a two-bar piano motif that I can't get out of my head and a simple bass guitar riff. These become the elements that get assembled in various forms and then have various cello and violin lines played on top. In this way the construction of the music mirrors the construction of the text and actions: repetitive motifs revisited and layered in different ways. In my delirious sleep-deprived state, the whispered lines from the text start to sound like the voices of ghosts amidst the static. When I get back to Scotland I start to think of the figures onstage in these terms, like souls in limbo trying to break back into the world by negotiating the possible lives of two characters, but only ever half in the world, trying but never succeeding to connect to it and each other.

Five, in a huddle with Graham, David and Ian after watching the first dress rehearsal of *Mainstream* at the MacRobert Theatre in Stirling. All week we have been joking about the (possibly spurious) fact that apparently the campus where the theatre is situated has the highest suicide rate of any in the country. David is looking worried, eventually stammering 'it's, er, not a warm production, is it?' And, looking back now, I'm thinking 'well, it did feature a recurring motif of someone achieving some sort of enlightenment by nearly freezing to death in a car caught in a blizzard. So, er, no, in that respect I guess it wasn't.'

Six, developing the ideas for *Lament*, we end up with a provisional structure for the show drawn as a shape on a sheet of paper. From a distance it reminds me of a diagram of a dinosaur skeleton, maybe a Diplodocus (appropriate for a show about lost things). The creature's spine consists of vertebrae (representing events or scenes along the show's timeline) separated by wider and wider gaps (pauses where scenes may fail and the action stop) until eventually the whole show/creature becomes one long gap (and here I have to let the dinosaur analogy go ...). Into this gap where all the scenes have failed we place a sort of rite, consisting of music, gesture, some singing, and virtually wordless apart from some very personal stories from the performers recorded live onto flatbed tape recorders, barely audible to the audience.

Looking back it is striking how many of our supposedly 'coolly minimalist' shows featured these unashamedly emotional sequences where almost liturgical imagery blended with the ghosts of spiritual practice – candle-lighting (*Timeless*), shrine-building (*Lament*), choral speaking before an image of perfection (*Airport*), shared gesture (all of them), music and singing, and it occurs to me that whilst we may have lost religion, ideology, our sense of selves, double-wrapped confectionary and the space race, as a group we were, and probably still are, yearning for something in their place.

Nick Powell co-founded Suspect Culture with David Greig and Graham Eatough at Bristol University. Nick is a composer for theatre, film and television based in London.

Productions

The following section presents information and production images, as well as graphic elements and contemporary reviews, of the complete archive of Suspect Culture work.

From 1997 onwards, Patrick Macklin was responsible for the company's graphic identity and promotional material, later becoming an artistic associate and collaborator on the shows themselves.

Top: Graham Eatough in *A Savage Reminiscence*;
bottom and opposite: posters for *Europe* and
A Savage Reminiscence.

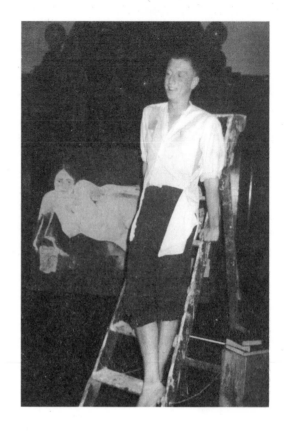

Early Years

A Savage Reminiscence

by David Greig, 1990

Performed by Graham Eatough

Premiered 24 April 1991, Hen and Chicken, Bristol.
Bristol University, Pinnar Arts Centre, Warwick
University, Bath Festival, Edinburgh Festival.

...and the opera house remained unbuilt

by David Greig, 1991

Performed by Graham Eatough and
Reno Pelakanou (Phil Collins in Edinburgh)

Premiered 17 August 1992, Roman Eagle Lodge,
Edinburgh. Bristol University, Edinburgh Festival.

The Garden

by David Grieg, 1992

Premiered 30 August 1992, St Columba's by
the Castle, Edinburgh. Bristol University.

Stalinland

by David Greig, 1992

Premiered 16 August 1992,
Roman Eagle Lodge, Edinburgh. Citizen Stalls, Glasgow.

An Audience with Satan based on Tony Parker's *Life After Life*

Performed by Graham Eatough and Alan Wilkins, 1992

Europe

A double bill of *Stations on the Border*, devised by the
company, and *Petra's Explanation* by David Greig, 1993

Premiered 6 July 1994 The Arches, Glasgow

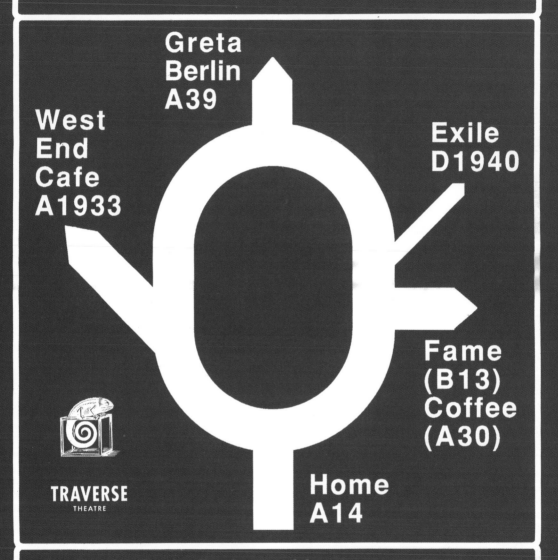

Suspect Culture Presents
One Way Street

Greta
Berlin
A39

West
End
Cafe
A1933

Exile
D1940

Fame
(B13)
Coffee
(A30)

TRAVERSE
THEATRE

Home
A14

By David Greig Performed by Graham Eatough
Traverse Theatre 2 Cambridge St Edinburgh
Wednesday 1 to Sunday 5 February 7.30
£6 / £3 Conc Box Office 0131 228 1404

Premiered 1 February
1995, Traverse, Edinburgh.
Glasgow 1995, Germany
(Magdeburg, Munich,
Chemnitz, Dresden) 1997.

Direction and Text
David Greig

Performer
Graham Eatough

Design
Katherine Lindow

Video
Sarah Ward and
Rachel Seffert

Director on tour
Guy Hollands

Top, bottom: Graham Eatough

One Way Street

A guided tour of ten short walks around the former East Berlin, exploring the idea of personal history as geography.

'*One Way Street* is a power packed, memorable little piece full of romance, imagination and promise.'
Scotland on Sunday

Playtext available in *Scotland Plays*,
Nick Hern Books, 1998.

Top: Poster by Central Design; **bottom:** Alan Wilkins;
opposite: Graham Eatough

Airport

An exploration of identity and language, set in
the glossy world of international travel.

Premiered 19 June 1995, Traverse 2, Edinburgh.
Performed in Glasgow, Edinburgh, Madrid, 1996; Basque
Country and Italy (Scotfest, Milan) 1998.

Direction
David Greig and Graham Eatough

Text
David Greig

Design
Evelyn Barbour

Lighting
Ian Scott

Music
Nick Powell

Performers
Graham Eatough
Cecilia Solaguren
Silvia Carmona
Jill Riddiford
Andrés Lima
Stuart Bowman
Alan Wilkins (on tour)

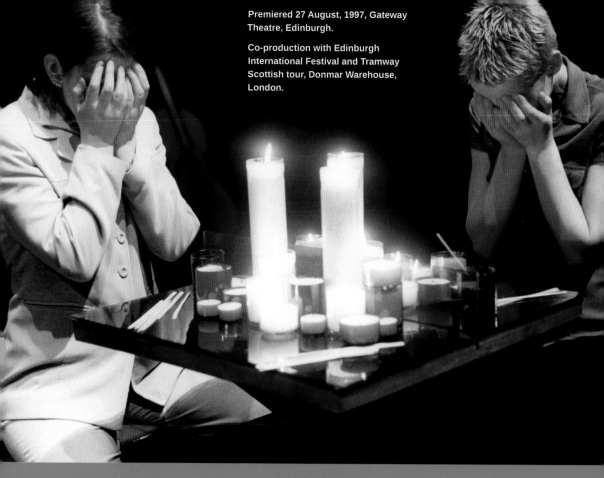

Premiered 27 August, 1997, Gateway Theatre, Edinburgh.

Co-production with Edinburgh International Festival and Tramway Scottish tour, Donmar Warehouse, London.

Winner of *Scotland On Sunday* Critics' Award 1997

'…director Graham Eatough, Greig and the company have made a work of world class.' *The Herald*

Timeless

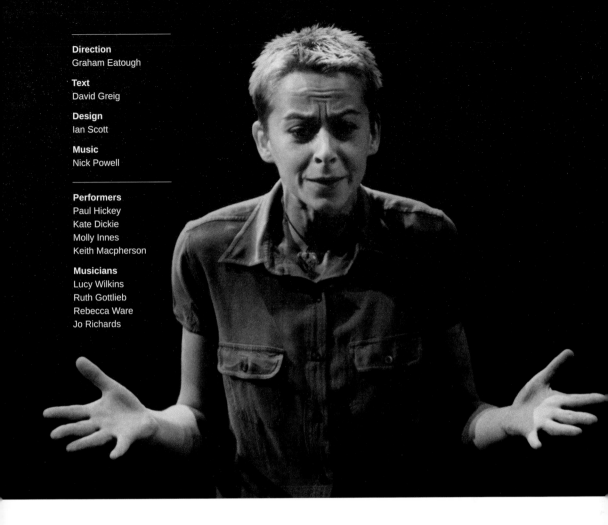

Direction
Graham Eatough

Text
David Greig

Design
Ian Scott

Music
Nick Powell

Performers
Paul Hickey
Kate Dickie
Molly Innes
Keith Macpherson

Musicians
Lucy Wilkins
Ruth Gottlieb
Rebecca Ware
Jo Richards

Timeless

Timeless tells the story of four friends whose present, past and future lives are delicately intertwined. They study their reflections in the window of a cafe, looking back on themselves nostalgically, dreaming of the perfect future, and failing to make contact with each other in the present.

Above left: Molly Innes and Kate Dickie; **above:** Kate Dickie; **opposite:** graphical elements by Patrick Macklin

79

Premiered 20 February, 1999,
MacRobert Arts Centre, Stirling
Co-production with the Bush
Theatre, London.

Scottish and English tour including
Bush Theatre, Edinburgh Fringe
and Dublin Fringe. International
tour to Greece, Croatia,
Bulgaria and Prague, 2000.

Direction
Graham Eatough

Text
David Greig

Design
Ian Scott

Music
Nick Powell

Performers
Kate Dickie
Louise Ludgate
Paul Thomas Hickey
Callum Cuthbertson
Gabriel Quigley (on tour)
Nathan Pope (on tour)

'This is a hard, cruel, beautiful show, almost mathematical in its precision. The coolness of the performance style is in perfect harmony with the piece's icy images.' *The Guardian*

Opposite: Gabriel Quigley, Louise Ludgate, Nathan Pope and Callum Cuthbertson; **below:** Kate Dickie

mainstream

Mainstream

This story of two people who meet in a three-star seaside hotel quietly and movingly unravels the fabric of two ordinary lives. They ask questions and let secrets slip. But in their desire to communicate they find that the more they tell, the less they reveal.

An elegant game with theatre and convention, four performers play either of the two characters. A single encounter breaks apart into any number of different possible stories. And as these stories unravel, so too does a drama of intimacy, disclosure and desire.

Cast members of *Local*

Local

The culmination of eleven workshop sessions with a variety of young people from all over Glasgow, *Local* deals with their relationships with the city through their aspirations and fears for the future. With projected video footage performed and produced by the participants in collaboration with Castlemilk Video Workshop.

Premiered 1998, Tramway, Glasgow

Produced in collaboration with Castlemilk Video Workshop

Direction
Graham Eatough

Text
David Greig

Design
Ian Scott

Video
Steve Jackson

Performers
Young people from Glasgow

Premiered 14 December, 2000,
Tron Theatre, Glasgow.

Co-produced with the Tron Theatre,
Glasgow, 2000.

Sergio Romano and Silval Soares

The Golden Ass

The Golden Ass

A wild satirical tale about the effects of wealth and power on modern-day society.

Following the adventures of Lucius – a Brazilian storyteller and magician – lost in the city of Glasgow, *The Golden Ass* is a wild and funny show about wealth and power in our society today.

An international production featuring members of the Gorbals community and performers from Italy and Brazil.

Devised with a group of participants from the Gorbals, Glasgow, including residents of the James Shield Project.

Direction
Mauricio Paroni de Castro
and Graham Eatough

Text
Mauricio Paroni de Castro

Design
Laura Trevisan and Giampaolo Kohler

Lighting
Dave Shea

Music
Nick Powell

Outreach Worker
Abbie Wallace

Performers
Sergio Romano
Silvia Soares
Members of the James Shield Project

Above: cast of *Candide 2000*;
opposite: Colin McCredie and Lucy McLellan

Candide 2000

A contemporary staging of Voltaire's classic story, set in the bright world of the modern shopping centre and developed with groups of young people from the cities visited.

A witty, extravagant and sometimes brutal exploration of innocence and knowledge at the beginning of the twenty-first century, *Candide 2000* combines live music with performances from a mixed cast of professionals and young people.

'A winningly ingenious adaptation of a literary classic and an admirable example of that most difficult of genres, young people's theatre.'
The Daily Telegraph

Premiered 8 March, 2000,
Old Fruitmarket, Glasgow.

Scottish and English tour.
Co-produced with Tramway.

Direction
Graham Eatough

Text
David Greig

Design
Ian Scott

Music
Nick Powell

Performers
Paul Blair
Grant Smeaton
Colin McCredie
Lucy McLellan
Jill Riddiford
and young people from
Glasgow, Edinburgh, Aberdeen,
Inverness and Newcastle

Musicians
Nick Powell
Lucy Wilkins
Colin Morrison

Casanova

Casanova

Casanova follows the travels of an internationally renowned artist curating the final exhibition of his illustrious career: an account of his life as the world's greatest lover. As the exhibition nears completion and the opening in his hometown approaches, a cuckolded husband's plan to avenge the loss of his wife also draws to an end.

Casanova raises questions about love, honesty and life lived in the pursuit of pleasure, and is an uncompromising examination of contemporary sex and morality.

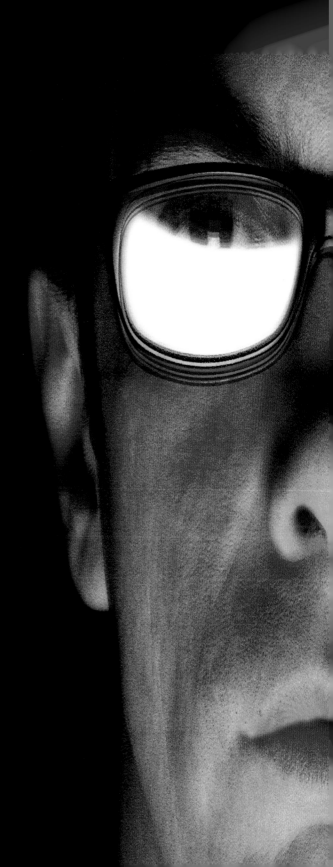

Premiered 14 February, Tron Theatre,
Glasgow 2001. Edinburgh Fringe
Festival, Dublin Fringe Festival,
Edinburgh Royal Lyceum, Paisley Arts
Centre, Stirling MacRobert, Aberdeen
Lemon Tree, Dundee Rep and
Newcastle Northern Stage.
Co-produced with the Tron Theatre,
Glasgow, 2001.

Direction
Graham Eatough

Text
David Greig

Lighting
Ian Scott

Set Design
Graham Eatough, Patrick Macklin

Music
Nick Powell

Performers
Gavin Mitchell
Paul Blair (on tour)
Mabel Aitken
Anne Marie Timoney (on tour)
Vicki Liddell
Louise Ludgate
Alan Williams
Callum Cuthbertson (on tour)

Playtext available in
Casanova, Faber, 2001

lament

Lament

Lament is a poem for the theatre. Funny and touching, honest and playful, it examines the sadnesses and absurdities of the state we're in today – or, at least, the state we think we're in.

Asked for their favourite sad song, their dream future, their assessment of current global politics, the answers of Suspect Culture's five performers unfurl as a succession of scenes and snapshots.

What emerges is a play which occupies the very present space between the personal and the political and acknowledges the heartfelt nostalgia we feel for a world today that perhaps never existed.

Premiered 4 April, 2002,
Tron Theatre, Glasgow.

Scottish and English tour.
Six Stages Festival,
Toronto, 2003.

'... this remains extraordinary
theatre – intimate and
universal, local and global and
as indulgently heart-warming
as the saddest song.'
The Guardian

Direction
Graham Eatough

Text
David Greig

Design
Ian Scott

Music
Nick Powell

Performers
Graham Eatough
Kate Dickie
Louise Ludgate
Paul Blair
Callum Cuthbertson
David Ireland (on tour)
Catherine Keating (on tour)

"ONE - TWO"...

Opposite: Faroque Khan and Sharon Smith; **left:** OSKAR

Part play, part gig, *One-Two…* harnesses the raw energy of live music and the emotional landscape of theatre to tell the story of what life would be like with your own personal soundtrack. Building a show around music, performance and video projection, *One-Two…* furthers the company's collaboration with musician Nick Powell and its ongoing exploration of different performance languages.

'…the music is mesmeric and the event as a whole is exactly the kind of adventurous overturning of form that we should be seeing…' *The Independent*

Premiered 7 August, Traverse, Edinburgh Festival, 2003.

Scottish and English tour.

Supported by CCA Creative Lab.

Direction and Text
Graham Eatough

Music
Nick Powell and OSKAR

Design
Ian Scott

Video
Shiona McCubbin

Performers
Jonny Dawe
Ruth Gottleib
Faroque Khan
Nick Powell
Sharon Smith
Sarah Wilson

Below left: Catherine Keating; **opposite left:** Selina Botack; **below:** John Macauley and Selina Botack; **right:** Paul Blair and Catherine Keating

8000m
EIGHT THOUSAND METRES

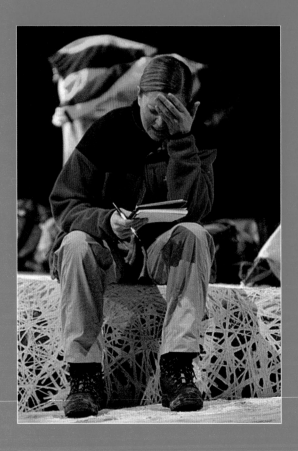

8000m

8000m dramatises the experience of climbing the highest mountains in the world – from start to summit and the return home.

It explores the desire to climb: the deep and strange impulse to go where no human being is supposed to be. It imagines people at their physical and psychological limits.

It examines the nature of communication between these extraordinary adventurers – in the multi-lingual community of international climbing, where technology is pitted against nature – and where every word weighs heavy in an oxygen deprived atmosphere.

8000m turns Tramway's Brook wall into the North face of Lhotse in order to dramatise the experience of climbing the highest mountains in the world.

'One of the most effective pieces of total theatre I've seen in recent years.' *Saturday Review*, **Radio 4**

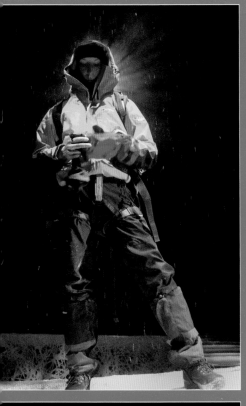

Premiered 24 February 2004,
Tramway, Glasgow.

Co-produced by Tramway.

Direction
Graham Eatough

Text
David Greig

Design
Ian Scott

Co-lighting design
Paul Sorley

Composer
Nick Powell

Performers
Selina Boyack
Eric Barlow
John Macaulay
Phil McKee
Matthew Pidgeon
Paul Blair
Catherine Keating

ESCAPOLOGIST

The Escapologist

The Escapologist follows a psychotherapist as he delves into the conscious and unconscious desires of his patients. Feeling increasingly sceptical about the powers of his own profession he starts to take flight into fantasies of the greatest escape artist of them all, Harry Houdini.

Inspired by the book *Houdini's Box* by Adam Phillips, *The Escapologist* is a celebration of theatricality, using live music, silent film and pitch-perfect dialogue.

'An intensely mesmeric affair…an elegant and profound piece of work.' *The Herald*

94

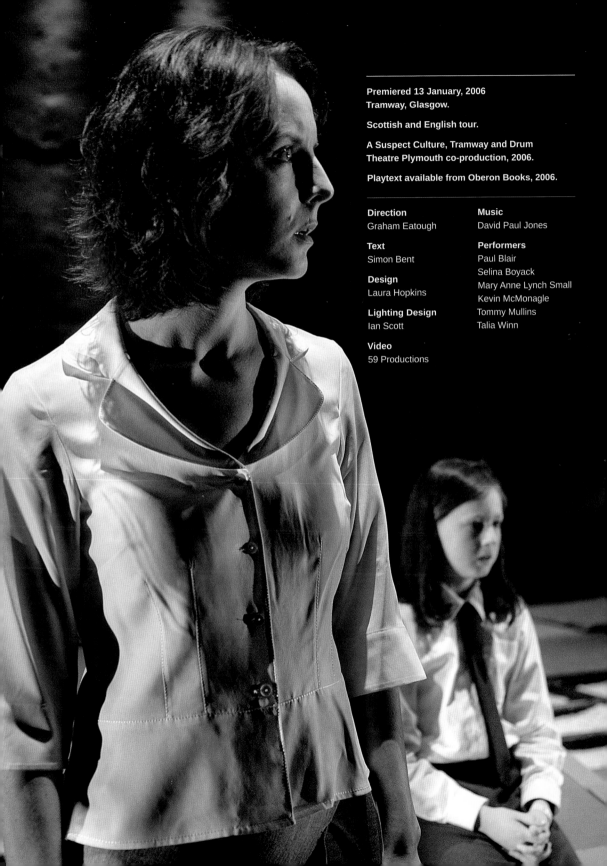

Premiered 13 January, 2006
Tramway, Glasgow.

Scottish and English tour.

A Suspect Culture, Tramway and Drum
Theatre Plymouth co-production, 2006.

Playtext available from Oberon Books, 2006.

Direction
Graham Eatough

Text
Simon Bent

Design
Laura Hopkins

Lighting Design
Ian Scott

Video
59 Productions

Music
David Paul Jones

Performers
Paul Blair
Selina Boyack
Mary Anne Lynch Small
Kevin McMonagle
Tommy Mullins
Talia Winn

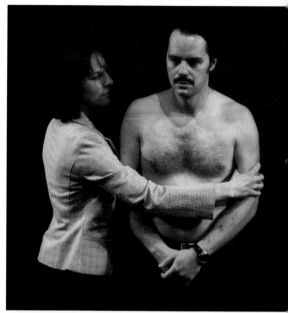

A Different Language

A Different Language is a before-love-story set in a world of internet chatrooms, life-coaches and easyJet. The story follows two single people, one Italian, one British, as they search for that one perfect person who will be their soulmate.

'Selina Boyack and Sergio Romano give two wonderful, relaxed yet searching performances under Graham Eatough's direction.'
★ ★ ★ ★ *The Scotsman*

A DIFFERENT_ _LANGUAGE

Premiered 28 February 2005, Tron Theatre, Glasgow.

Scottish, English and Italian Tour.

Co-production with Il Rossetti – Teatro Stabile del Friuli Venezia Giulia.

Direction
Graham Eatough

Text
Renato Gabrielli

Design
Luigi Mattiazzi

Sound Design
Kenny MacLeod

Performers
Sergio Romano
Selina Boyack

FUTUROLOGY
A GLOBAL REVUE

uturology

darkly comic musical looking at the state of
e planet and our seeming inability to effect
eaningful change.

e future's coming towards us at a hundred
es an hour. Do you ever feel like a rabbit
ught in the headlights? The oil's running out,
e climate is changing, China's on the rise.
eanwhile we're left wondering how to act now.
here something we should be doing? Is it OK
be doing nothing?'

urology explores the big questions in a
kly comic show packed full of song, dance,
ntriloquism and Suspect Culture's trademark
atrical style.

Premiered 10 April 2007,
SECC Glasgow.

A Suspect Culture, National
Theatre of Scotland and Brighton
Festival co-production, 2007.

Scottish tour and Brighton Festival.

Direction
Graham Eatough

Dramaturgy
David Greig and Dan Rebellato

Design
Patrick Macklin and Ian Scott

Music
Nick Powell

Arrangements
Nick Powell and the band

With contributions from
Suspect Culture's associate
artists Renato Gabrielli,
Mauricio Paroni de Castro,
Andrés Lima and Sergio Romano

Video
59 Productions

Performers
Raphaelle Boitel
David Carr
Angela de Castro
Callum Cuthbertson
Robert Melling
Robert Moss
Robert Owen
Maria Victoria Di Pace
Jon Thorne
Grant Smeaton
Sharon Smith
Morag Stark
Warren Speed
Edd Muir
Catriona Paterson

'Bold, original, confident...
Futurology is a present-day delight.'
★ ★ ★ ★ *The Guardian*

KILLING
TIME

Killing Time: an exciting fusion of performance, sculpture and installation at Dundee Contemporary Arts. This co-production by DCA and Suspect Culture involved a unique artistic collaboration between the company's director Graham Eatough and visual artist Graham Fagen.

The *Killing Time* publication, Dundee Contemporary Arts, 2006, is available from DCA.

Opened 9 September 2006, Dundee Contemporary Arts.

'*Killing Time* is undoubtedly one of the most compelling and exhilarating Scottish visual arts projects in recent years.' ★ ★ ★ ★ ★ The List

'*Killing Time*, then, is made of powerful stuff. It illuminates four well-known plays, and it will change the way you think about art, performance and the space between the two.'
The Herald

Vincent Friell

MISSING

Missing

Suspect Culture's short film *Missing* examines the experience of those left behind when a loved one disappears without warning or explanation.

It follows Rachel through a day in her life without Paul, her husband who's been missing for eight years. We see her trying to come to terms with the insurmountable fact of not knowing; why he left, where he is, and if he's ever coming back. *Missing* explores the painful imaginings that fill this vacuum and the stories we tell ourselves when we just don't know.

'This is excellent work, beautifully shot in a variety of locations, with a real depth. Based on *The Missing* by Andrew O'Hagan, this is a haunting piece'
★ ★ ★ ★ *Eye for Eye*

Premiered at the Edinbugh International Film Festival in 2007. A co-production with Digicult/ Scottish Screen.

Written and directed by
Graham Eatough

Producer
Kat Calton

Director of Photography
Oliver Cheesman

Art Director
Amanda Currie

Music
Nick Powell

Performers
Barbara Rafferty
Vincent Friell
Callum Cuthbertson
Charles Donnelly
Morag Stark
Marion Sangster
Caroline McKeller
Ian Sexon

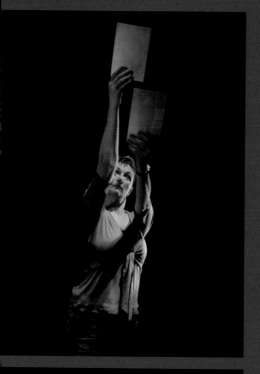

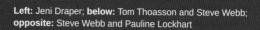
Left: Jeni Draper; **below:** Tom Thoasson and Steve Webb;
opposite: Steve Webb and Pauline Lockhart

STATIC

GRAEae
THEATRE COMPANY

A STORY OF LOVE, LOSS AND COMPILATION TAPES

Static

Static: a unique collaboration with London-based Graeae theatre company follows the story of a young woman who loses her husband.

Fusing music, dialogue, sign language and audio description, *Static* is a complex response to the ways in which we deal with love and loss.

Nominated for the John Whiting Award, the playtext is available in *Static*, Oberon Books, 2008.

'A blistering meditation on the nature of love, grief and the importance of compilation tapes.' *Financial Times*

'*Static* is always about what fills the gaps between words. It makes signing an art form and suggests that when words fail us in times of grief, music can speak straight to our battered hearts.' *The Guardian*

Premiered at Glasgow Tron
Theatre, 14 February 2008.

Scottish and English tour.

A co-production by
Suspect Culture, Graeae
Theatre Company and
Theatre Royal Plymouth.

Direction
Graham Eatough & Jenny Sealey

Script
Dan Rebellato

Design
Ian Scott

Sound
Kenny Macleod

Performers
Jeni Draper
Pauline Lockhart
Tom Thomasson
Steve Webb

STAGE FRIGHT

Stage Fright

Stage Fright was an exhibition of new artworks by Luke Collins, Graham Eatough, David Greig, Patrick Macklin, Sharon Smith & Felicity Croydon (Max Factory), Nick Powell & Jonny Dawe (OSKAR) and Dan Rebellato.

The exhibition was co-produced and co-curated with the Centre of Contemporary Arts and was presented at CCA over the course of April and May 2009. The show explored the ways in which visual art and theatre feed off of each other as well as ideas around authenticity, reproduction and the positioning of the viewer in relation to the work.

Opened 4 April 2009, CCA, Glasgow.

'... Characteristically inquisitive, cerebral and witty ...'
★ ★ ★ ★ *The Guardian*

'... endlessly thought provoking.'
The Herald

Complete Texts

The following section presents the complete texts of three Suspect Culture productions: *Timeless*, *Mainstream* and *Lament*.

Suspect Culture productions were conceived by Graham Eatough, David Greig, Nick Powell and Ian Scott. They were directed by Graham Eatough, and the texts were written by David Greig. Nick Powell composed the music, and Iain Scott designed the sets and lighting.

A NOTE ON THE TEXT

The text was written specifically for the Suspect Culture production of *Timeless* which premiered at the Edinburgh International Festival in 1997. I would like to thank Graham Eatough, Nick Powell, Ian Scott, Kate Dickie, Paul Hickey, Molly Innes and Keith MacPherson for their contributions to the final text.
David Greig

SETTING

A cafe, in a city, recently

CHARACTERS

Ian
Martin
Veronica
Stella

ACT ONE: THE PRESENT

I.

_____

[Ian and Martin.]

IAN: It's unbelievable.
       I mean … It's … big. It's a big thing … I mean it's …
       But truly, I can't tell you what it is.

MARTIN: OK.

IAN: It's earth shattering.

MARTIN: Right. Earth shattering.

IAN: But I can't say more than that.
       It's just too … universal.

MARTIN: OK.

IAN: Wipe it out of your mind.

MARTIN: OK.

IAN: I never mentioned it. I never spoke.

MARTIN: I understand. OK. That's fine.

[Beat.]

IAN: It is worrying though. I can't help worrying about her.

MARTIN: Ian. I'm Stella's friend. I'm your friend.
          We go back a long way.
          And a friend's job, a friend's purpose Ian …
          If you're worried if …
          A long way, Ian, so when she comes in …
          It's going to be 'Hello. Stella. Long time no see' and so …
          If this is big Ian, if this is 'earth shattering' …

I should be up to speed.
You know.
For her sake. Ian.

IAN: No. You're right. I should …

[Ian wants to show something to Martin.
Martin wants to see it.]

Only I don't know.
This is not my place. I don't feel good about doing this …

MARTIN: This is some kind of picture.
What you have in your pocket.
It's a photograph?

IAN: Yes.
Look.
The more you go on about this, the worse the situation gets.
Because I can't tell you. OK.
So let's stop talking about it.
We'd better forget it.
…
How's Veronica?

MARTIN: Veronica's fine, Ian. Veronica's terrific.
Fuck Veronica.

IAN: I shouldn't even have told you what I've told you.

MARTIN: OK. Let me get this right. Just in my head.
You have a picture in your pocket?

IAN: I didn't say that.

MARTIN: Yes you did.

IAN: Well I shouldn't have.

MARTIN: This is a picture of Stella?

IAN: I probably made a mistake.
It probably isn't even her.
Just someone who looks like her.

MARTIN:	So. Where did you get the picture?
IAN:	It was in one of those … Actually no. No way. This is just too … jesus. I've gone too far. Let's just stop. OK.
MARTIN:	OK. We'll stop.
IAN:	Good.
MARTIN:	And we'll talk about something else. All right?
IAN:	All right.
MARTIN:	So how's things? How's … you working? Or are you still …
IAN:	I've got a few things coming up. You know. Just some stuff.
MARTIN:	Good.
IAN:	You?
MARTIN:	Busy. You know. Too busy. I spend my life in airport hotels. I go business class. It's not my image of myself. I fucking hate myself.
IAN:	Inevitably.
MARTIN:	But what can I do. It's where I am. Air-conditioned. Trying to communicate in some fucking foreign language.
IAN:	Yeah.
MARTIN:	I haven't got you a drink. I feel like my throat's been cut here. Do you want a drink?
IAN:	I'm OK.
MARTIN:	Have one. What do they do here? A bottle of something. What are you having?
IAN:	I don't know. A beer?

MARTIN: They do one. It comes from the Slovak Republic. I can't pronounce the fucker's name but it tastes OK.

IAN: Cheers.

[Pause.]

MARTIN: So. Stella said she's coming?

IAN: Yeah.

MARTIN: Good. That's good.

IAN: Yeah.

MARTIN: Long time since I've seen Stella.

[Pause.]

IAN: All right. OK. But only because this is a big thing.

MARTIN: What?

IAN: Look, I like Stella. I love Stella.
            We go back a long way. Like you say.
            We're her friends.

MARTIN: She's a mate. No doubt about it.

IAN: So.
            OK.
            So I shouldn't but…
            Because it's too earth shattering but…

MARTIN: Maybe we can help her or something.

IAN: Exactly so… this is between you and me.
            I so much shouldn't be doing this.
            If I seem like I'm smiling it's because I'm nervous.
            I'm not really smiling.

MARTIN: No. I recognise that Ian.

IAN: Because this is serious.

MARTIN: That's obvious.

IAN: OK. Here.

[He gives Martin a folded-up page from a colour magazine.
Martin carefully unfolds the page.]

MARTIN: (Laughs.)
              Hello Stella.
              (Laughs.)
              Long time no see.
              (Laughs.)

IAN: OK. So … look, you'd better give it back before she gets here.

              2.

              ————————

VERONICA: I'm so sorry. I'm sorry. (Kisses Martin. Kisses Ian.) You know I really hate being late.
              I'm out of breath so I can't speak. I mean I knew I was pushed for time so first
              it was a taxi, and then the guy was so slow. I mean he was creeping through the
              traffic and I wanted to say, 'I don't have time', please, 'I don't have any time mister'.
                  And then it was that I didn't have any money and I said I needed to get out at
              a cash machine and so the man was going off his head. He was quite an old man
              for a taxi driver. I mean I thought he's going to chop me up. He's going to rape
              me in his taxi and then chop me up and deposit me in a bin bag by the side of a B
              road in the country. Anyway, he follows me to the cash machine on the corner so
              I give him the money and then he starts counting out change so, of course, I start
              running.
                  So I'm running and everyone thinks I'm a robber, you know, or a member of
              a girl gang, and they're shouting 'Stop Thief!', you know and I can't breathe, I
              actually feel my lungs shrinking and shrinking, and people are shouting, 'That's
              her! She's the one!' and my body's so empty of air that my brain's starting to cave
              in on itself and I'm thinking 'I've got to run, because I'm late, and everyone's
              waiting for me. And I thought:
                  What right's that bastard taxi driver got to interfere with the timing of my
              life? But then I thought – you know that thing people say – that if you're late for
              something it's an unconscious indication that you don't want to be there at all.
              Your unconscious is rebelling against your conscious action in the way you use

time? Well I thought … here I am. I'm late. But I really don't want to be late. It's just circumstance. I'm genuine. Even unconsciously I don't want to be late and suddenly the whole idea of psychology seemed really unfair.

Listen I must just go to the loo before I sit down. Does anybody want a drink?

3.

———

IAN:	OK. So, quick, maybe you should just give it back …
MARTIN:	This is hot property. Ian.
IAN:	This is between you and me. Not even Veronica.
MARTIN:	Where did you get it?
IAN:	It was just in a magazine.
MARTIN:	You get magazines like this?
IAN:	Not really. Sometimes.
MARTIN:	That's not my image of you. Ian.
IAN:	OK. I know.
MARTIN:	She looks sexy … The way she's captured here.
IAN:	Yeah.
MARTIN:	Did you … ? You know.
IAN:	What?
MARTIN:	I'm just curious.
IAN:	What?
MARTIN:	It's a pornographic picture. I mean. It has a purpose. You must have bought the magazine for a purpose.

IAN:	So.
MARTIN:	The picture. Did you … You know use it?
IAN:	No.
MARTIN:	You did.
IAN:	No. No way. I was … I couldn't.
MARTIN:	She looks stunning. It's a tempting prospect.
IAN:	Yeah. Well. I did. You know, once.
MARTIN:	You're sick.
IAN:	No … I mean I …
MARTIN:	Calm down Ian. I'm only joking.
IAN:	Right. OK. The thing is. If you look at it. Her hair. The way she is. She's younger. This picture is from a while ago.
MARTIN:	Must be.
IAN:	Poor Stella.
MARTIN:	What do you mean?
IAN:	Well. I feel sorry for her.
MARTIN:	Why?
IAN:	Just. Well not sorry for her but she looks so … in the picture. She's naked. She's … it's … Inevitably it's a sexual thing but …
MARTIN:	Inevitably.
IAN:	She's naked but the picture seems, I don't know – poignant.
MARTIN:	You mean sad?
IAN:	Yes … well no. She looks so happy.

It's such an intimate moment.
I found it moving.

MARTIN: I bet you did.

IAN: The caption says ...
'This lovely redhead is on fire with desire.
Her fantasy is to have sex with two men at the same time ...'
Then the editor has written in italics ...
'No shortage of volunteers. Ed.'
Of course they make those comments up but still ...
They shouldn't write that.

MARTIN: Why?

IAN: Well they shouldn't make stuff like that up.

MARTIN: They make the comments up?

IAN: I think so. Don't they?

MARTIN: I don't know Ian.
You seem to be the expert in this particular area.

4.

VERONICA: Where's Stella?

IAN: She's not here yet.

MARTIN: She'll be late. She always is.

VERONICA: I can't wait to see her. How long is it?
It's been absolutely years.
Ian.
Ian Ian Ian. Look at you!

IAN: How are you Veronica?

VERONICA: Me. OK. Yeah. I'm moving along.
It's so good to see you. We haven't talked!
You must have so much news.

MARTIN: Veronica's been in the country photographing birds.

VERONICA: I've been working.

IAN: Right.

VERONICA: I haven't spoken to another human being virtually for three days. I'm sort of all over the place.
You?

IAN: Me?

VERONICA: How are you? You look good. You're getting a bit of a belly.

IAN: Am I?

VERONICA: No. It's nice. I like it. Suits you. So what are you up to?
You working, or are you still…

IAN: I'm OK. Stuff coming up. You know.

VERONICA: Good. Martin don't do that.

MARTIN: What?

VERONICA: He fiddles with his hand.
Have you noticed that?
He does it when he's nervous.

IAN: I do it when I'm bored.

5.

_____

[Stella arrives.]

STELLA: Hello.
What?
What?
Do I look older or something?
I am older.
I'm entitled to look this way.
Besides I'm hungover.

So are we staying?
Or are we going?

[time break]

6.

————

IAN: There's a really brilliant film I saw where they do this.
What we're doing.
Ha ha.
Because you do. Don't you? People do.

STELLA: You're looking at me.

IAN: The whole film's just people looking at each other.
It's long.
You know, they don't know quite what to say.

VERONICA: We're looking at Stella because we've not seen her.

MARTIN: Stella's looking good.

VERONICA: And she's looking back at us. It's so normal Ian.

IAN: It's a very self-conscious film.
The camera focuses on really small things.
Like the ashtray.
Or a person's ring.

VERONICA: I'd like to see it.

STELLA: Sound's good.

MARTIN: Who's drinking? I'm buying.
There's a lager from the Slovak Republic they do.
You can't pronounce the fucker's name but it tastes all right.
Drink?

VERONICA: Mineral water for me please. Why don't you call the waitress over?

IAN: It is a good film. It's quite well known.

STELLA: I've given up going to films.
Actually I've given up art totally.
I read women's magazines instead.
You still smoking?

MARTIN: I had to give up.

VERONICA: He's been clean six months now.

IAN: I'm still trying, I'm trying but…
I think I'll stop next year.

STELLA: Is that what happens when you hit thirty?

IAN: What?

STELLA: You stop trying.

IAN: …

MARTIN: You're looking serene Stella. Money suits you.

7.

———

STELLA: I think I'm drinking too much. I'm getting a pain in my side. Where my kidneys are or liver or whatever else organ it might be. I'm getting hangovers recently like I've been beaten up. A couple of days ago I finished off a bottle of wine. Actually I do that a lot of times. Since my mum died especially. Did you not know that. Oh god. It was about a year ago. Don't worry I'm actually quite over it.

But anyway I usually drink a bottle of wine in front of the telly to help me sleep as much as anything else. And there was some left in the bottle, less than a glass. I wanted to drink it but I wouldn't let myself. I thought…if I drink that half glass then I must be an alcoholic. I will not drink that half glass. That half glass is a test. So I left it sitting there and went to bed. I felt quite good about myself as a matter of fact, and I had this dream…

I dreamt that I was standing in the middle of some destroyed landscape surrounded by broken trees and the sky's like totally black with rain waiting to pour down on me. And the rain mixes with the ash on the ground and makes black water and it's all over my face and I'm crying and it looks like I'm covered in running mascara. And my dress is black with ashes and I keep thinking I'll never ever get it clean. Not ever again.

Don't ask me what the dream means but it freaked me out like fuck. The next morning I was still shaking so I drank the half-glass for breakfast. I'm obviously on a downward spiral. Still. Like Ian said, I've got till I'm thirty before I really need to worry about it.

8.

IAN: This is just too ... isn't it?
Can you talk to her?
I mean, I can't talk to her.

MARTIN: Why?

IAN: The whole thing's distracting.

MARTIN: The picture?

IAN: Of course the picture. What else?
I'm talking to her but I'm seeing her naked.
Maybe we should say something.

MARTIN: People do things. Not everything's important Ian.
Calm down.
Most people would think this whole photograph incident
is completely insignificant.

IAN: I know but. She's been exposed ...

MARTIN: So exposure. What's wrong with exposure?
We all have exposure. It's just different levels.

9.

———

VERONICA: I brought pictures. I thought it'd be nice.
This is us.

…

This one's people you don't know.

…

This is us again. With that friend of yours from L.A.

…

I don't know what that one is.

…

This is one from the time we went to the beach.
I took it with a self-timer.
I had to run towards you over the stones in my bare feet.
That's why I'm looking flustered in the picture.

MARTIN: Look at the clothes.
If I could get away with that now.

STELLA: We look so happy.
How happy do we look?
It's sickening.

VERONICA: Look, you've got your arm around me.
We'd only just met.

STELLA: Fast work.

VERONICA: You must have fancied me even then.

IAN: This is the beach.
That beach we went to that one time.
When we had the fire?

VERONICA: The fire. Yeah.

IAN: I thought you … I thought that that was a different time.

VERONICA: No. It was that time. That's when he seduced me.
Didn't you Martin?

MARTIN: Sometime round then.

VERONICA: It was very romantic. In the moonlight.

IAN: Right. That must have been great.

STELLA: Look at that. I'm beautiful.
Why does nobody fancy me?
I fancy me. Looking at that.
Do you fancy me? Not now but then?
Was I pretty?

IAN: Yeah. You were. I mean are. You are still.

MARTIN: As a matter of fact you're very ugly.
But I'd shag you.

STELLA: I don't like photographs. I don't like looking at photographs.
There's always something you don't want captured.
Look at the way I smile. It's repulsive.

VERONICA: I think you're very photogenic Stella.

STELLA: If I got murdered. Which photograph would they use on the news? To sit behind
the newsreader's head?

IAN: They like to use snapshots.

VERONICA: That is absolutely sick.

IAN: They use a badly taken snapshot. It has to be badly taken because it shows that
even though you've been murdered, you were a real person. Just like a member of
the general public.

STELLA: They always use smiling photographs. People in swimming
costumes. Or people at Christmas.

IAN: Because it's poignant.

STELLA: When I see photos of me at Christmas I can't help but visualise my own death.

MARTIN: If you were murdered. Stella. I'm sure we could find a picture that would be
poignant. A snapshot for the press.

VERONICA: I don't understand why this one's so dark.
Maybe the flash wasn't working.

IAN: I like it that way. Can I keep it?

VERONICA:	Do you want it?
IAN:	I have a wall at home which is covered with pictures that never came out properly. It's a project.
MARTIN:	You could frame it. Veronica's an artist.
IAN:	Even pictures that don't come out capture something.
MARTIN:	If you framed it it would look like one of those gallery fuckers.
VERONICA:	It's just darkness. It would just look like a frame around nothing.

10.

_____

MARTIN:	Remember we had the fire and we hunted.
STELLA:	You hunted and …
MARTIN:	We tried to make a spear …
STELLA:	We tried to make a spear out of wood.
VERONICA:	The power station. This is when we went to the beach?
IAN:	When we had the bonfire.
MARTIN:	And we thought we'd try to catch some animal fucker and cook it.
STELLA:	You wanted to roast it or something.
MARTIN:	We never caught anything.
STELLA:	No.
IAN:	You were never going to catch anything.
STELLA:	I nearly hit a rabbit's skull. I nearly broke it open with a stone.
MARTIN:	Your face.
VERONICA:	I like rabbits.
STELLA:	I was like some Amazon queen or something.

MARTIN:	You attacking some rabbit fucker.
IAN:	It was a timeless event.
MARTIN:	It was fucking prehistoric.
STELLA:	You tried to organise us. You wanted to be leader.
IAN:	It was weird. It was like that thing where children go mental and form tribes.
MARTIN:	You have to be organised if you want to catch anything. That's why we evolved language. Over millions of years of time. Because if you want to catch a rabbit you have to be able to say … 'go over there, the fucker's running away.'
VERONICA:	It was pretty. The lights of the power station. Was it a nuclear power station?
IAN:	I think it was just an ordinary electrical power station.
MARTIN:	Those films you watch. The books you read. Even your fucking bird pictures. It's just a more sophisticated way of saying – 'go over there, the fucker's running away.'
STELLA:	I just remember it being so serene when the sun went down. It was dark, but we had the fire, an actual fire out of actual wood, so even the dark seemed OK.

11.

MARTIN:	You know, sometimes I think people look at me, and they see an easy guy, they see business, they see hardness. But what gets me is there's no understanding of, what would you call it? 'Cleverness' you know, or 'hard work', or just 'thinking.' So for example Carter asked me to go to Moldova. So at first I'm 'Carter – where the fuck, or what the fuck is Moldova when it's at home.' It's a gorgeous place as it happens. I mean it's ruined with concrete and the roads are totally to fuck but the company provide you with a jeep and a driver. We had this wee guy with a Michael Jackson 'Thriller in Bangkok' T-shirt. So I bought the fucker a beer. What I'm saying is my colleagues are looking for child prostitutes or they're steaming in the hotel sauna and I'm walking the streets with this guy, was actually

walking in the Moldovan streets. I talked to people in shops. I asked questions. I drank beer with other Moldovan guys. I asked them about their wives. I had insights. They said to me stuff like – 'Martin you're not like those other Western guys. You're a good guy.

'I declare you an honorary Moldovan.'

All I'm saying is – I loved Moldova. You should go if you get the chance. It's a very real place. I'm thinking of going back. The sense of history they have there. You don't get that in this country. I mean they had tram lines and willow trees on the street. Cafe's filled with smoke and people talking in a friendly way. This guy put his life on the line for me and I bought the fucker a beer. That's how it is over there.

12.

_____

[A long silence. People have run out of things to say.]

13.

_____

VERONICA: Why don't we do it again!
Why don't we have a picnic again!
We're only sitting here.
And we're all together.
A fire again! The beach we went to by the power station.
We could go just now.

MARTIN: We could…

STELLA: I suppose.

IAN: If people are into it then…

VERONICA: How long is it? Since any of us just relaxed.
Took our shoes off.
Am I being stupid?

You know just took a walk on a beach with some friends.

…

It's like the feeling of wanting to jump into a pool on a hot day.

IAN: Yeah.

MARTIN: Uh huh.

STELLA: It is quite hot isn't it.

VERONICA: This is a hot day. What I'm saying is there's too much smoke in here and too much, I can't even breathe, slumping around.

IAN: If people think beach we could get the car.

MARTIN: I'm waiting for a call. Carter said he was going to call me but why don't you three go.

STELLA: If you're waiting for a call we should …

VERONICA: Come on. How long is it since we did something we hadn't planned for. It would be good.
I mean it could rain but that's the point isn't it.
We don't know. Let's just …

IAN: I'm up for it.

STELLA: If everyone else is.

MARTIN: OK. Where do you want to go Veronica?

VERONICA: Why don't we go to the same place again.
The electrical power station.
We can get Indian food again from that shop.

STELLA: Does booze exist in this plan?

VERONICA: If we're going to do it we should do it now.

MARTIN: I'm waiting for a call.

VERONICA: If we go now the traffic won't be so bad.

IAN: We could go in your car.

STELLA: We wouldn't all fit.

VERONICA:	We could just squeeze in. Remember you sitting in my lap.
IAN:	Yeah.
VERONICA:	Singing that song … what was that song … you know …
IAN:	I don't remember.
VERONICA:	You remember Martin … you know the one I mean …
MARTIN:	Which one …
VERONICA:	How did it go …? doo doo doo doo doo doo doo doo …
IAN:	Oh yeah. I remember that one.
VERONICA:	How did it go? Martin sing it.
MARTIN:	I …
STELLA:	No sing it Martin.
MARTIN:	…
IAN:	doo doo doo doo doo doo doo doo.
MARTIN:	That's it. That's the one.
VERONICA:	I'm just saying. You could sit on my lap.
IAN:	Yeah.
MARTIN:	You could.
IAN:	I could go home and get some food if you want.
VERONICA:	We'll pick stuff up on the way. We were just driving and decided to have a picnic. We could get Asian food from that shop.
IAN:	We'd want nice stuff though.
VERONICA:	Forget all that. Let's just go now. If we don't go now we'll never go.
STELLA:	I need to sleep. I've got a long drive tomorrow.
VERONICA:	Just stay as long as you can then.

IAN:	All I'm saying is I could make a pasta salad.
	I've been making a lot of different types of salad recently.
VERONICA:	There's no time to do anything special.
	Last time we just went.
	That's what makes it so good.
STELLA:	It's just how will you all get home?
VERONICA:	In the car.
STELLA:	Only it's my car. So if I go…
MARTIN:	Maybe we should do it some other time.
STELLA:	I can plan around it. Maybe get a B and B.
IAN:	Or camping.
	I'd like that.
STELLA:	I don't know about camping.
MARTIN:	Whatever. It'd be good.
VERONICA:	Yeah. You're right.
MARTIN:	We really should do it.
STELLA:	Next time we're together.
IAN:	Yeah.
STELLA:	It's a pity but…
VERONICA:	You probably need better weather for it anyway.
	…
	Remember it was really beautiful when the sun went down.
	And the power station looked just wierd.
	And we had a bonfire and pakoras from the shop.

[time break]

14.

————

IAN: I'm working on a project. With some friends. Well, they're artists. Some of them are from America. It'll probably be shit you know. People are talking about New York but… I'm the… well it was really my idea.

It's all about… it's difficult to say what it's about. It's about – on one level it's about drowning. It's also about breath, and breathing, and the way that we have to breathe to live but on the other hand breathing is totally unconscious. But on another level it's just a story. About a man and a woman who have a thing about having sex in water. They're on a beach. A beach with stones. And the idea comes to them.

Only she's really afraid that she's going to have a prolapse, because the movement in the water can create a vacuum. I don't know if you knew that. So anyway he has to persuade her. But then these menacing children in swimming trunks come down to the beach and start taunting them, you know, calling them cunts…

And so obviously the guy gets really upset. He's really nervous because he can't defend the woman. And it's all getting ugly and out of hand. There's a bit where he fantasises about having a machine gun and taking out the suntanned little fuckers you know splattering the little fuckers' brains all over the stones, and rubbing their blood over his face till he looks like a fucking cannibal.

…and he's going 'I am the big guy!' 'I am the total big guy!' And then there's just like… silence… So eventually the woman takes her clothes off and walks into the sea and beckons him, you know 'Venus' and so they do it. They have sex in the water. And of course they drown. It's a ten minute thing.

15.

————

VERONICA: Why are you showing me this picture?

MARTIN: Because it's funny. The caption. Don't you think it's funny?

VERONICA: She's a friend Martin. Of course it's not funny.
Do you buy these type of magazines?

MARTIN: No.

VERONICA: So where did you get it?

MARTIN: Never mind that. The point is Stella must have sent it in.

VERONICA: I do mind. I didn't know you wanted to look at these things.

MARTIN: Ian gave it to me.

VERONICA: Ian did? I don't believe you.

MARTIN: I'm telling you he did. He buys that stuff. He's well into it.

VERONICA: Are you saying you want me to do this kind of thing?
               You want me to pose naked?
               Is that what you're telling me?

MARTIN: No. Why do you fancy it?

VERONICA: No.

MARTIN: I just thought it was good gossip.
               That's all.
               I thought you'd be interested.
               Don't take it so seriously.

16.

IAN: Have I said something. Veronica? I didn't… did I say something? You just seem.
               Are you annoyed about the picnic? We could go. You and me. Tomorrow even.

VERONICA: I'm fine.

IAN: Honest.

VERONICA: Honest.

17.

STELLA: So do you still fantasise about other women?

MARTIN: Yeah.

STELLA: I knew.

MARTIN: But I don't do anything. Not for a while anyway.

STELLA: Inevitably.

MARTIN: We're thinking of getting married?

STELLA: Congratulations.

MARTIN: Thank you.

STELLA: You're very lucky. You should be very happy.

MARTIN: Me happy. When?

STELLA: You have everything.
Look at me. I've got fuck all.

MARTIN: Yeah.

STELLA: I know you Martin.
This is not you.

MARTIN: Maybe.

STELLA: I know.

MARTIN: OK. All right. It's not me.

STELLA: As long as you're happy.

MARTIN: Happy. Not happy. It's all the same fucking thing.
...
What about you? How are you, Stella?

STELLA: You know. OK.

MARTIN: Really?

STELLA: Content. You know. Which is a start. Isn't it.

MARTIN:	Yeah.
STELLA:	You should come and visit sometime. I never see you.
MARTIN:	I'm busy. Too busy.
STELLA:	A weekend. Sometime.
MARTIN:	Yeah. Sometime.

18.

———————

IAN:	She's talking about drinking you know. And her mum dying. Did you know that? She never told me.
VERONICA:	Martin told me.
IAN:	I didn't know. And when she's telling us… I don't want to know that stuff. You know. Stop talking. You need to be a trained person to listen to that kind of stuff. Because she was… And I'm. Aaaah. No. You know. Feelings.
VERONICA:	Maybe she just wanted someone to talk to.
IAN:	I suppose.
VERONICA:	Sometimes that's all people want.
IAN:	Of course. I know.
VERONICA:	She's had a really low year. Those pictures of her. From the beach. She looks so young. She's still young.

But you know. She's reaching out.
You shouldn't be so...

IAN: God no. I'm joking. I mean obviously I didn't.
I mean I listened. You know. Christ.
I'm not that bad.
I just felt. Inside... stop talking.

VERONICA: She'll have sensed that.

IAN: I don't think so. I hope not.

VERONICA: People do.
People know more than you think.

IAN: Yeah. You're right.

VERONICA: You should really work on some of that fear.

IAN: Yeah.

VERONICA: You've got so much fear Ian. You really do.

IAN: Yeah.
(Mock startled.)
Ahhh!

VERONICA: You make it a joke Ian.
But that doesn't make it go away.
I know you too well.
I've known you too long.

IAN: I love you. I need you. We should get married.

VERONICA: Yeah.

IAN: No. We should.
Have an affair. Go to France.
Ha ha.
I tell jokes. It's this self-deprecation thing.
It's joking but...
Can I tell you something I've never told anyone.

VERONICA: Yes.

IAN: I'm actually in treatment for depression at the moment.
             I'm in treatment.
             So I'm fucked up officially now.
             I haven't told anyone because they'd only make something
             out of it.

VERONICA: People aren't like what you think Ian.
             People are much kinder inside than you think.

IAN: Yeah.

VERONICA: So you shouldn't only look at the surface.

IAN: Right.

             19.

             ─────────

MARTIN: So. Are we doing anything?
             We could go back to ours or …

STELLA: We could carry on.

MARTIN: We could get some wine and carry on at ours.

IAN: Whatever anyone else is doing. I don't mind.

MARTIN: C'mon. We'll get some drink.

VERONICA: Why don't you two get some drink.

STELLA: I don't mind going.

VERONICA: Martin'll go. He's got the money. Ian can help him carry.

MARTIN: Whatever.

IAN: Just whatever.

[time break]

20.

[Veronica is holding the picture of Stella.]

VERONICA: I hope I've done the right thing. Telling you about this. It's probably a shock isn't it? Martin said you must have sent the picture in yourself but I saw the way you're looking at the camera. I take pictures. It's the work I do. And I know when an image is… real. I know when something's happening and people know they're going to be looked at. They have a particular way of looking.

STELLA: Is it a nice picture, Veronica?

VERONICA: Nice?

STELLA: You're a photographer.

VERONICA: It's quite badly taken.

STELLA: But is it nice?

VERONICA: No. No. I don't think it's a nice picture.

STELLA: Describe it to me.

VERONICA: I don't think you want to know.

STELLA: Tell me what you see.

VERONICA: It'll upset you. I just thought you ought to know.

STELLA: I'm actually quite OK.

VERONICA: You might think that Stella, but maybe it hasn't hit home yet.

STELLA: No really. I'm quite OK. Describe it.

VERONICA: It's just a picture of you.
You're naked in it.
I'm sorry.

STELLA: Don't be sorry.

VERONICA: This must be an awful shock.

STELLA: My face. Does it have an expression?

VERONICA: What?

STELLA: In the picture. Am I smiling?

VERONICA: Yes.

STELLA: Does it look real? Does it look like a real smile?

VERONICA: No. I don't know … yes.

STELLA: My skin. What does my skin look like?

VERONICA: Nice.

STELLA: Does it look glowing? Are there tones of colour in it?
Or does it look dry and dead.

VERONICA: It looks nice.

STELLA: So where are we, Veronica?

VERONICA: How do you mean?

STELLA: The location. What's the location of the picture?

VERONICA: A bedroom. The curtain's are drawn.

STELLA: What kind of bedroom.

VERONICA: Just an ordinary bedroom.
Look maybe we should talk about this.

STELLA: We are talking about it.

VERONICA: I know but this is …

STELLA: Whose bedroom is it?

VERONICA: Anyones. I don't know.

STELLA: Is it a bedroom you recognise?

VERONICA: I don't know. It seems vaguely familiar.

STELLA: Vaguely.

VERONICA: You can see for yourself if you want.

STELLA: You look at it. You tell me. The sheets.

VERONICA: What about them?

STELLA: What colour?

VERONICA: It's hard to tell. I mean it's not lit well. The light's deceptive.

STELLA: Try.

VERONICA: Stella, maybe I shouldn't have told you about this.
This is the wrong moment. I didn't think of the emotional impact this would have.
We should go somewhere. You need time.

STELLA: I don't need time.
I remember that picture. Veronica.
I was smiling.
When that picture was taken.
Because I was lost in a very happy moment.
I hadn't planned for it, or expected it to happen, but it seemed perfect at the time.
Perfect that somebody should take a picture.
To preserve the moment.
Because I felt very beautiful at that moment Veronica.
And I don't feel that way very often.

…

Do you recognise the bedroom?

VERONICA: It's Martin's old bedroom.

STELLA: Yes.

VERONICA: Martin took this picture.

STELLA: You know, you shouldn't let things get to you so much Veronica. People do what they do and you can't affect it. Things break up don't they? Nothing lasts. You have to take what you can when you can and forget about the rest or else you just end up screaming outside in the snow and nobody likes people like that, do they?

VERONICA: When did he take the picture?

STELLA: Before.

VERONICA: I didn't know that.

STELLA: Of course you didn't.

VERONICA: Take it.

STELLA: You should keep it.

VERONICA: Take it back.

[Stella exits.]

STELLA: Why don't you have it?
As a memento.
A keepsake or something.

[Veronica alone.
Martin enters.
He looks at her, doesn't move.
She looks at him, doesn't move.]

ACT TWO: THE PAST

1.

————

[Ian alone.
Nervously smoking.
Arranging himself in the reflection.]

2.

————

[Stella arrives.
Catches sight of herself in the reflection.
She lights up a cigarette. Offers one to Ian.]

STELLA: Fuck I look savaged. I look pornographic. You all right? Fag.

IAN: I've just put one out.

STELLA: I mean for me.

IAN: Oh.

[He gives her a cigarette.]

STELLA: I love you. I need you. We should get married.
              Smile, Ian, the look on your face …
              I actually nearly feel sick so I shouldn't be smoking at all. My insides are
swimming with poisons. By rights I should be attached to some kind of a life-
support system. Girl takes lethal cocktail. Ban everything. By rights you should all
be praying for me to come out of some type of a coma, you know.
              So I went back to Martin's after the pub. Where did you get to anyway? Martin
had a bottle of rotten whiskey he'd stolen from a shop, and somebody else had
some type of grass only I thought it was more likely oregano or something but I

think it must have been grass because right now it feels like there's a small monkey trapped in my brain trying to stab its way out. So then the whole night just kind of went on until I was so completely fucking savaged I was virtually a vegetable and the only thing I can remember about how I got home is that birds were singing and it was cold. I'm still suffering. How are you?

IAN: OK. You know. Fine.

3.

————

[Martin arrives.
He looks at his reflection.]

MARTIN: All right?

IAN: Big night?

MARTIN: Big.
            Universal.
            Timeless.

IAN: Sounds like an event.

MARTIN: Stella was …

STELLA: I know I know. I'm beaming.
            How red is my face.

MARTIN: She was savaged. She was bloody.

STELLA: So were you.

MARTIN: I know nothing. Stella.
            I remember nothing.
            Where did you get to?

IAN: I left. I didn't see you. I …

STELLA: He's being serene or something.

MARTIN: He insists on being serene. It's inevitable.

IAN: No. I just. I felt tired.

MARTIN: Oh yes.

IAN: Truly.

MARTIN: Truly?

IAN: I'm sorry. I'm boring. I'm vacuous. I went home.

MARTIN: You got a fag?

STELLA: Here.

MARTIN: I love you. I need you. We should get married.
            So what are we doing?

STELLA: I don't know. Are we doing something?

IAN: I'm … there's a friend who I said …
            She said she might come along or something.

STELLA: A friend?

IAN: Yeah.

MARTIN: A friend who's a woman?

IAN: I suppose.

MARTIN: Is this some sort of sexual event you've got planned for tonight. Are we invading
            your space?

IAN: Oh god. Totally not. She's just a friend.

STELLA: Who?

IAN: Just a person.

STELLA: A person?

IAN: I don't think you know them.

STELLA: A new person?

MARTIN: Ian likes meeting new people.
            That's why he works in a shop.

IAN: She just said she might turn up. I don't know.

STELLA: OK. Don't mind me. Subject me to your person.
I'm only dying.
My skull's only cracked open.
My skin's only seeping out poisons
But I can cope.
Fuck. Sorry. I've got to get out of here.
I need privacy.

[Exit Stella in order to puke.]

MARTIN: I cannot live this way, Ian, I'm telling you.

IAN: Yeah. No.

MARTIN: These poor bones can't take the punishment.

IAN: Me neither.

MARTIN: I'm getting old. I feel so old. Truly.

IAN: I know how you feel.

MARTIN: Have you got any money, Ian?

IAN: I'm just in between cheques at the moment I'm sorry.

MARTIN: Leave it. Forget it. I shouldn't have asked.

IAN: No it's fine. It's just I don't…

MARTIN: Don't worry. It's understood.
The man has problems.
The man is walking hard roads.
It's understood.

IAN: Sorry.

MARTIN: Don't be sorry. Listen Ian. If you want… space with your friend.
I can divert the Stella you know.
Because a sexual event requires space. I understand the need for that.

IAN: No. God no. It's quite OK.

MARTIN: Do I look good. Ian. I feel good.
I don't mean healthy. I mean in a spiritual way.

I mean … fucking … all-conquering. All-consuming.
I feel good in a philosophical way.
Do you know what I mean.

IAN: I wish.

MARTIN: Truly universal Ian.

IAN: It's probably the after-effects of drugs.

[Stella returns.]

STELLA: How do I look? Do I look OK.
Am I pale?
Are my pupils OK …

MARTIN: You look all right Stella. You look good.

[Veronica arrives.]

IAN: Veronica! Over here!

VERONICA: Hello. Hi. Hi. Sorry am I late?

IAN: No. God no.

VERONICA: Only I got lost on the way and this guy I know stopped me to say hello and what
with one thing and … well … sorry anyway.

IAN: Eh … this is Veronica.

VERONICA: Hi.

IAN: This is Martin.

MARTIN: I think we've made contact before.

VERONICA: We have. We've seen each other around.

IAN: Eh …
Well Stella Veronica Veronica Stella.

STELLA: All right Veronica.

VERONICA: Hi.

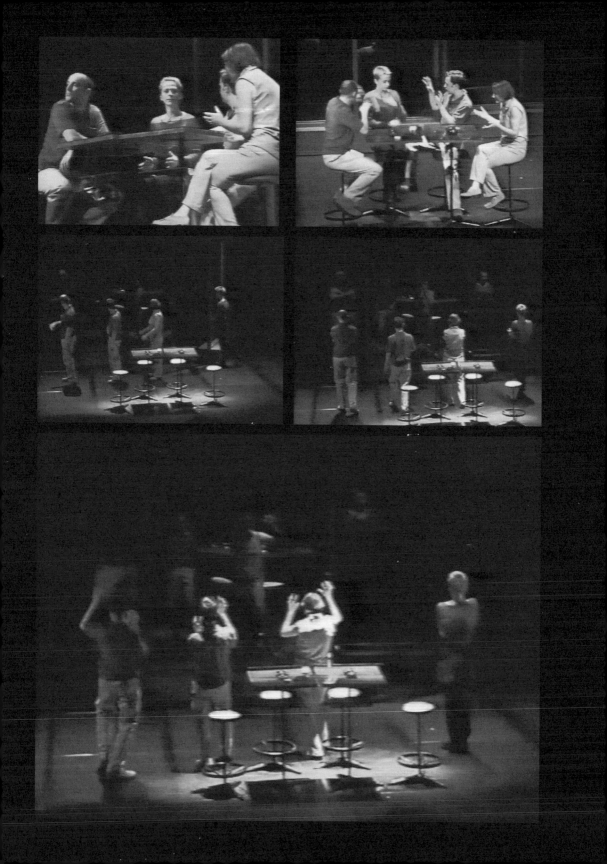

IAN: 'Hi. I'm Ian pleased to meet you…'
Ha ha.

STELLA: He's so inevitable.

VERONICA: So.
Does anybody want a drink or anything?

MARTIN: Vodka and coke for me. Cheers.
Do you smoke Veronica?
You wouldn't have a fag would you?

VERONICA: I'm sorry… I don't smoke.

MARTIN: It's quite all right. Don't apologise.

[Veronica leaves.]

STELLA: Veronica.

IAN: Yeah.

MARTIN: As in Veronique.

IAN: Right. She's OK actually.

MARTIN: As in Ronnie…

STELLA: So why's she here?

IAN: Last night we… so I suggested you know…
She said she'd be around so…I was meeting you so…

MARTIN: Did you fuck her last night?

IAN: No.

MARTIN: Did you really try?

IAN: It wasn't like that.

MARTIN: You're so inevitable Ian.

STELLA: So you were with her last night?

IAN: We watched a video. We just sat on the sofa. No sexuality.
It was very serene.

STELLA: I thought we didn't like her.

IAN: She's all right.

STELLA: I thought she was combat trousers.
I thought she hung about with the girl's brigade.
I thought she was supposed to be vacuous.

MARTIN: She's all right.

IAN: We got talking. About films as a matter of fact.

STELLA: Inevitably.

IAN: She said some interesting things.

STELLA: She's a film buff.

IAN: As a matter of fact not. She has quite fresh ideas.
She has quite a lot of insight I think.

MARTIN: Insight. Fresh ideas. It's pornographic. Listen has anybody got any cash. I've got cash coming on Tuesday but I'm at the end of my tether. If anyone could lend us a couple of quid or something. Just for fags. Because I can't stand asking.

[time break]

4.

———

IAN: I was saying to Veronica, we were talking about exactly this and I was saying 'There's just so much that is truly bullshit about stuff.' You know. And it weighs you down. It presses you down. That's all I was saying. I mean, just as a for instance, you're supposed to train, or something before you can do something. I mean did so and so train? Did the guy who did the thing about death and chess… did he do a training course. Was he qualified? Of course not. So much so because he was making art. He was following a … a … I don't know need or instinct or something. All-conquering. All-consuming. He wasn't pressed down. You know. So these courses they keep demanding of me are vacuous in the extreme. I want to say. I want to just go up to these people. I sometimes think I should go up to one of these so-called people and say 'You can't be trained to suffer. You can't be trained to have thought. Excuse me but I train by being alive. By simply surviving. Life is my course. OK.'

That's pretty much what I said. Isn't it?

VERONICA: Yeah. Something like that anyway.

5.

———

[Stella and Martin.]

STELLA: We're not... are we OK?

MARTIN: What?

STELLA: After last night. After...

MARTIN: We're OK.

STELLA: Truly?

MARTIN: What?

STELLA: I just don't want... I mean OK so we do something which...
We did do something.
It's important to me that it's not important. You know what
I mean.

MARTIN: Right. OK. It's so much not important.

STELLA: Because I was happy. I was... and you were...

MARTIN: Don't worry about it.

STELLA: I was lost, really happy, Martin. Seriously.

MARTIN: Seriously.

STELLA: But not because I love you.
Don't think that.
I'm not coming after you.

MARTIN: Of course. Me neither.

STELLA: We're friends.

MARTIN: Look. That's the purpose of a friend, isn't it? To make each other happy.

STELLA: So we're OK?

MARTIN: We are serene.

STELLA: Are we going to …?

MARTIN: What?

STELLA: No. It doesn't matter. Forget it.

MARTIN: No say.

STELLA: It's fine.

MARTIN: OK.

STELLA: I'm just thinking …
            We could do it again?

MARTIN: Again?

STELLA: Only for a laugh …

MARTIN: Inevitably.

STELLA: We maybe shouldn't though. Should we?

MARTIN: No. Maybe not.

STELLA: It's just easier isn't it?

MARTIN: Yeah. It's easier.

STELLA: No. I mean with us. The whole sexuality thing. It's easier than … with other people. Easier than going through the whole ugly/beautiful thing. You know?

MARTIN: Truly.

STELLA: No guessing. No disgust.

MARTIN: Do you want to again?

STELLA: No.
            I mean.
            No.

MARTIN:	Yeah. It's a shame but. Just one time. One universal memory and then leave it.
STELLA:	Yeah.
MARTIN:	Still. You were …
STELLA:	We're so much bad for each other, Martin.
MARTIN:	We're good for each other.
STELLA:	Good. Yeah. The two of us.
MARTIN:	We save each other from ending up vacuous or something.
STELLA:	I was savaged.
MARTIN:	It was good though.
STELLA:	It was. Wasn't it?
MARTIN:	Timeless. It was timeless.

6.

———

[Veronica and Ian.]

VERONICA:	I've seen them about but I've never talked.
IAN:	They're OK.
VERONICA:	Are they together?
IAN:	No. No way. They just …
VERONICA:	They seem like they're together.
IAN:	No.
VERONICA:	Martin's a funny guy isn't he?
IAN:	He can be yeah.
VERONICA:	He's got a kind of something about him … the way he speaks even.
IAN:	Yeah.

VERONICA: It seems like it's addictive.
You're really lucky to be all together.

IAN: We're just. I don't know. We just sort of. Ended up like this.

VERONICA: And Stella.

IAN: She's actually OK. You know. You have to sort of get to know her.

VERONICA: It's good that a man and a woman can be friends.
It's more interesting than lovers don't you think. More intense.

IAN: Yeah. Quite intense.
That's kind of what we're like.

VERONICA: You should make a film about it.

IAN: Do you think so?

VERONICA: Yeah. You should.

IAN: I've been thinking about it but…

VERONICA: Don't think about it. Just do it.

IAN: I should.

VERONICA: I think that's what you have to do.

IAN: I'm too. I get very… I don't know I'm too introverted or something.

VERONICA: I don't think you're introverted. I think you hold back.

IAN: Yeah. Inevitably. Probably.

VERONICA: I think you're keeping things to yourself, Ian. I think you're
waiting for the right time.

IAN: So much so.

VERONICA: I think you'll make your moves when the time's right.
I get that sense from you.

IAN: You're so much right. You really get that sense from me?

VERONICA: I promise you.

IAN: I love you. I need you. We should get married?

VERONICA: What?

IAN: You know. We should get married. It's a sort of joke or something. We say it sometimes.

7.

————

MARTIN: You get older. Inevitably. So when are you supposed to stop? There's so many drinks I haven't tasted. So many women, never mind men. Never mind different varieties of women I have yet to make contact with, you know or something. Time passes. Things change. You do what you do and you take what you can and good luck to you. But I'm not there. I'm somewhere else. I'm taking a different road or something. I hate this idea that you're supposed to stop or switch off. Fuck that. Serene and vacuous like what? Like a fucking field of grass or something. Is that what I'm supposed to be? I'm taking a different road. I envision myself walking into the fire. I envision that guy whose arms and legs have been amputated with disease but he still asks the nurse to stuff a lit fag in his mouth or something. He can't breathe and his heart's jumping back and forth but he still asks the nurse to do something pornographic. That's living. That's a timeless image.

STELLA: Never stopping.

IAN: Just going on.

8.

————

STELLA: So are we doing anything?

MARTIN: I don't know.

STELLA: We've got a whole night to play with.

IAN: Veronica. You said you were …

VERONICA: I was thinking … Well.

STELLA: What.

VERONICA:	You probably wouldn't be …
STELLA:	Say. You can't not say.
IAN:	She can.
VERONICA:	It's all right. I was thinking it's a beautiful evening. It's warm. I was thinking of going to the country. But I was just going to go. I mean … if you want to come. I was going anyway.
MARTIN:	In a car.
VERONICA:	If there's a car.
IAN:	I could get my car.
STELLA:	The country. Why?
VERONICA:	No reason. I just … sometimes go up to the beach. Just to relax. To calm down.
STELLA:	The beach.
MARTIN:	I don't think I've been to the country ever.
STELLA:	Not willingly. I've been through the country, inevitably, but not actually in it.
MARTIN:	Except that time we went to look for magic mushrooms.
STELLA:	That was beside a motorway.
IAN:	I'd like to come. If it's all right.
VERONICA:	Fine.
MARTIN:	It's night, Veronica. This excursion … do you have a tent or something.
VERONICA:	We could make a fire.
MARTIN:	An actual fire?
STELLA:	With actual wood?
VERONICA:	Yeah. Just sit by the fire. It's …

IAN: People can do that?
Is it legal?

VERONICA: It's just a beach.
Only if people want to.

STELLA: This fire. This night time thing ... I'm right that you've done this before?

VERONICA: A few times.

STELLA: On your own?

VERONICA: Yeah. Sometimes. Sometimes with friends.

MARTIN: Total serenity.

VERONICA: I watch birds.

STELLA: At night? Darkness birds?

VERONICA: At dawn.
I take photographs of them.

IAN: Really?

VERONICA: Yes.

MARTIN: That is almost pornographically serene.

STELLA: I'm not convinced.

VERONICA: I've always done it. My brother used to take me and now I do it myself. It's just a thing I do.

STELLA: Birdwatching.
Do you know the names of the birds?
Like 'wader' and 'puffin' and that kind of thing?

VERONICA: You don't have to come. I'm just saying.

IAN: I want to come.

[time break]

9.

———————

STELLA: So there's the day, and you see people and you talk to people or something and you do your work or whatever you do and all the time you're thinking 'I'm stuck in this,' you know? 'Am I stuck in this?' And then there's the night and you either watch telly or you drink or maybe you fuck somebody. And it's 'I'm definitely stuck in this.' Do you know what I mean? You're stuck in your own body. Your own life. Whatever you've done or not done. You can't even run away. You know? So the only thing I think when I look at that situation is I imagine owning some kind of a car and just getting into it and driving off to the furthest place away I can think of. Like fucking Russia or fucking Alaska and my skin's going to crack open like one of those snakes or lizards or something and a new Stella's going to slide out of my skin and fall onto the snow.

VERONICA: You think that way? God.

MARTIN: Only when she's hungover.

VERONICA: No. I think that's amazing. I get that exact same thing.

10.

———————

MARTIN: Your hair Veronica.

VERONICA: What about it?

STELLA: It's dyed. Isn't it?

MARTIN: I like it.

VERONICA: I just…

STELLA: Is it dyed?

VERONICA: Yeah.

STELLA: Right.

IAN: It looks great. Maybe I should do it…
Ha ha.

VERONICA: I just did it myself. I just…

IAN: You did that yourself. That's … wow.

STELLA: I wish I could get away with that look.

MARTIN: It's a …transformative look.

IAN: Yeah.

MARTIN: Because it's saying… this could change any minute.

IAN: Yeah. Exactly.

MARTIN: One day it's this, the next it's different. It says 'temporary'. It's good.

VERONICA: Oh it's just. Something you know. I don't even really think about it.

MARTIN: Exactly. That's what it says. It says you're above style.

VERONICA: Maybe I should have … does it look messy or something.

IAN: God no.

MARTIN: Don't touch it. It's perfect.

STELLA: I'm thinking of a change. I'm thinking maybe, I'll go blonde.

MARTIN: No. Blonde's not you. You're red. Red's who you are.

STELLA: Just for a change. Maybe sometime.

VERONICA: I think you'd look stunning Stella. If you went blonde.

STELLA: Maybe.

VERONICA: No you would. You really would.

11.

————————

MARTIN: Trust me. She wants to make physical contact with you.

IAN: I don't know. I hope so.

MARTIN: The signs are there.

IAN:	You think so.
MARTIN:	Truly.
IAN:	I don't know. She …
MARTIN:	You want her.
IAN:	No. But. You know. I'm … Yes.
MARTIN:	She looks good. Don't be embarrassed.
IAN:	You think she's vacuous.
MARTIN:	No. Would I lie to you?
IAN:	OK.
MARTIN:	If we do this birdwatching or something. This fire at night thing she's into. That is the moment. Serene. Romantico. Al fresco. So …
IAN:	I should get my car.
MARTIN:	Get your car. Then at some point. You know when the night gets cold. You say, 'are you cold?' and she says … yes I am. And you say. 'Here, take my jacket.'
IAN:	No way. That's so overblown.
MARTIN:	Overblown is what does it with a girl like that. Truly. So you drape the jacket over her shoulders. Both of you look into the fire. You're in some distant place. You're considering the depths of life in the flames and then you shiver. As if you've had a chilling intimation of death or something.
IAN:	Inevitably.
MARTIN:	And she says … 'now you're cold.' And you say … 'no, I'm OK.' And you hold yourself, because now you are

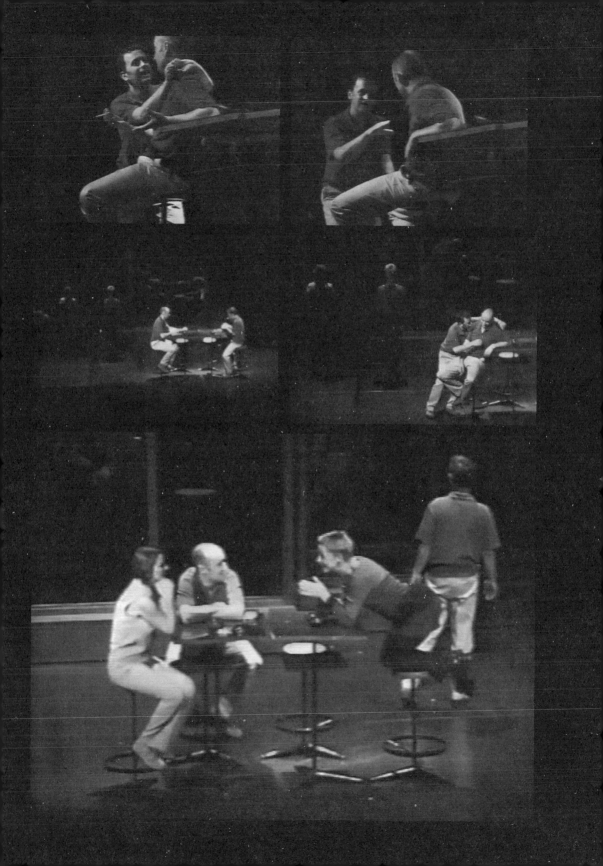

	cold. And she say's 'let's share the jacket.' And you huddle up together.
IAN:	I can't huddle. I get nervous.
MARTIN:	This is so easy. This is just so easy Ian. When the sun goes down, you huddle up and you say… 'Baby, I wish I could sing.'
IAN:	Why do I say that?
MARTIN:	Because… You say 'because Baby, the things I feel about you just now. You can't put them in ordinary words. But I'm thinking maybe… just maybe… if I could sing then I could find the right words for the things that are in me now…

[Martin sings.]

> Blah blah blah blah blah blah…

[Pause.]

> She doesn't speak. She's choked up. She can't speak.
> And then, that is the moment, you look into the fire and you say
> 'Veronica. I hope you don't mind me saying this,
> but I would very much like to fuck you.'

IAN:	You say what?
MARTIN:	That's what you say.
IAN:	I could so much not say that. I will go to my grave an old man and I will not have said that. That's how much it's not going to be said.

12.

———————

VERONICA:	The beach has stones. It's not so much sand as small stones. And there's some woodland. It's just a place you can breathe. I can never breathe in the city, you

know, after a while my lungs feel like they're collapsing. But on the beach you can breathe. I think it's because the air comes off the sea. So it's sharp, you know, it cuts away the dirt from inside you.

We can get food on the way there's a shop that sells Asian food. It's run by a terrifically happy man and his wife and children. He always tells me a joke and describes which food is best for which occasion. And there's a nuclear power station or something nearby so you can see the lights it's very beautiful even though it's, you know, manufacturing poison. Then we can smoke some stuff and drink a few beers and talk and then when the dawn comes we can watch the birds. I've seen them take fish out of the sea.

I've done it loads of times with loads of different people and it's always… people always talk about it. People find it emotional. It's a guaranteed emotion.

13.

STELLA: So you're thinking you're in love with her.

IAN: I think I might be. Truly.

STELLA: I know you too well. You're too visible.
I can't see the attraction. But then…
You obviously can.

IAN: She's not what I thought. She's…

STELLA: She's new. You're a man.

IAN: She's different. Her attitude is…

STELLA: So she talks about nature. She's a nature girl.
See through it Ian.

IAN: This thing she has about watching birds. I'm so jealous of that.

STELLA: It's a pose.

IAN: It's such a pure thing. Her brother took her to watch birds at dawn. I've never had a thing like that. A thing I do. I've never
had a memory of something natural like that. Something not

to do with sex or drink or cruelty. She takes photographs of birds. That's the most attractive thing I think I've ever heard.

STELLA: Men are so inevitable.

14.

VERONICA: So are we going because … if we're going to go we should go now.

IAN: I'm coming.
Is there anything we need?
Maybe someone should bring a camera?

VERONICA: I've got a camera.

STELLA: Are we going to get booze?

VERONICA: We can get it on the way. But we should go.

STELLA: OK. So …

MARTIN: Yeah well. Why not.

IAN: Something different.

MARTIN: An event.

IAN: Yeah.

STELLA: OK. So are we going in your car.

VERONICA: If that's all right.

IAN: It's good. It's fine.

MARTIN: So you'd better get your car.

IAN: Yeah.
What? Now?

STELLA: Veronica says we need to go now so …

IAN: Right.

MARTIN: Veronica, why don't you go with Ian.
           You can keep him company.
           We'll wait here for you.

IAN: Would you mind?

VERONICA: No. It's OK.

IAN: Right. OK. We're all set.
           I'm really looking forward to it.
           Something to look back on. You know?

15.

———————

[Martin is holding a photograph.]

STELLA: Let me see it.

MARTIN: You look truly good, Stella.

STELLA: Do you think I look OK?

MARTIN: You look on fire.

STELLA: My skin looks like it's glowing.

MARTIN: Yeah.

STELLA: That's cos I'm happy.

MARTIN: I just thought you'd probably want it.

STELLA: Do you not want it?

MARTIN: You should have it.

STELLA: We're so bad for each other.
           We're such bad influences. Aren't we?

MARTIN: Yeah.

STELLA: Taking a picture. Doing a thing like that and taking a picture.
           What were we thinking of. I'm beaming.

MARTIN: Don't. You shouldn't be embarrassed. I imagine myself being old and looking at that picture and thinking 'fuck yes.' You know. I was there. I did that. With that woman. And she was my friend. 'Fuck yes.' It's worthwhile to have been alive. Obviously I'm exaggerating but you know.

STELLA: Yeah. I know.

MARTIN: Are you OK Stella?

STELLA: I'm OK. Yeah.

MARTIN: Really?

STELLA: Truly.

MARTIN: So are we going to do this beach thing or something.

STELLA: Why not? Ian wants to fuck her. It's too poignant to keep them apart.

MARTIN: Exactly.

STELLA: She's vacuous but she seems OK.

MARTIN: She seems OK.

STELLA: We'd better go.

MARTIN: They'll be waiting in the car.

STELLA: Wait. Martin.

[She turns him to face his reflection in the window. They both look at their reflections together.]

MARTIN: What are you doing?

STELLA: I just want to look at us.

MARTIN: Why?

STELLA: So I can remember everything.

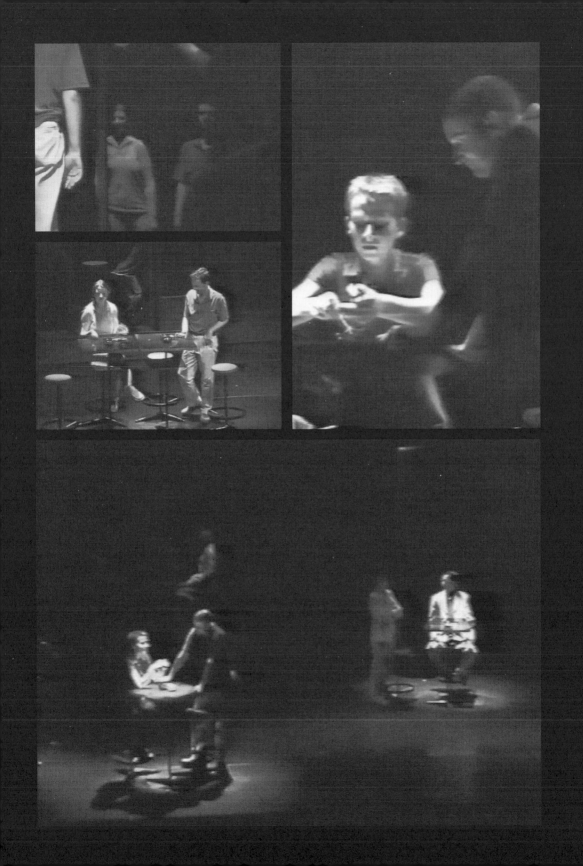

ACT 3: THE FUTURE

[Lines in brackets are spoken thoughts.
Lines in italics are sung.]

I.

———

[Martin and Stella are sitting.
Ian is standing looking at his reflection.]

IAN: Yeah. Good.
                Bit of this. Bit of that.
                Busy.
                I'm actually doing…
                I'm involved in a…

[He turns to them.]

                I'm part of a project with some people in London.

MARTIN: That's great Ian. Terrific news.

IAN: New York people. People from New York.
                L.A. people, who're based in New York.

STELLA: It sounds good.

IAN: But they've come over to London and they're staying in extremely lavish hotels.
                So yeah. You know.
                I'm serene.
                I've made contact.
                You know me…
                (Very casual, remarkably casual.)
                Beer?

MARTIN: Cheers Ian. I can't…

IAN: I'll pay.
               Can I get you a beer?
               Maybe we're in France.
               Un bière, s'il vous plait!
               England
               Snifter for you?

STELLA: Thank you.

[He returns to his reflection.]

IAN: Because baby, let me tell you. I need a drink.
               I feel like my throat's on fire.
               Jesus. I'm about to cut my throat here.

[He turns back to them. Martin stands up.]

MARTIN: Ian. Good to see you.

IAN: Marty. Marty baby.
               You're looking good like I knew you would.
               Take a seat.
               (Let me see your dead face.)

[Martin sits down.
Ian sits down.]

IAN: Busy?

MARTIN: No.

IAN: Shame.
               I've got a job as it happens.

MARTIN: What doing?

IAN: Doing what I want to do.
               Which is projects. (Mainly.)
               I spend my life in jet aeroplanes.
               UK LA NYC OK?
               Jesus I hate Heathrow.
               Beer?

MARTIN: Cheers.

IAN: Un bière, s'il vous plait.
               Where's Veronica?

[He returns to his reflection.]

               I want to buy Veronica a beer.
               I want Veronica.
               Because I'm about to cut my throat here as a matter of fact.

[Veronica enters.
He turns from his reflection.]

IAN: Veronica!
               Veronica as in Veronique.
               Ronnie.
               Ronnie baby.
               My Ronnie.
               My very own special Ronster.
               Veronica…
               I hope you don't mind me saying this.
               Casually.
               But I would very much like to fu…
               I would very much like to fuh…
               Fuh.

[Martin laughs.
Ian turns to his reflection.]

IAN: Jesus I hate Heathrow.

VERONICA: Ian Ian Ian Ian Ian.
               Good to see you.
               How are you?
               We haven't talked.
               What are you up to these days?

IAN: I'm part of a project as it happens.
               So…travelling.
               (Eyes.)

VERONICA: Ian, you have such sad eyes.
I've never noticed that before.
But I just did. Just now.

IAN: You know they did a profile on me in the paper where they said exactly the same thing.
They said my wife…
(You're my wife.)

VERONICA: How was LA.

IAN: I don't want to talk about LA.

VERONICA: I've missed you Ian.
Ian when you're away travelling I feel… split apart… the way…

IAN: (Freezing water splits rock on a mountainside.)

VERONICA: Freezing water…

IAN: (Cry.)

[Veronica cries quietly.]

IAN: Did you get my letter?

VERONICA: It was beautiful Ian.

[Martin laughs.
Ian turns towards his reflection.]

VERONICA: Ian has such sad eyes. Have you noticed that?
He writes to me, you know, when we're split apart.
The way freezing water splits rock on a mountainside.
He writes me tender letters from LA.
He's working on a project.

[Ian turns towards them.]

ALL: Tell us more. Ian. Tell us more about your project Ian.

VERONICA: What's it about?

Ian: It's about
It's hard to say what it's about.

[They turn away from him, to their own reflections.
He tries to hold on to them.]

> (What's it trying to say.)
> That's hard to say.
> It's a ten minute thing.
> Actually it's more of a feature length thing.
> It's about…
> A man and a woman who…
> A man and a woman who…

[He turns to his reflection.]

2.

――――――――

[They are all sitting together.
Stella enters.
Walks straight towards Martin.
Starts to hit him.
As she hits him she speaks full of fury.]

STELLA: What?
What?
Do I look older or something?
What did you say?

MARTIN: Sorry.

STELLA: I am older.
I'm entitled to look this way.
What did you say?

MARTIN: I'm sorry.
I'm sorry.
I'm sorry.
Stella.

[*She stops hitting him.*
She goes to her reflection.
She turns out again.
She sits down.
Martin turns towards her.]

MARTIN: How are you Stella?
Are you OK?

STELLA: I'm fine Martin.
I don't have anything to say to you…

…

(I'm actually quite emotional.)

MARTIN: Are you OK?

STELLA: Sit down.

[*Stella sits.*]

MARTIN: How are you Stella?

STELLA: Oh, you know. Happy.
Not happy.
But content to be unhappy which is…
A start, Martin, which is a new departure for me.

MARTIN: Stella. I saw the picture.

STELLA: You saw it?

MARTIN: It reminded me of you.
As a matter of fact you're very ugly.
But I'd shag you.

STELLA: What did you say?

MARTIN: Stella. How are you? Are you OK?

STELLA: I'm fine Martin. Happy.

MARTIN: You're not. Stella. Are you? You're not really happy.

STELLA: No Martin. I'm not.
(I'm actually quite emotional.)

Actually my skin has cracked open and pure
fucking emotion's oozing out of me.
Which is a start.
Which is a new departure for me.

MARTIN: So are you fucking happy now?

[Stella turns to her reflection.]

Are you happy now you fucking alcoholic wilderness?
Because it's about fucking time you got sorted out?
Isn't it.
Because who'd have you?
Who'd have you?

[Stella turns back to them.]

STELLA: Did I tell you I sent a pornographic picture of myself to a men's
magazine?

IAN: I saw that.

VERONICA: I saw that as well.

STELLA: Did you fancy me in it?

IAN: Very much so.

VERONICA: You looked good in it.

STELLA: I was naked, Martin took it.
(That's why it was badly taken.)

VERONICA: You looked beautiful in that picture Stella.
You looked gorgeous.

STELLA: I don't normally look good in pictures.
Normally I'm repulsed by my own reflection.
But in these pictures I looked good.
I looked reborn.

MARTIN: How are you Stella?
How are you really?

STELLA: I'm in fucking Siberia Martin.
I'm in fucking Alaska.
To tell you the truth, Martin, I'm alone in the wilderness
and I can't hear my own screaming over the sound
of the wind.

MARTIN: I'm sorry.

STELLA: That ugly body you gave me. Martin.

MARTIN: I remembered you from the picture and I was sorry.
Stella I was sorry.

STELLA: That ugly grief.
The look on your face can't reach me now.

[They turn away.
She tries to get them back.]

I've spent far too long in that particular wilderness.
I've thrown that particular hope onto the fire.
Because it's too late.
The moment's passed.
I'm lying born on the snow in a pool of my own mess.
So you might as well save your breath.

[She is looking at her reflection.]

3.

[Martin enters.
Veronica sits apart.
Martin lights a cigarette.]

MARTIN: Cry.

[She cries quietly.
He reaches out his hand.
He withdraws it.]

MARTIN: Don't cry.
               Please don't cry Veronica.
               I'm here now.
               You don't have to cry.
               You can stop.
               (I reach out my hand, with a kind of infinite slowness,
               And say the perfect thing)

[He reaches out his hand.]

MARTIN: Blah blah blah blah blah blah.

[Veronica laughs and sniffs.
She looks at him.
She looks away.
She starts to cry quietly.
He sits near Veronica.
Veronica is crying quietly.]

MARTIN: Don't cry. Veronica.
               Don't cry because …
               Don't cry Veronica because …

[Stella turns from her reflection.
She sits crying quietly.
He looks at her.]

               Don't cry Stella.
               Please don't cry because …

[Martin reaches his hand towards Stella.]

MARTIN: Blah blah blah blah blah blah.

[Stella laughs and sniffs.
She cries quietly.
He reaches his hand towards Veronica.]

MARTIN: Blah blah blah blah blah blah.

[Veronica laughs and sniffs.
She cries quietly.]

[Ian enters. Martin goes to him.]

MARTIN: So what the fuck am I supposed to say?

IAN: She's crying?

[Veronica cries quietly.]

MARTIN: She's crying on her own in some dark place.

[Stella leaves.]

IAN: What the fuck are you supposed to say to that?

MARTIN: Exactly.
                   You arrive and you say...
                   Don't cry.
                   Because now that you're here she doesn't need to cry any more. You light a
                   cigarette.

IAN: I thought you'd given up.

MARTIN: You can't. You have to smoke for this.

IAN: Of course you have to smoke.
                   Fucksake. Who told you not to smoke.
                   You have to smoke because...

[Martin turns to his reflection.]

MARTIN: Because...
                   The smoke winds. It winds round your bodies.
                   And you...
                   (My touch is able to transmit comfort.)
                   So you...
                   The smoke's winding and...

[Veronica is crying quietly.
Martin reaches out his hand.]

IAN: Why is she crying?

[Martin withdraws his hand.]

MARTIN: She's crying because of the reasons women cry.

IAN: She's crying because of cruelty.

MARTIN: Exactamundo.
            She's crying because without ever meaning it I've been
            unthinkingly cruel to her.

IAN: Unthinking?
            What the fuck are you supposed to do about that?
            Jesus.

MARTIN: The smoke winds and … (my touch can transmit love as well.)

[Martin reaches out his hand to Veronica.]

MARTIN: Blah blah blah blah blah blah.

[Veronica laughs and sniffs.]

VERONICA: It's all right Martin. It's all right.

[She cries again.]

IAN: It's poignant. Martin.
            Her look is poignant.
            It's such an intimate moment.

[Ian gets up, walks over to Stella.]

MARTIN: We observe the smoke from my cigarette winding …
            My touch … (comfort.)
            It's dark. So her face is reflected in the window pane.
            (Go back.)
            Stop crying.

[They stop crying.]

            So OK. I arrive like a ghost.
            Smoke winds.
            Touch – comfort.
            It's dark so her face is reflected in the window pane.
            Her look is poignant.
            She's telling me she's accepted things.
            She says my hand, which she had noticed on her shoulder is the hand of …

IAN: The hand of a man who has walked these hard roads alone.

MARTIN: Exactly.
             (I should really phone Ian.)
             And I say…
             Yes.
             That's so true.
             You know me too well baby.
             My eyes.
             (She looks into them knowingly.)

[Veronica does so.
Martin reaches out his hands for both women.]

             These eyes have seen things it's not given every one to see.
             I've seen things that aren't pretty like a woman.
             I've seen things that aren't as pretty as you are baby.

[They laugh and sniff.
They cry again.]

MARTIN: The crying goes on.

IAN: It's fucking non-stop.

[Stella, Ian Veronica look away.
Martin tries to regain them.]

MARTIN: It's fucking non-stop tears with me baby.
             That's what you signed up for when you bought the package.
             So no dice baby. OK.

[Martin looks at his reflection.
He reaches out his hand.]

             Blah blah blah blah blah blah.

4.

[Veronica is outside the cafe. Looking at them through the window.]

VERONICA: I feel easy. That's the only word for it.
            My lungs feel full and my breathing feels easy.

[Martin and Ian enter together, happily. They go over and stand in conversation at Stella's table. Veronica stands but does not move.]

VERONICA: This is the moment when I see everyone.
            This is the moment when I glide across the floor as easily
            as a bird rising off water.
            This is the moment when I kiss them.
            This is not a jumping on tables situation.
            This is not a blushing moment.
            My voice is not high and crackly.
            This is just a chance to be together with some friends.
            So this is the moment when I go forward…

STELLA: She's a right fucking nippy bitch Veronica. Isn't she?

MARTIN: Tell me about it.

IAN: She's a right nippy high-pitched hysterical bitch.

STELLA: Tell me about it.

MARTIN: She talks about nothing. Nothing. All the time.
            It's like her lungs are half empty and she's got to fill them with
            some kind of hysterical high-pitched nippy gas.

VERONICA: (I'm looking through the window and they're laughing.)

[They laugh, happily.]

            This is the moment just before I open the door.
            I can breathe.
            I'm breathing normally.
            And there's no question that I feel easy.

MARTIN: She's a right fucking nippy…

STELLA: High-pitched…

IAN: Shrieking hysterical…

VERONICA: (Not today.)

[They laugh, happily.]

My voice is not high. My voice is not crackly.
Today God has reached down and pulled all the stupid words from my throat.
He's taken them to the beach we went to that one time.
And he's thrown them on that fire.
So this is the moment when I open the door.
And I feel easy.
This is the moment when I say.
This is the moment when I turn and say…
Hello.

ALL: Hello Veronica.

VERONICA: Hello.
I don't blush now.
I don't feel need.
Their faces are turned towards me and I glide across the floor
towards them as easy as a bird rising off the sea…

STELLA: Can you believe the fucking cheek of the bitch.

VERONICA: (Not today.
Not today please.)
Hello.

ALL: Hello Veronica.

VERONICA: We're all together.

ALL: Yes Veronica. We've all come together.

VERONICA: For a reunion?

ALL: For one last reunion Veronica.

VERONICA: It's a surprise. It's a surprise for me?

IAN: We arranged it behind your back Veronica.

MARTIN: We didn't let on.

STELLA: All that time you thought we thought you had a high and crackly
            voice.

IAN: All that time you wanted to be found dead by the side of a B
            road in the country.

ALL: We were planning this surprise.

VERONICA: And I had absolutely no idea that anything was going on.
            You were doing this for me.

STELLA: Out of friendship Veronica.

IAN: Because we love you like our favourite sister.

MARTIN: Because we only stay with you out of pity Veronica.

[They turn away.
Veronica looks at her reflection.]

5.

———————

STELLA: I walk into the place and … and see him … and
            I look at my face in the window and… Fuck I look reborn.
            I'm lying born on the snow in Russia, born on the snow
            in Alaska.
            And I'm watching the snow turn red as I slide out of my body onto it.
            And I can't hear my own shouting over the sound of the wind and …
            I am the wind.
            This time I am the fucking wind.
            I'm the wind and I blow into the place scattering tables.
            I explode into the place and gather him up.
            I throw him against the window.
            And he smashes through his own reflection.
            And I gather him up and
            I pick the glass out of his eyes and …
            I wipe the blood out of his eyes and …

We can't speak and I say …
Remember the fire …
The beach we went to that one time.
We bought pakora from the shop.
Got pissed and watched the sun go down.
And even though it was just some fucking picnic.
Something happened to us all.
That was the time Martin.
I know that was the time.

IAN: Dear Veronica.
I wrote this letter sitting in some LA hotel room.
Looking out across the city.
The hotel is lavish.
The city is covered in that haze … you know. The LA haze.
And I'm writing about that fire.
Because the city was burning.
Because it's burning and so I took out the hotel paper and …
I wrote the letter during a fire in LA Veronica.
And there was an angry mob outside the hotel.
And they very much wanted to kill you.
And I took out the hotel paper from a drawer and …
The city was in fucking uproar Veronica.
And I took out the pen you gave me …
And I wrote you this tender letter.
To tell you about my new project.
Which I hope you like.
Because it's about the fire.
The beach we went to that one time.
We bought pakora from the shop.
Got pissed and when the sun went down.
And even though it was just some fucking picnic.
Something happened to us all.
Because that was the time Veronica.
I'm sure it was the time.

MARTIN: She's crying in a dark place.
Ghost. Smoke winding around our bodies.
My touch transmits … ease so …

You know Stella Veronica. I've been with so many women.
I've been with … I've felt uneasy with so many women.
I've made so many women feel uneasy.
I've been with and felt uneasy and my dreams have
been haunted by so many women.
And Veronica Stella … Veronica Stella …
Let me tell you …
It's not all right. No way.
My brain and heart are steeped in a pretty black sink.
I've seen things that aren't as pretty as you are baby.
I've walked hard roads.
So don't cry. Please don't cry …
Because I've been unthinkingly cruel to uneasy women.
But … If I could reach out my hand and say …
If I just had that touch.
A touch that could transmit that thing you want.
That thing women want which is …
Whatever it is.
I would.
Veronica Stella.
I would transmit that.
And it'd be like the fire.
The beach we went to that one time.
We ate pakora from the shop.
Got pissed and watched the sun go down.
And even though it was just some fucking picnic.
Something happened to us all.
That was the time Stella Veronica.
That must have been the time.

VERONICA: So they're probably late.
Any minute now. They're on their way and I'm …
Maybe I'm late.
I'm late.
God I'm late, as usual …
They're all waiting for me.
And I can't breathe and, not today,
Today I walk towards them so easily …

I'm dying here.

I can't breathe, not today.

Today I don't blush.

Except charmingly.

My hands do not attempt to cover my body.

Not today.

Today their kind words, their witty conversation, their clever thoughts are like currents of warm air and I'm a seabird gliding above them all. Supported by the warmth of their words.

And when I'm flying I'll say…

I'll say…

Remember the fire?

The beach we went to that one time.

We bought pakora from the shop.

We got pissed and watched the sun go down…

And even though it was just some fucking picnic.

Something happened to us all.

I'll say,

Remember that time? When we were all together.

I want to go back…

I just want to go back and…

[They all enter.]

IAN: It'll be dark. It'll be warm.
I will be casual. Remarkably casual.

STELLA: I'll look at myself in the flames.
And I'll be reborn.
Which will be a new departure for me.

MARTIN: My touch will be able to transmit ease.
My touch will be able to stop tears.

VERONICA: This is the moment when I feel easy.
This is the moment when I breathe easily.

IAN: I'll look at everyone.

STELLA: I'll look at everyone.

MARTIN:	I'll look at everyone.
VERONICA:	I'll look at everyone. And we'll glide upwards together on the warm air of our conversation.
IAN:	And we'll get pissed. Because our throats feel like they've been cut here.
MARTIN:	We'll reach out our hands with a kind of infinite slowness. And we each say the perfect thing.
STELLA:	And we'll unpack the grief from the boot of my car. And throw it into the sea.
VERONICA:	And I'll say d'you remember:
ALL:	*The beach we went to that one time.* *We bought pakora from the shop.* *Got pissed and watched the sun go down.* *And even though it was just some fucking picnic.* *Something happened to us all.*
VERONICA:	I'll say remember that time. When we were all together.
STELLA:	And we'll make a fire.
VERONICA:	We'll watch birds rising off the water.
IAN:	And even though we've been split apart the way frozen water splits rock on a mountainside.
VERONICA:	We'll look into the fire.
MARTIN:	And we'll each say the perfect thing.
ALL:	Blah blah blah blah blah blah blah.
IAN:	And it will be a timeless time.
STELLA:	That we can never get back to.
VERONICA:	That we'll always come back to.
MARTIN:	Something nice to look back on.

THE END

Mainstream was created with the intention that four actors, two male and two female, would randomly be assigned the roles of A & R and Personnel in each scene. This has the effect that in any given scene the performers could be two men, a man and a woman or two women. It is not necessary to perform the text in this way but it informs a reading of the text and may influence production decisions to know the circumstances of its creation.

SETTING

A hotel near the sea

CHARACTERS

A & R
Personnel

1.

_____

A & R: They told me after, it had been two days I'd been there.
         I had something like frostbite. I was only just alive. All the heat in my body had
         retreated inside me, away from my skin, away from my arms and legs. There was
         only the faintest detectable pulse being sent out from some deep core. So quiet it
         was hardly anything at all. Like one of those radio signals sent through space that
         just says, 'I'm here.' 'I'm here.' 'I'm here.'

[Break]

2.

_____

PERSONNEL: Can I ask you something?

A & R: Anything.

PERSONNEL: Would you take your clothes off for me?

3.

_____

PERSONNEL: I wonder if I could begin by asking you a few questions?

A & R: Why?

PERSONNEL: I just want to find out a little bit about you.

A & R: Sure. Go ahead.

PERSONNEL: Really just to get an idea about – who you are.

4.

―――――

PERSONNEL: Close your eyes.
What do you see?

A & R: You.

PERSONNEL: Do you see my face?

A & R: No.

PERSONNEL: My body?

A & R: No.

PERSONNEL: What do you see?

A & R: You.

5.

―――――

A & R: I'm thirty-three currently living in Scotland, Glasgow … I work in the music
industry. But you know that already.

PERSONNEL: Don't assume that I know anything.

A & R: OK.

PERSONNEL: You work in the music industry.

A & R: The music biz.
It's not glamorous. I used to be in a band.
Now I work in A & R.

PERSONNEL: What does A & R stand for?

A & R: Artists and Repertoire.
I basically talent spot, you know, I look for bands, I try to find hit records.

PERSONNEL: You're thirty-three?

A & R: Do I not look it?
          That'll be the drugs.

PERSONNEL: Do you take drugs?

A & R: Do you?

PERSONNEL: Do you?

A & R: I have done. Not now. Not for a few years now.
          I had a breakdown.
          I was in hospital for a while.
          I had to stop.

PERSONNEL: It doesn't say any of this in your file.

A & R: That's because it's a secret.

6.

_____

PERSONNEL: Can I take your photograph?

A & R: Where? Here?

PERSONNEL: Just here. Lean on the sea wall. Wear your shades … look at me – just be yourself.

A & R: I'll smile. I don't ever smile in pictures. I'm going to smile.

PERSONNEL: Watch the birdie! Say cheese!

A & R: Cheese.

PERSONNEL: Lovely.

7.

_____

PERSONNEL: What type of music do you like?

A & R: All types. It's my job.

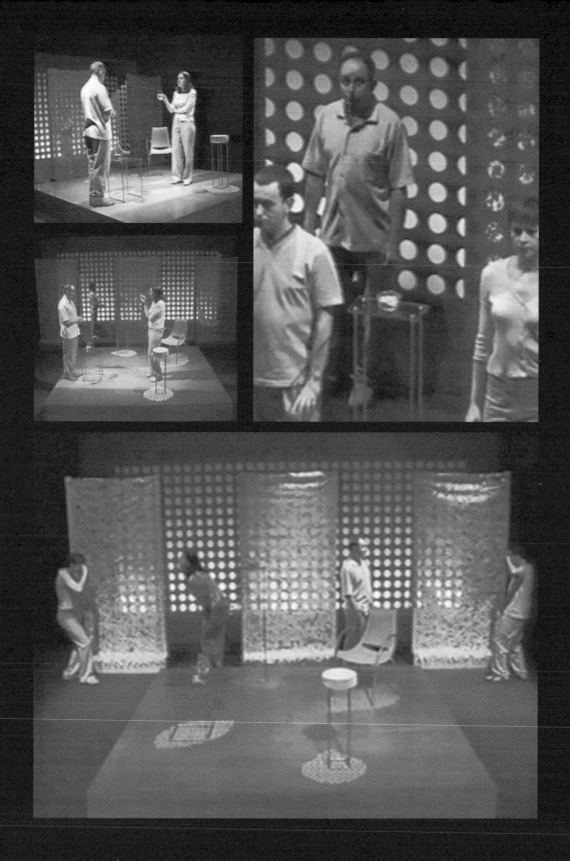

PERSONNEL:	Particularly?
A & R:	Particularly? God I could just go on ... I mean ... what do I like? I like rock. I like pop. I like jazz. I like country. I like folk. I like classical ... I ... what do you mean 'particularly'?
PERSONNEL:	What do you like the best?
A & R:	It depends on the situation. The mood I'm in.
PERSONNEL:	If you were on a desert island ...
A & R:	A desert island disc ...
PERSONNEL:	What music would you choose?
A & R:	God. I don't know. I mean ... the choice ... what a choice! If I was on a desert island ... I've thought about this. I would choose as my luxury ... a machine that could allow you to project your thoughts into holographic form. So, you know, if I wanted to remember some happy occasion or even imagine something – conjure something up – I could just think it and it would appear. What music would you choose?
PERSONNEL:	I would choose *Blue Eyes Crying In The Rain* by Willie Nelson.
A & R:	God! That's an astonishing record. That's an amazing record. That's definitely one of my favourites of all time. I can't listen to that song without crying. Good choice. ... I would never have had you down as a Country Music person.
PERSONNEL:	What type of person would you have me down as?
A & R:	I don't know ... something more ... mainstream.

8.

———

A & R:	Morning.
PERSONNEL:	Morning.
A & R:	How are you feeling?

PERSONNEL: OK.

A & R: You don't sound sure.

PERSONNEL: No. I'm fine.

A & R: Did you sleep well?

PERSONNEL: Not really.
That noise outside my room kept me awake.

A & R: What noise?

PERSONNEL: The gull ... you must have heard it.

A & R: I didn't hear anything.

9.

———

PERSONNEL: If you don't mind, I'll begin by asking you a few questions?

A & R: Fire away.

PERSONNEL: How much do you earn?

A & R: I'm on about thirty grand a year.
In a good year.

PERSONNEL: Is this a good year?

A & R: No.

10.

———

PERSONNEL: The sea looks very grey this morning.

A & R: It does doesn't it.

PERSONNEL: Not very inviting. Grey sea.

A & R: I suppose it must always look grey at this time of the morning.

PERSONNEL: Yes.

A & R: At this time of year.

PERSONNEL: It must do.
             When they told me I was interviewing you here,
             Can you believe this?
             I didn't even know it was by the sea.

A & R: Really?

PERSONNEL: Really.

A & R: I've been here before.

PERSONNEL: I have no… It's just an area I'm blank on – where things are in the world…

A & R: I drive so much, getting to gigs, whatever, I get to know places.

PERSONNEL: I follow certain particular routes.
             House. Tube. Office.
             I don't know anywhere else.

A & R: Brass monkeys at this time of year.
             That sea.
             I'd say.

PERSONNEL: What's that?

A & R: What?

PERSONNEL: What you said – brass monkeys.

A & R: – it's an expression.

PERSONNEL: Oh right.

A & R: It means cold.

PERSONNEL: I've never heard it.

A & R: I don't really – it's…

PERSONNEL: Where does its meaning come from?

A & R: It's cold enough to… It's a London thing I think.
             Last night… did you… you left?

PERSONNEL: You fell asleep.
I just went back to my room I ...

A & R: It's all right.

PERSONNEL: I just –

A & R: It was very late.

PERSONNEL: I was very drunk.

A & R: I was drunk. I slept.

PERSONNEL: I was a bit stupid, when I got back to my room, you know,
because I drank the champagne in the minibar.

A & R: Last of the big spenders.

PERSONNEL: Just in the hope of getting some sleep.
Because of the noise.
The bird. A seagull. Just outside my window.
All night.
Cawing away.
Squawking away.
I tossed and turned.
I put my pillow over my head.
I wanted a gun just to kill it.

11.

———————

PERSONNEL: How long have you been working in A & R?

A & R: Three or four years.

PERSONNEL: Do you enjoy it?

A & R: That's a difficult question to answer.

PERSONNEL: Why?

A & R: Because – I don't enjoy anything.

12.

———

PERSONNEL: I work in Personnel – why? Because I like people. I know it sounds naff but it really is that simple. I think people are ... broadly speaking ... good. I think people try. I think they want to do their best and it's just that the paths that they take can lead them to positions where – their best isn't good enough. And that creates a bad energy. Because their colleagues, who want to like this person, feel let down. And the person feels guilty and resentful and defensive and they put up barriers you know so the workplace becomes – me versus them. The harmony of the workplace is really difficult to maintain when someone isn't ... isn't in the right position for them to contribute. I see my job as putting people on the right path. Reaching down and taking people out of these bad energy situations and putting them onto a path which will lead them to a good energy situation. I think that's an important job for the organisations I'm working for. I think it maximises the efficiency and the profitability of those organisations but you know what? I think there's something else. I think, in a small way, I'm helping people. I'm helping people be happy.

[Break]

13.

———

PERSONNEL: Do you mind if I ask you a few questions?

A & R: Why?

PERSONNEL: It's a survey.

A & R: What for?

PERSONNEL: We're surveying the attitudes of our employees.

A & R: Why?

PERSONNEL: You seem very suspicious.

A & R: I'm not being suspicious. What makes you say I'm suspicious?
                Are you going to note that down? That I'm suspicious ... because
                I object I ...

PERSONNEL: I'm not noting down anything.
                I just ... want to get to know you a little.

A & R: Get to know me. What – be my friend?

PERSONNEL: It's what a personnel officer is there for ... to know the people
                who work for the organisation.
                There's really nothing to be concerned about.

A & R: You've got a CV what's wrong with a CV?

PERSONNEL: A CV only tells me so much.

A & R: What else do you need to know?

PERSONNEL: I need to know what you're like – as a person.
                Your needs.
                Your wants.
                Your hopes.

A & R: OK. So ... do I have any choice.

PERSONNEL: Of course.
                You don't have to answer if you don't want to.

A & R: Only if I don't.
                You'll note that down.
                You'll say I was un cooperative.

PERSONNEL: I'll just note down that you chose not to respond.

A & R: I get a call. I get a call to come to this – what – glorified seaside hotel. This ... to
                come and participate in a ... personal dynamics interview ... I say what's that all
                about? Nobody's able to tell me. I get here. They tell me to come up to this room.
                To see you. And now you're ... what ... psychoanalysing me?

PERSONNEL: All it is – is a few questions.

A & R: Fire away.

PERSONNEL: Let's start with you telling me a little bit about yourself.
How old are you?
Where are you from?

A & R: I'm 33, currently living in Scotland, Glasgow… I work in the music industry. But you know that already.

PERSONNEL: Don't assume that I know anything.

A & R: But you work for the fucking company.
It is a record company.

PERSONNEL: I'm not actually employed by your organisation.
I'm employed by a different organisation.
But we're brought in to – help.
We're personnel consultants.

A & R: Right.

PERSONNEL: It's better because when we meet staff… we're objective.
We have no preconceived ideas about who they are.

A & R: OK.

PERSONNEL: So…

A & R: What's your first impression then…
Objectively?

PERSONNEL: I think you're very intelligent. Very driven. Very troubled.

A & R: Really?

PERSONNEL: It's just a first impression.

A & R: God.
…
That's…
There you go.

14.

PERSONNEL: Can I ask you something?

A & R: Sure.

PERSONNEL: It's … it's … I don't know what you'll think of me …

A & R: I don't mind. Fire away.

PERSONNEL: Would you …
           No I can't.

A & R: Go on.

PERSONNEL: Forget it. I shouldn't have …

A & R: Please. I don't mind.

PERSONNEL: I'm embarrassed.

A & R: Don't be.

PERSONNEL: Would you …
           …

A & R: What?

PERSONNEL: I – just can't.

A & R: Have a drink.
           Don't worry about it.
           Trust me.
           I'm unshockable.
           You can ask me anything.
           Look let's both have a drink.
           We'll come back to it later.

15.

—————

PERSONNEL: What type of music do you like?

A & R: I like country music. I listen to country when I'm driving. I have cassettes in my car. I tune in to local stations. Almost every local station has a country show. Some DJ you've never heard of playing country music. It's strange because – you know – the bands I'm looking out for, the music I'm looking for – it's … aimed at – a certain person – 14-25 years old, plenty disposable income, they watch early evening TV, they're worried about their looks, they live at home, both parents still alive, they drink alco pops, they have sex regularly, if they're not having sex – they think about sex. That's who I'm trying to please. But, in my car, I listen to the country music stations. It's like, when I see a band, and I like what they do, I know I'm not going to sign them. I know they're not – mainstream enough.

16.

—————

A & R: Morning.

PERSONNEL: Morning.

A & R: How are you feeling?

PERSONNEL: OK.

A & R: Did you sleep well?

PERSONNEL: Not really.
The noise outside my room,
Kept me awake.

A & R: What noise?

PERSONNEL: The gull.
You must have heard it.

A & R: I didn't hear anything.

PERSONNEL: You must have.

A & R:	I'm a heavy sleeper.
PERSONNEL:	Really? I couldn't sleep at all.
A & R:	Why don't you join me for breakfast? Only if you want.
PERSONNEL:	I'd like to.
A & R:	If you don't feel comfortable – I understand.
PERSONNEL:	I normally eat breakfast alone.
A & R:	So do I.

17.

PERSONNEL: I did an exercise once, at a conference, a sort of a fun thing, it's a thing they've started doing in the states called a self-realisation exercise and what you do is you make up a CV for the sort of person you would most like to be. And so we all did that – you know so I put better grades – and more interesting hobbies, and different experience – I said I'd been travelling. I said I took a year out on a round the world air ticket – that sort of thing – and then the CVs all got discussed by the group – you weren't allowed to say which was yours – and the group decides which part of the organisation the candidate is best suited for. So we were discussing my one. And I was smiling – thinking they must know it's me, they must know – I mean I was laughing.

And the group decided – in the end – that the department that I was best suited to be in was personnel. So – no surprises there.

18.

A & R: We can never talk about this to anyone.

PERSONNEL: Never.

A & R: Never tell a soul.

PERSONNEL: Never.

A & R: From now on.
              We can't even refer to it between ourselves.

PERSONNEL: It never happened.

A & R: It happened in your head.

PERSONNEL: It happened in my head.

A & R: You imagined it.

PERSONNEL: It never happened.

A & R: It's your secret.

PERSONNEL: My secret.

19.

———————

PERSONNEL: You look beautiful.
              Your eyes.
              Your skin.
              Your lips.
              You look perfect.
              I can hear the sea.
              I feel as though …
              If I put my hand out to touch you,
              You would disappear.
              The room would disappear.
              And I'd be standing on a beach.
              In the dark.
              In the wind.
              And this maybe never happened.

20.

———————

PERSONNEL: How would you say you rate your relationship with your colleagues?

A & R: OK. They're OK.

PERSONNEL: Are they good at their jobs?

A & R: Some are. I think … well, you know, sometimes you're irritated aren't you by some little thing but – no, generally, they're great.

PERSONNEL: Do you think you're good at your job?

A & R: I get results.

PERSONNEL: Does that mean you're good?

A & R: Good. Or Lucky. One of the two.
I've had the hits.
So.
Yes. I am good.

PERSONNEL: Do your colleagues respect you?

A & R: Have they said they don't?

PERSONNEL: Do you think they would?

A & R: I think – let me tell you what I think – what I think is – this conversation – this – if you ask enough questions – you'll break anybody apart – if that's what you're trying to do here. That's what I think.

PERSONNEL: Do you think they like you?

A & R: Do you like me?

PERSONNEL: I'm only just getting to know you.

A & R: Would you go for a drink with me?

PERSONNEL: Would you go for a drink with your colleagues.

A & R: No.

PERSONNEL: Why not?

A & R: Because I've got better things to do with my life.

PERSONNEL: Hobbies?

A & R: I have other interests.

PERSONNEL: What sort of thing.

A & R: Watching TV.

21.

_____

A & R: I like country music. I listen to it when I'm driving. I have cassettes in the car. I
              buy all my own music on cassette.
                   Also I tune in to the local stations. All the local stations have a country music
              show. Some DJ you've never heard of playing country music. There's a gadget I
              have… it attaches to the car radio… it observes what you listen to and it builds up
              a profile of you… then, when you're driving it automatically tunes to the station
              that's playing the type of stuff you like. Isn't that wild? I love this gadget. It finds
              me all the country music shows.
                   …
              You know I used to think I was the sort of person who liked Radio 4.
              Until I had this gadget.
              It taught me who I really am.

22.

_____

A & R: You look worried.

PERSONNEL: I don't mean to.

A & R: I don't bite.

PERSONNEL: I know.

A & R: Have another drink.

PERSONNEL: Thanks.

A & R: What's your favourite drink?

PERSONNEL: Gin.

A & R: And tonic.

PERSONNEL: In summer.

A & R: Guinness.

PERSONNEL: Cold or normal.

A & R: Normal. I hate it cold. Sets my teeth on edge.

PERSONNEL: I like champagne.

A & R: So do I.

PERSONNEL: The cocaine of drinks.

A & R: My favourite drink is a whisky.
A whisky.
A bottle of whisky.

PERSONNEL: Malt whisky.

A & R: Any fucking whisky.

PERSONNEL: Do you have it with anything?

A & R: Yes.
I have it with whisky.
You're smiling.

PERSONNEL: Tell me what you were telling me before.
About the car.
About the ice.
About being buried in the ice in the car.

A & R: All this time, and we've talked about me.
That's what I'm like.
I talk about myself all the time.
And then I wonder why no one listens.
Tell me about you.

PERSONNEL: What about me?

A & R: I don't know …

PERSONNEL: If you knew me, you wouldn't like me.

A & R: How do you know?

PERSONNEL: I've met people like you before.
I so much admire people like you.
The way you talk. The way you – throw ideas, you throw subjects up into the air
and then you talk about them. You like to argue. You have opinions. I sit and listen.
People like you despise people like me.

A & R: That's not true.

PERSONNEL: It is.
You don't notice us.
And then, when we come into your lives,
for whatever reason,
We annoy you.

A & R: I like you.

PERSONNEL: Tonight.

A & R: Always.

PERSONNEL: Can I ask you something …

A & R: Fire away.

23.

————

PERSONNEL: I have a nephew, my sister's boy, I visit them. They have this warm house – I mean
it's literally warm, you know because they keep the central heating turned up. It
has to be on, because people are at home during the day – the house is inhabited.
When I visit them. I look at my nephew, everything he sees, everything he does he
enjoys.
I look at him.
He's perfect.

I think he might disappear.
He takes my breath away.
You know why?
Because he's made no wrong choices.
He has done, absolutely nothing, wrong.
He has no secrets.

[Break]

24.

_____

PERSONNEL: Do you mind if I smoke?

A & R: Go ahead. Please.

PERSONNEL: Do you want one?

A & R: ...Yes. Please.

    ...

I'm actually supposed to have given up.

PERSONNEL: I don't think I can eat.

A & R: Maybe, you should at least eat something.

PERSONNEL: No. It's all right. I'm not hungry.

A & R: They say stress can affect the appetite. Some people eat a lot.
Some people eat nothing.
It's different coping strategies.

PERSONNEL: How do you cope?

A & R: I cope by...
I...
It doesn't really make any difference to how I eat.

PERSONNEL: The sea looks very grey this morning.

A & R: Last night.

PERSONNEL: I feel very ashamed about last night.

A & R: You shouldn't. Neither of us should feel ashamed.

PERSONNEL: We broke the rules.

A & R: I don't care.
No.
I care.
But I don't regret it.
It's not our fault.
It's the fault of the rules.

25.

A & R: You know, when they told me your name – that I was to see you. I didn't know whether to expect a man or a woman.

PERSONNEL: That happens a lot.

A & R: It just – threw me.

PERSONNEL: Were you disappointed?

A & R: Quite the opposite.

PERSONNEL: It helps to keep people – on their toes.

A & R: It's an unusual name.
Is it foreign?

PERSONNEL: It's actually quite traditional.

A & R: It's very … it's … distinctive.

PERSONNEL: I chose it. It's actually my middle name.
I hate my first name.
I don't use it anymore.

A & R: What's your first name?

PERSONNEL: Promise not to laugh?

A & R:　　　　I promise.

[Personnel whispers the name.
A & R laughs.]

26.

——————

PERSONNEL:　Do you mind if I smoke?

A & R:　　　　Go ahead, please.

PERSONNEL:　Do you want one?

A & R:　　　　I've actually given up.
　　　　　　…
　　　　　　Yes please.

PERSONNEL:　I don't think I can eat anything.

A & R:　　　　Cigarettes won't help.
　　　　　　They take away your appetite.

PERSONNEL:　Really?

A & R:　　　　Nicotine is an appetite suppressant.

PERSONNEL:　I didn't know that.

A & R:　　　　You should really eat something.

PERSONNEL:　I'm just not hungry. That's all.

A & R:　　　　They say stress can affect the appetite some people eat a lot.
　　　　　　Some people eat nothing.
　　　　　　It's just different coping strategies.

PERSONNEL:　How do you cope?

A & R:　　　　I cope by…
　　　　　　I…
　　　　　　It doesn't really make any difference to how I eat.

PERSONNEL: The sea looks very grey this morning.

A & R: It does, doesn't it.

PERSONNEL: Not very inviting. Grey sea.

A & R: I suppose it must often look grey at this time in the morning.

PERSONNEL: Yes.

A & R: At this time of year.

PERSONNEL: It must do.

A & R: In summer, on a summer's morning, it's probably, very blue.

PERSONNEL: Would it be a different colour in summer?

A & R: I think so. I think...
Apparently it's the quality of the ambient light that gives
the sea its colour.

PERSONNEL: I didn't know that.

A & R: When you come to think of it.
Water has no colour.

PERSONNEL: No.

A & R: So it must be – the rest of everything – that makes it grey or blue
or whatever.

PERSONNEL: You know these things?

A & R: I'm just assuming really. I don't – know.

PERSONNEL: I think you do know.
You seem like a person who would know things like that.

A & R: Do I?

PERSONNEL: Nicotine. Ambient.

A & R: I'm sorry.

PERSONNEL: Knowledgeable.

27.

––––––––––

PERSONNEL: If you knew me you wouldn't like me.
I'm dull.
I know nothing.
I do this job.
I can't talk about anything else.
I'm uninteresting.
I'm ugly.
I have an ugly face.
You can't do anything with my hair.
I never understood clothes.
I'm rude to people.
All the time.
But not rude in that way where people say you're forthright.
I'm rude in a backhanded way. By accident.
I'm rude clumsily.
Like an evil type person.

A & R: Don't say these things.
If you say them you start to believe them.
And then you become that thing.

PERSONNEL: It's too late.

A & R: When I see a band. I want them to sell themselves to me.
I know they're just some bunch of kids making a racket
but… if they say they're great, if they believe they're great,
you feel that coming off them. From the stage.
If they think they're shit.
Then they most probably are.

PERSONNEL: I think I'm shit.

A & R: Tell me your strong points.

PERSONNEL: I…

A & R: Tell me what you like about yourself…

PERSONNEL: I'm trying.
I can't.

28.

————

A & R: I like country music. I listen to it when I'm driving. I have cassettes in the car. I buy all my own music on cassette.

Also I tune in to the local stations. All the local stations have a country music show. Some DJ you've never heard of playing country music. When I'm driving, it's the only time I get a feeling of – peace. As if the interior of the car has become me. The music, the heating system, the seats, I'm no longer confined to my body but I've expanded to fill this metal skin. The windscreen is the border between me and the rest of existence. The music, country music, fills the car, fills me.

29.

————

PERSONNEL: Your boss.

A & R: What about her.

PERSONNEL: What do you make of her?

A & R: She's good. She's smart. She's … people say she can be testy.

PERSONNEL: Testy?

A & R: That's not necessarily what I think.

PERSONNEL: She's testy with, what, colleagues? Clients?

A & R: People say she's not the sort to …

PERSONNEL: Suffer fools gladly?

A & R: Yeah.
I like her though.
As a person.

PERSONNEL: As a colleague?

A & R: I value her input.
Do you talk about me this way?
Have you had this conversation about me?

PERSONNEL: We canvass opinion. It's part of the job.

A & R: What opinions did you get about me?

PERSONNEL: You're well thought of.

A & R: Who did you talk to?

PERSONNEL: I can't tell you that.
You wouldn't want me to tell you that…

A&R: Am I how you imagined?

PERSONNEL: In what way?

A & R: Only, you know,
You've talked to people.
You've seen my CV.
Have you?

PERSONNEL: I've seen it.

A & R: So, you know all about me now.

PERSONNEL: A CV's nothing. It tells you nothing.
It's just a way of recording certain information.
I don't know you at all.

A & R: I'm just wondering if I live up to your expectations.
You know my school record, you know my personal interests,
you know my history. In a way we're quite intimate.

PERSONNEL: I know you're married.

30.

A & R: When you drive on the motorway, you notice, everything around you moves slowly, gracefully. Because all the speeds are relative. Cars move past you, they take ten minutes to overtake, gliding back and forth, passing briefly into each other's worlds. It's a very elegant way to experience life.

If you've ever had a breakdown on the motorway then you're suddenly catapulted from this world of grace into an alien place full of speed and cold and darkness and noise. When I had my breakdown, that's what it felt like.

PERSONNEL: You had a breakdown?

A & R: I had a mechanical breakdown.
I also had a mental breakdown.

PERSONNEL: That isn't mentioned on your file.

A & R: That's because it's a secret.

31.

─────────

A & R: I'm sorry, I was too defensive – I overreacted.

PERSONNEL: I hate this job.
Can I tell you that?

A & R: I didn't mean to snap – I'm sorry

PERSONNEL: I hate it.
Sitting here, asking questions.
People are afraid of me.
They think I'm after them.
You start asking questions and people think they've done some bad thing.
They don't know what it is they've done.
But they know it must be bad.
I hate that.
I want to help people.
I don't want to scare them.
Take people at face value.
That's all I want to do.

A & R: It's not your fault.

PERSONNEL: And so you ask questions.
                You – pick. They make you – pick at people.
                And people – they don't like it.
                You follow a path of questioning till the end.
                You dig things up.
                It's horrible.
                It's – it's repulsive.

A & R: It's the rules. It's the rules of the organisation.

PERSONNEL: Maybe I'm in the wrong organisation.

A & R: Maybe.

PERSONNEL: I'm in the wrong job.

A & R: Isn't everyone.

PERSONNEL: On the wrong path.

A & R: That old wrong path – we all take it.
                You're not alone in that.

PERSONNEL: I know but –

A & R: Why don't you have a drink with me.
                C'mon. Fuck this.
                Let's go down to the bar.
                Let's, drink. Let's just, chat.
                You can fill in this form, some other time.
                Make it up.
                I don't care what you put down.

PERSONNEL: We should complete the interview.

A & R: C'mon. Who cares. It's all … statistics, it's all … just information.
                We've nothing better to do.
                Let me buy you a drink.

PERSONNEL: You're a kind person.
                You know that.

A & R: No. I'm …

PERSONNEL: I wouldn't have had you down as a kind type person.

A & R: What would you have had me down as?

PERSONNEL: A – difficult type person.

A & R: I can be difficult.

PERSONNEL: A bitter type person.

A & R: OK. You got me. That's what I'm like.

PERSONNEL: But you're also kind.

A & R: I don't think I'm especially kind.
I think I'm just showing a normal concern for … another person.

PERSONNEL: It isn't normal to show a normal amount of concern.
It's rare.

A & R: Should I put it on my CV?

32.

_____

PERSONNEL: We're sitting, in the dark, in a hotel bedroom.
And we've been drinking.
Drinking and drinking.
And I know this person.
I know them very well.
And I don't know them at all.
The radio's playing.
And I ask them to take off their clothes.
And I ask them to lie on the bed.
And I sit in the hotel chair.
And I ask them to come for me.
And I ask them to imagine me as they come.
And I watch.
The only light is moonlight off the sea.
The sound of the sea.
The music on the local station.

As they shut their eyes.
And make in that moment
A present for me,
A memory.
Of somebody
Alone
Somebody alone with me.
And then I watch that person till they are asleep.
And then I go back to my room.

A & R: What music do you hear – on the radio?

PERSONNEL: Blue eyes.

A & R: Blue eyes crying in the rain?
              Does the person have blue eyes?

PERSONNEL: I've never noticed.

[Break]

33.

PERSONNEL: What does A & R stand for?

A & R: Artists and Repertoire.
              I basically talent spot, you know, I look for bands, I try to find hit records.

PERSONNEL: You're thirty-three?

A & R: Yes.

PERSONNEL: You don't look it.

A & R: Thank you.

PERSONNEL: Don't take this the wrong way.
              But you look … older.

A & R: That'll be the drugs.

PERSONNEL: Do you take drugs?

A & R: Only prescription drugs.

PERSONNEL: They make you look old?

A & R: Really I don't know.
             I didn't know I looked older.
             I don't want to talk about it.
             I don't see what right you have to ask me about drugs.

PERSONNEL: It's important for us to know if the employees of the organisation are dependent
             on substances…

A & R: I'm an alcoholic.

PERSONNEL: I see.

A & R: I'm dependent on alcohol.

PERSONNEL: That isn't on your file.

A & R: That's because it's a secret.

34.

A & R: I was on the motorway, driving back from some gig by some band, and it was
             snowing heavily. It was whiteout. I was warm in the car. Listening to some DJ on
             a local station. Just in the car. Just… and then, something went wrong with the
             engine, it cut out, it kept cutting out and so I pulled over. I got out of the car to
             look for a phone but – the noise, the speed of the lorries, the cold, the dark. I was
             only wearing a kind of Hawaiian shirt. So I got back into the car and I switched on
             the radio and the heating system and I thought, I'll wait for the snow to stop. I'll
             wait here. I sat in the car and watched the snow fall.

35

A & R: Why don't you join me for breakfast?
Only if you want…

PERSONNEL: I don't know…

A & R: If you don't feel comfortable joining me I… understand.

PERSONNEL: I normally eat breakfast alone.

A & R: So do I.

PERSONNEL: Do you eat meat?
Are you going to be having meat?
I don't… I can't… the way I feel I couldn't look at meat just now.

A & R: I've ordered a cooked breakfast – so – well it's going to have
sausage and bacon so – is that a problem?

PERSONNEL: Look if you've ordered.

A & R: I can easily change the order. I…

PERSONNEL: Don't be ridiculous. I'm…

A & R: No. I will.
Because, you know…

PERSONNEL: … overreacting.

A & R: …cholesterol, heart attacks, I should eat –

PERSONNEL: Really.

A & R: No it's OK.

PERSONNEL: It's just the smell of meat. In the morning. I often feel nauseous in the morning
and…

A & R: I'll have cereal.
Cornflakes.
No – no fruit.
Yes. A melon.
They have melon here.

PERSONNEL: Do you mind if I smoke?

A & R: Go ahead. Please.

PERSONNEL: Do you want one?

A & R: ...
No.
...
Yes please.
I'm actually supposed to have given up.

PERSONNEL: Oh don't then, don't start if you've stopped.
I'd hate to be responsible for ...
Something like that.

36.

———————

A & R: I sat in the car and watched the snow fall on the windscreen.
It was a big thing. The radio was reporting this blizzard as a big thing. The whole road was ... stopped with snow. And it was all around the car and it was all over the bonnet and it kept falling.
I don't know if I was mostly asleep or if I was mostly awake.
I just ...
Sat.

37.

———————

PERSONNEL: I like your shirt.

A & R: Thank you.

PERSONNEL: It suits you.

A & R: I think so. I like it. Some people think it's tacky.

PERSONNEL: Which people? Who thinks that?

A & R: My… well some people… for example my partner says that for an A & R person to wear a Hawaiian shirt is a… tacky statement. I just like it. I just think it's me. With the shades. You know.

PERSONNEL: In winter.
It's brass monkey weather and you're wearing your shades.

A & R: Shades cover your eyes.
They give you an air of…

PERSONNEL: Who's under there?
What colour are your eyes?
Can I take your photograph?

A & R: I don't think you should.
I think it's better not.
Don't you?

PERSONNEL: How's it better?

A & R: I think it's better we just keep this in our head.
No records.
Nothing they can put on file.

38.

_____

A & R: By the time the sun came up. It had stopped snowing.
The car was buried. I only knew it was morning because the quality of the light changed. The snow had a bluish grey tinge. Some of it was melting. I watch the little ice crystals break off and slide down the windscreen. The radio was very quiet. I couldn't hear anything. I was cold.

39.

_____

PERSONNEL: The way you hold hands – you curl a finger in my palm.

A & R: Do I? I suppose I do.

PERSONNEL:	It's comforting. I like it.
A & R:	I never thought about it. It just seems natural.
PERSONNEL:	I've never met anyone else who does that. It's unique. It's you.
A & R:	I should put it on my CV.

40.

―――――

A & R:	Very quiet music.
	I seemed to inhabit the whole car.
	As though it was my metal skin.
	The blue snow on the windscreen.
	Drifting in and out of sleep.
	Very quiet.
	Some DJ on a local station you've never heard of.

41.

―――――

A & R:	Can I ask you something?
PERSONNEL:	If you want.
A & R:	Are you … in a relationship just now?
PERSONNEL:	No.
A & R:	Right.
PERSONNEL:	I've never been in a relationship.
A & R:	Never?
PERSONNEL:	Never.
A & R:	Not even a one-night stand?

PERSONNEL: I've had one-night stands.

A & R: You don't want a relationship?

PERSONNEL: I can't have one.

A & R: Why not?

PERSONNEL: You really want to know?

A & R: Really.

PERSONNEL: I can't have a relationship because…
If I think a person really likes me,
I feel nothing but contempt for them.

A & R: You're sure about that?

PERSONNEL: I know myself.

A & R: You… have you tried to get help for this thing?

PERSONNEL: Why should I?

A & R: Because it would make you… it might make you happy.

PERSONNEL: I don't believe that.

A & R: But…

PERSONNEL: I know who I am.
It's OK.
I'm fine.

A & R: But…

PERSONNEL: Don't try to make me into – whatever. Whatever it is you
think.

A & R: I'm sorry.

PERSONNEL: Can I ask you something?

A & R: Sure.
Of course.

PERSONNEL: Do you like me?

42.

_____

PERSONNEL: I was a bit stupid when I got back to my room because I drank the champagne in the minibar.

A & R: Right.

PERSONNEL: Just in the hope of getting some sleep.
Because of the noise.
The seagull.
Cawing away.
Squawking away.
I wanted a gun just to kill it.

A & R: I didn't hear a thing in my room.

PERSONNEL: You were sound asleep.

A & R: Dead to the world.
In dreamland.

PERSONNEL: Did you dream?

A & R: Last night?

PERSONNEL: Yes.

A & R: I don't think so. Now you come to mention it.
Although they say you always dream.
It's just. If you wake up at a particular time in the sleep cycle – the dream's forgotten.

PERSONNEL: You're very knowledgeable.

A & R: No. I'm just … I assume these things … I don't – know.

PERSONNEL: I think you do know.
I think you look like a person who knows things.

A & R: What about you?
Did you dream?

PERSONNEL: I spent the time just … drifting …
It's very dark.

That time of the morning.
You feel like you might never emerge.

A & R: I wish I'd ... been with you.

PERSONNEL: I wished that.

A & R: You left the room. If you'd stayed, you could have woken me.
We could have talked until it got light.

PERSONNEL: I didn't seem right for me to sleep in your bed.

A & R: It's only a hotel bed.

PERSONNEL: Still. Your bed.

43.

A & R: When you stay absolutely still for a very long time.
You lose a sense of where you begin and where you end.
Your mind wanders.
At first you observe the way it wanders.
Hold a mirror up.
Watch the thoughts drift past.
Then, after a while.
You stop even noticing the thoughts.
And after a while.
You stop even thinking.
And there's just.
Peace.
The sound of the music playing very quietly.
The blue snow on the windscreen.
A trickle of grey water.
Cold.

[Break]

44.

PERSONNEL: When I got dressed.
Only the moonlight.
I had to look for my clothes where they'd fallen.
In the dark.
In bare feet.
Holding my shoes so as not to make a noise in the corridor.
Scared of bumping into someone.
I felt like a child.

A & R: You should have just stayed.

PERSONNEL: When I shut the door to my room.
I was panicky. Out of breath.
I thought – it felt like –
Something's happened.
Something really bad has happened to me.
But I couldn't pin down exactly.
What the bad thing was.

A & R: Do you want to talk about what happened?

PERSONNEL: I don't know if it's sensible to talk.

A & R: No.

PERSONNEL: I don't think we should ever refer to this.

A & R: Never.

PERSONNEL: Not even between ourselves.

A & R: No.

PERSONNEL: It can be our secret.

45.

PERSONNEL: How would you rate your level of fulfilment in your work?

A & R: Very low.

PERSONNEL: Do you want to expand on that?

A & R: I drive up and down motorways to crappy hotels to watch kids make a racket. See if the racket's something I can sell. It's disgusting. I watch them play their songs you know, and the – they're doing it to – it's absolutely the right thing for them to be doing – expressing themselves.

And this evil creature stands at the back with a whisky and drinks them in. What kind of way of spending your time is that for a human being? Standing there I feel like the fucking lord of darkness. It's disgusting. Honestly. And then, if you think they've got that – whatever – that – quality that taps into the mainstream then you – what? Do you feel good about it? No. Because you know that whatever human quality it is that these children possess you're going to turn into fuel and burn it. So that all the rest of us can have some human heat and light until it's all turned to ash. And then the only thing those burned kids are capable of is becoming people like me who go out and find other children playing guitars in crappy hotels. More fuel. More heat. More light.

PERSONNEL: That's a very pessimistic view of the music industry.

A & R: You asked me the question.

PERSONNEL: If that's what you think. Why do you do the job?

A & R: I've spent too long going down the one road.
I'm just waiting till I get to the end now.

46.

PERSONNEL: Can I ask you something?

A & R: Anything.

PERSONNEL: Do you want me?

A & R: Honestly?

PERSONNEL: Honestly.

A & R: Yes.

PERSONNEL: Would you …
No.

A & R: Ask.

PERSONNEL: I can't … I shouldn't have even. Forget it.

A & R: Ask.

PERSONNEL: Would you take your clothes off for me.
Would you lie on the bed.
I want you to come for me.
I want you to think of me.
I want to watch you.

47.

———————

PERSONNEL: How would you rate your level of fulfilment in your work?

A & R: Very high.

PERSONNEL: Do you want to expand on that?

A & R: I enjoy it. I mean. It's not even a real job is it. I get to travel up and down the
country. See different places and – I get to watch these young bands. You know,
you're in some hotel somewhere and there's a stage and you're at the back with
a whisky in your hand, you feel like god or something, and the kids are playing,
they're belting out some song they've written you almost want to cry at the
sheer fucking beauty of it. Even when they're no good, there's something – it's
absolutely right that they should be there, on that stage, at that moment, just –
pure expression. And if they're good, you know, if you see that quality, whatever it
is that you think taps into the mainstream, then – what a buzz. Because you know
that you're going to be bringing this human warmth, this human light to people.
You know? And these kids are going to become – stars.
That's an amazing feeling.

PERSONNEL: That's such a nice way of … thinking about it.

A & R: Well, you know, I care about it.

PERSONNEL: Would you like to see yourself progressing within the organisation?

A & R: I don't know. It's a vocation. As long as I have contact with the music. As long as I can wear my Hawaiian shirts and my shades. Then yeah. I suppose.
What about you?

PERSONNEL: Me?

A & R: Is this what you see yourself doing.
Is it fulfiling?

PERSONNEL: Not in the way that you describe it.

A & R: Would you say it was fulfiling at all?

PERSONNEL: You know, I ask these questions all the time, nobody's ever asked me?

A & R: I am. I'm asking.

PERSONNEL: Why?

A & R: I'm interested.

PERSONNEL: Why do I do this job? Well …
I took a road and … I'm just waiting to get to the end of it.

A & R: Do you ever think of getting out. Changing.

PERSONNEL: I can't imagine what else I could do. Where I could go.

A & R: Anywhere.

PERSONNEL: No.

A & R: Really.
Believe me.
You can just – leave. Just walk up to your boss and say, I'm sorry, I'm leaving. You know. Free yourself. Find out who you really are.

PERSONNEL: I wish it was like that.

A & R: It is.
People don't see this.

I see this.
Look.
I had a breakdown.
A mechanical breakdown which sort of led to a mental breakdown. And, I… saw.
That you could just leave things.
Take a step.

PERSONNEL: What did you leave?

A & R: It doesn't matter.
A previous life which seemed … like it was the only possible life.
I had a breakdown.
And I just.
Took a step onto a different path.

PERSONNEL: You had a breakdown?

A & R: Yes.
I was alcoholic.
I was on drugs.
I was pretty low.

PERSONNEL: It doesn't say any of this on your file.

A & R: That's because it's a secret.

48.

———

A & R: What's your favourite TV show?

PERSONNEL: *Friends*.

A & R: *Star Trek*.

PERSONNEL: What's your favourite sweet?

A & R: Jelly Babies.
Or. No… wait… no definitely Jelly Babies.

PERSONNEL: Liquorice All Sorts.
What's your favourite mode of transport?

A & R: Car.

PERSONNEL: For me it's ships.
             I love ships.
             Ferries. Ferries to islands. Especially.

A & R: I don't mind a ferry.
             As long as I'm in a car.

PERSONNEL: What's your favourite record of all time?

A & R: … anything. I don't have one.
             Something by Willie Nelson maybe.

PERSONNEL: No way – same as me.

A & R: What's your favourite drink?

PERSONNEL: Gin.

A & R: And tonic?

PERSONNEL: Definitely.

A & R: Guinness.

PERSONNEL: Cold or normal.

A & R: Normal. I hate it cold.
             Or whisky.

PERSONNEL: With anything.

A & R: With whisky.

PERSONNEL: You ask one.

A & R: OK. What's your favourite …
             What's your favourite …
             Sexual position.

PERSONNEL: My favourite sexual position?

A & R: You don't have to say if you don't want to.

PERSONNEL: Promise you won't tell anyone?

A & R: It's our secret.

PERSONNEL: I like to…
             No.
             I can't say.

A & R: Go on.

PERSONNEL: I've always wanted to…

A & R: What?

PERSONNEL: I've never done it.
             But I've always wanted to…
             Watch someone come.

A & R: Watch them fuck?

PERSONNEL: No – on their own.

A & R: Watch them… oh right.

PERSONNEL: I'm embarrassed now.

A & R: Don't be.

PERSONNEL: You'll think I'm a pervert.

A & R: No. It's normal. It's…

PERSONNEL: What's your favourite sexual position?

A & R: Underneath.

PERSONNEL: Is that it?

A & R: Tied up.

PERSONNEL: That's better.

A & R: Gagged.

PERSONNEL: Better still.

A & R: Made to… do things.

PERSONNEL: What things.

A & R: Whatever you might want.

PERSONNEL: I want another drink

A & R: I think I could manage one

PERSONNEL: I think I might need one.

49.

_____

PERSONNEL: My flat is empty. I come back to it. I can hardly bear to open the door sometimes. I watch TV. I have to force myself to cook. I knock back a bottle of wine. Once I did an evening class in Swedish. Can you believe it. I thought I'd – I don't know – go to Sweden and talk to them. I stuck it about three weeks before I realised that all the Swedes speak English anyway so what was the point. Once a month I look after my nephew. I take him to the zoo. I go to work. I come home. That's what I do. I can't imagine doing anything else. Maybe take up the piano.

50.

_____

A & R: Let me get this right.
You're from a different organisation to my organisation.
And you – what parachute in? To ask me questions.
You fill out these forms.
You – psychoanalyse me.
And then what?
I get fired.

PERSONNEL: We try to build up a personnel profile of the whole organisation.

A & R: Fuck it. Fuck that. Forget it.
I'm not taking part.
I'm going.

PERSONNEL: You don't have to take part.

A & R: I don't want to.

PERSONNEL: The aim of this is – ultimately – to help you.

A & R: I don't need help.

PERSONNEL: OK. That's fine.

A & R: Look at you.
Fucking standing there.
What the fuck do you look like.
Christ.
Saying nothing.
Waiting for me to spill my fucking guts.
Well you can forget it.
I have nothing but contempt for this sort of …
Bullshit.
This … psychological …
What – study my handwriting why don't you.
Who the fuck are you?
That's what I want to know.
Who the fuck are you?
Nobody.

PERSONNEL: I'm sorry.
I …

A & R: Shit.

PERSONNEL: Excuse me.

A & R: What?

PERSONNEL: Excuse me please.

A & R: What? What have I said?
Shit.
Look. Wait.
Forget it.
Just -
…
…
I'll participate. I'm just …
Sorry.

51.

———————

PERSONNEL: Would you take your clothes off for me.

A & R: Don't ask. Tell me.

PERSONNEL: Take your clothes off.

...

Lie on the bed.
Lie down.
Close your eyes.

...

I can't do this. I can't keep up the act.

A & R: You're doing fine.
Don't talk so much.

PERSONNEL: Stay still.
Stay absolutely still.
Think of me.
Imagine me.
Conjure me up.
Touch yourself.

[Break]

52.

———————

A & R: Do you have central heating?

PERSONNEL: I just have a gas fire.

A & R: You should think about it.
If you get central heating you can set it to come on just before you get in.
That way the house is warm when you come home.

PERSONNEL: Is that what you do?

A & R: Yeah. That's what I do.

53.

A & R: Are you sure you're not eating?

PERSONNEL: Sure I'm sure.

A & R: Look.
               I have to …
               I really have to go.

PERSONNEL: Of course.
               Me too.
               Get back to …

A & R: Where are you parked?

PERSONNEL: Just along the front.

A & R: I could … walk you to your car.
               We could go for a walk.

PERSONNEL: The amount we drank.
               We probably shouldn't be driving at all.

A & R: We could stay another night.

PERSONNEL: We could.

A & R: We could … stay for the rest of the week.

PERSONNEL: We could …
               Just …

A & R: We could stay for a week and then drive to … Sweden.

PERSONNEL: They all speak English there.

A & R: Nobody knows who we are.

PERSONNEL: We could just turn up.

A & R: We could.

PERSONNEL: We could.

54.

_____

A & R: When they dug me out. They took me to hospital. They said after, I'd been buried
            two days. I was very close to being dead. They asked me how I was. I said OK.
            Glad to be rescued. But you know … I wasn't. The truth of it is that in the car
            under the blue snow I was … OK.

55.

_____

A & R: Look.
            I have to …
            I really have to go.

PERSONNEL: Of course.
            Me too.
            Get back to …

A & R: Where are you parked?

PERSONNEL: Just along the front.

A & R: I could … walk you to your car.
            We could go for a walk.
            When do you actually have to leave?

PERSONNEL: Soon. Not that soon but still soon.

A & R: Me too.
            Look. You're going home. I'm going home. So this is a – what happened – it's –

PERSONNEL: It's OK. You don't have to say anything.

A & R: It's safe because – there's no route forward, there's nothing to be done so – it's not an affair. It's just. It only exists in our heads. We both did something at a particular time and now it's gone. So, you know, we're unlikely even to see each other again. We'll go for a walk. And then we'll go back to … and all the rest is only in our heads.

PERSONNEL: You know what's surprising?

A & R: What?

PERSONNEL: I was thinking, last night.
That fucking bird squawking away outside my window.
I was thinking.
I would never have had myself down as the sort of person who would do this sort of thing.

A & R: Me neither.

56.

————

PERSONNEL: Just a couple of final things I need to know –
Do you have any history of mental illness?

A & R: No.

PERSONNEL: Clean driving licence?

A & R: Clean.

PERSONNEL: Fine. Great. Well.
Thanks very much for your co-operation and
…
Nice to have met you.

A & R: Is that the form finished?

PERSONNEL: That's it.

A & R: My personal dynamics profile.
What happens to it now?

PERSONNEL: We process it.
We put the information on computer.
We put it together with all the other information.
And then
It goes into your file.

THE END

LAMENT

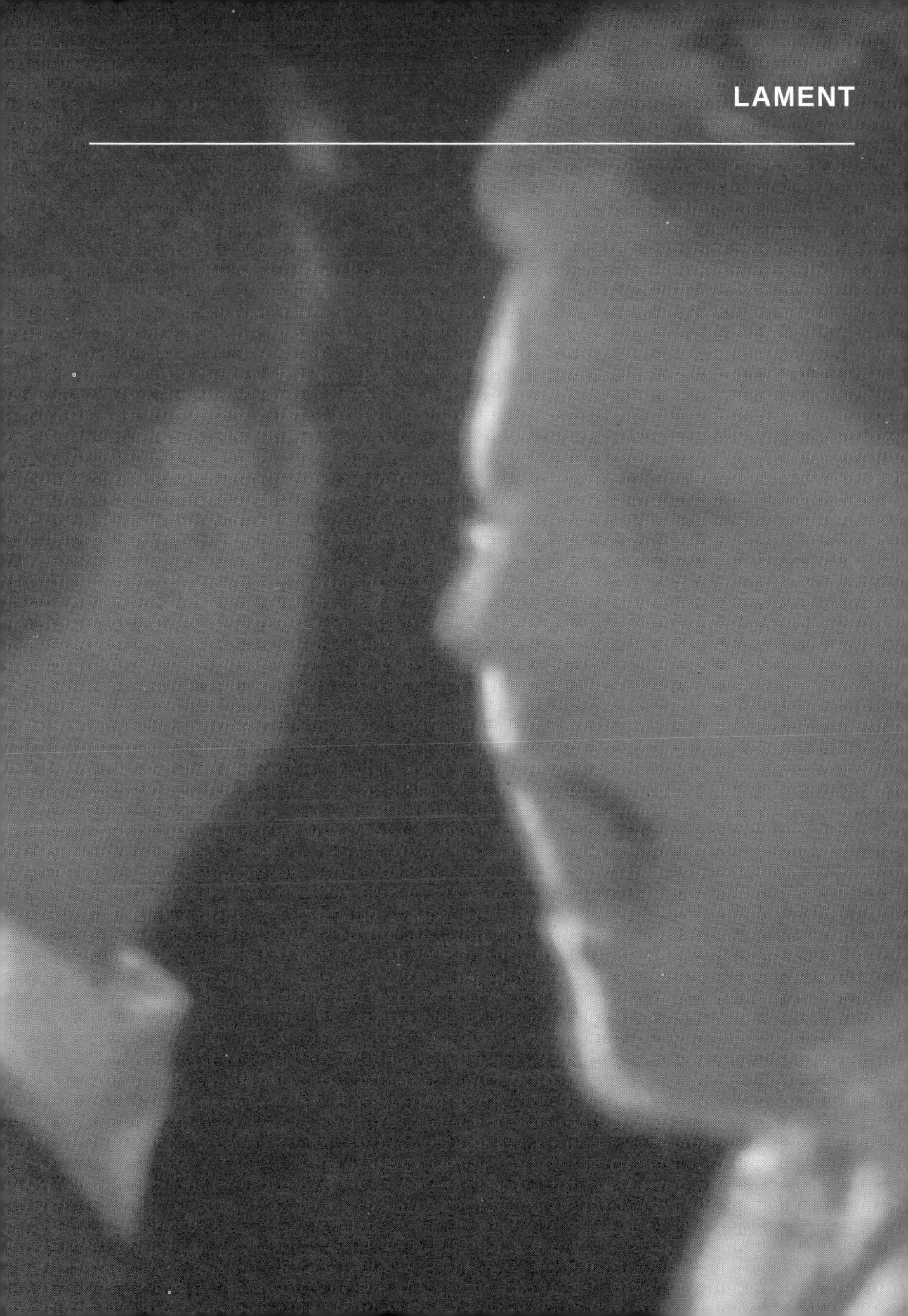

A NOTE ON THE TEXT

Lament was first presented by Suspect Culture in 2002.
The artistic collaborators Graham Eatough, David Greig,
Nick Powell and Ian Scott devised the show with the
performers.

SETTING

2002

CHARACTERS

Graham
Callum
Nick
Paul
Louise
Kate

Prologue

[A series of talking heads on a video wall at the back of the stage.

Louise, Kate, Callum, Paul and Graham are on stage listening to themselves answering questions on the video.]

GRAHAM: *(Pointing to coldsore)* Does my coleslaw look really obvious?

CALLUM: I think the thing I would feel most comfortable in would be a pair of 501s, a pocket Gap T-shirt and a checked shirt, some kind of flannel shirt.

KATE: A pair of flares or baggy trousers, trainers and a wee vest top or something like that.

NICK: Erm … black is the main feature I think. A leather jacket? Kind of what I'm wearing now.

PAUL: I'm probably just comfortable in jeans or a shirt. I like the kind of mix and match. The formal and the informal.

LOUISE: Usually something tight on top. *(Laughs.)*
Possibly low-cut. Possibly not. I've kind of steered away from that recently …
Probably because it's winter.

GRAHAM: My outfit is, I suppose, a pair of beige cords, a navy blue V-neck and a short-sleeved white shirt.

KATE: *(Sings.)*
I can't live if living is without you.
I can't give.
I can't give anymore.
Neilson. I have many favourite sad songs. All my favourite songs are sad.

CALLUM: *Men with broken hearts* by Hank Williams.

PAUL: I've just been listening to lots of Tom Waits songs again so …
Tom Waits songs kind of make me sad. But there's quite a few. Off the top of my head … *Martha*.

GRAHAM: *(Sings.)*
And if a double-decker bus

Kills the both of us
To die by your side
It's such a heavenly way to die.
There is a light and it never goes out.
There is a light and it never goes out.
Fade.

LOUISE: *(Sings)*
May you never lay your head down without a hand to hold …
… I can't remember the rest.

KATE: I lament that sometimes I don't stop enough and just be pleased with what I've got. And I'd like to look in the future more rather than just harking back to the past.

CALLUM: I'd like to write a novel, you know, and I've got like bits of one lying about. Most days I look at it and think I really must get round to finishing that. It's called *The Unfolding*. It's very slowly unfolding.

GRAHAM: I'd like to be more considerate. Not just in relation to other people but in how I conduct myself. I wish I thought more.

LOUISE: Quite a lot.
Not having a stop button. No motivation. No mental stability. The list goes on.

NICK: I lament not having taken care of myself physically, and possibly having fucked up my health basically.

PAUL: What I do lament is … I don't know if I actually was … but the feeling of being young and for the first time ever really getting involved politically and stuff and, you know, the idea that then … it's probably to do with youthful naivety and stuff, but I think things were slightly different and the feeling that there's another way, you know, and this far off notion that things could turn on their head, you know, and maybe become fair.

KATE: A few places, but I spent … until I was 9 I grew up on a big estate. My father was a gardener on a big estate. Near Couper Angus. And I was quite like *Stig Of The Dump* really. I ran about in pants. I only wore pants, if I was lucky, and my dad would hide Opal Fruits in the greenhouse and tell me the fairies had left them and tell me lots of stories.

CALLUM: When I was growing up it was the time of the space race you know and that was very exciting. Men going to the moon, you know, and I used to follow that very

keenly. And there was an enormous sense of optimism about that, that we would go into space. And that's lost now.

KATE: It's just very open. You didn't lock your doors. You were there for your neighbours and had time to have proper conversations with people.

LOUISE: It was much greener then. There was a lot more … Because I kind of lived down by the river and lots of fields and there would be a huge park and there wasn't so many houses. Now there's something like 20,000 new houses being built and it's just like … spread.

PAUL: Loads of kids in the house and noise and, you know, and all that sort of stuff and … I think that's really important and that's not a part of my life anymore. It's just not there.

GRAHAM: I think lots of people are really considerate, but I think it would be hard to give it that title, that we live in a considerate society. But there are amazing examples of consideration at every level in society. So … er … yeah … probably not a considerate society but I do think there are great examples of consideration.

PAUL: The first house that I lived in. Has been demolished.

CALLUM: I think we've lost quite a lot already. We don't even know we're in the process of it. I think there's quite a lot that's gone and … I don't see how we can get it back.

PAUL: I suppose as well though I think there is no sense anymore of the possibility of real radical change. That things could, you know, be revolutionary. That, you know what I mean, things could really change. Everything just seems to be about … well … this is it.

NICK: There's just raging injustices going on and I think … economic decisions lead to human rights abuses all over the world and I think we're all implicated.

GRAHAM: No, it's just that *The Guardian* is the … *The Guardian* feels … it's actually because *The Guardian* is closest to me because it's the newspaper out of all of them that I would choose. Which is why I think it frustrates me the most. So, do you know what I mean, if it was *The Daily Mail* you kind of wouldn't worry because obviously, you know, *The Daily Mail* is full of rubbish. But because it's the one where people go 'Oh well, at least there's *The Guardian*', and yet … yeah …

KATE: Food mountains annoy me as well actually. Because I heard lately right … you know how you've been told for ages that olive oil is very good for you? Well seemingly it was just a lie because they had a big olive oil mountain and really vegetable oil is better for you.

PAUL: Ordinary people. The people who make the stuff who create the company who make the wealth are the ones who get fucked first. But that's just the way it goes I suppose isn't it?

KATE: *(Laughs.)* A big mountain of food. I imagine … do you know what I imagine actually, and it's completely made up, is just like huge big colossal barns filled with piles of potatoes and margarine.

LOUISE: I think the threat of nuclear war with him in power has got as big as it was when Reagan was in and I think that's … He seems to be inciting other countries to … war …

CALLUM: I don't know an enormous amount about the issues, about the economics of it. All I know is that there are many Third World countries that owe an awful lot of money to the major powers. And these debts are crippling them. And they can't get out from under these kind of debts. And that tends to create a tremendous amount of social injustice.

NICK: Well yeah I would club global capitalism to death with an iron bar. But my feeling about global capitalism is that it's won, and I will never be in that room with it, and I have no bar so all I can do is eat at the same table, and feel shit about it.

CALLUM: Kind of despair and sadness and anger as well but … I don't know, anger is not very … it's not a very constructive feeling I don't think.

GRAHAM: To live in Madrid as a classical guitar maker.

KATE: I would either be a photographer in Madrid or … that's maybe a bit much. I would live in Puerto Pollensa in Mallorca and I would own a glass-bottomed fishing boat and I would do my garden. I would drink cortados every day and eat … the tomatoes there are like the best tomatoes I've ever tasted and I would eat them all day. With some oil and pepper and salt.

LOUISE: I would like to work in a Kenyan reserve looking after all the wild animals. The lions and tigers and things.

CALLUM: To Venice. I'd like to be a novelist living in Venice living on the Grand Canal. In a little house with a little terrace overlooking the Grand Canal.

GRAHAM: But to lots of makers this stage is the most vital to them and they taste the wood, they bite the wood and you know they kind of lick it. They have to become completely intimate with the qualities and properties that this particular part of the guitar has.

PAUL: The thing that pops into my head is that I met a couple once who lived in Alaska and they stayed so far away from … I think it might have been Anchorage in Alaska. But they had their own plane that they would … Sorry they'd two small planes.

LOUISE: I'd just have a quick reccie around the area and just make sure that everything was alright – make sure there's no poachers about. Then go back with my mate … (*Laughs.*) … with my mate. Actually I think he's more than a mate.

KATE: Very good. I'm very content and I want for nothing. I'm very content. That's what I would like, and want for nothing.

Well I was stuck between having a nice, quiet, idyllic life and having an absolutely nutting … I mean, not nutting … a nutty life.

LOUISE: Oh god, you've got to have guns.

No we don't kill the animals. I look after the animals. I'm kind to the animals. I'm Dr. Loulittle.

KATE: I'd like to be a photographer. I'm not very good with photos just now you see. I take photos and I never get them developed. So I would like to get into photography.

Yeah I think she has a lover. That she calls upon whenever it suits her. She has a nice lover but she's not in a serious committed relationship, which is very nice but I think she's quite fancy free.

GRAHAM: Maybe we're a little bit cynical about believing in stuff, that it's somehow unfashionable. I don't even necessarily mean religion. I just mean that kind of enthusiasm that can be kind of embarrassing when people express it for a bigger idea.

LOUISE: I wouldn't have to jam everything in. And I think that's kind of part of it – I want to do everything all the time, I want to see people all the time, get things all the time, I always want things.

NICK: I think we're presented with such colossal problems of perspective and scale in terms of information we're given, what's available to us, that it's... the ability to do the right thing – and this is in terms of everybody in the world – eludes us.

GRAHAM: Most technological things... *(Points at camera.)*

The Maelstrom

The shipping forecast... Rockall, poor, rising more slowly, Malin Force 7 poor, rising...

zap

(A Yoga Demonstration)
And breathe in...

zap

(A Reporter on Lewis speaking to camera on a windy, wet, cliff.)
This is the harsh north Atlantic ocean. Somewhere out there, forty miles to the east of this lonely spit of rock, the Tanker 'Spirit of 76' is drifting. Out of control. Towards the Rockall where she will surely break up under heavy seas and that can only mean one thing for the people of this isolated settlement... catastrophe.

zap

And breathe out...

zap

(A sportsperson being interviewed while still sweaty after the game)
I don't know what happened. We just lost it. Full credit to them they came out and did what they had to do but... at the end of the day it's up to us I don't make any excuses we just have to –

zap

(A bomb falls nearby)

zap

And breathe in…

zap

(*A gardening advice programme. Presenter and Expert discuss soil.*)
So this soil is a sandy soil?
That's right,
So what can Jenny do to improve a soil like this?
Well.
I think I know what you're going to say.
What I always say –
Compost.
You must lay down compost.

zap

(*A bomb falls again. Nearer this time.*)

zap

(*An old person speaking in Gaelic, as they speak another voiceover translates their words at the same time. The old person's mouth moves but the voice comes from elsewhere.*)
We used to take the cattle up to the sheilings in the summer time, it was always a time of great fun for the children then because there was singing and great activity. You know. The whole village would gather –

zap

(*A bomb falls. A woman loses her head completely.*)
Oh my god
Oh my god oh my god…

zap

(Strikers gathered round a brazier. Cheerful, cold, defiant. A reporter nearby to camera.)
The strike is now in its eighth week, and the strain is beginning to tell on the workers on this picket line in Hull.

zap

(A video diary recorded high on a mountain by a young climber, in his tent.)
I'm just amazed by the Sherpas, I mean me and Sam have been carrying loads up the mountain, probably half what they've been carrying and we're … f-ing knackered but the Sherpas just – they just seem to carry on … and they're still cheerful. It's a … it's some kind of … it's … –

zap

A violent kicking.

zap

(A striker talking to the reporter.)
Striker – It's not easy no. Because obviously the money's very tight and I'm having to say to the kids not to get trainers you know which is very hard – but it's what we have to do – if you believe in it, you have to fight for it.

zap

(A young woman holding a bottle of tomatoes. A voiceover.)
For centuries the women of Giorgininato Family have been bottling tomatoes to preserve the ripe, juicy goodness and flavour of the sun. They kept the recipe secret for generations … and then Maria came along –
(Woman gives a sheepish/sexy/aren't I naughty sort of look.)

zap

(A novelist and an interviewer on a literary show.)
How long did it take you to write?
Ten years.

That's a long time.
I wanted to get it right.

zap

(The young woman holding the tomatoes. Voiceover.)
Del Pomodoro – The Secret's Out.

Y.W.:   Don't tell my mother.

zap

(The literary show.)
The book's been translated into over twenty languages, it's sold millions of copies ... I suppose you must feel that's a vindication if you like of the time you spent on it.

No. I don't really see it that way. I wrote this book for myself. I don't need you know sales as a vindication. This was ... something I needed to write.

We're running out of time. Perhaps you could just read a passage for us ...

Sure. 'We mourn uneasily, guilty, unsure what to do or say unsure if maybe we are at fault. Bill loosens his tie. And then tightens it again ...'

zap

(A doctor on a mid-morning show.)
We recommend you check your testicles every morning by cupping them in your hand and lifting them gently ...

zap

(Someone is shot dead.)

zap

(A reporter running dust through their fingers.)
This is the dusty soil in the northern Sahel region of Sudan which is the surest sign of a drought that's claiming –

zap

(Gritty made for TV Drama on ITV.)
– Don't say that.
– It's the truth.
– No.
– She's never coming back. Say it.
– …
– SAY IT.

zap

(An advert for the Irish Tourist Board. Irish music and voiceover.)
There is a place where the song goes on forever, where sparrows quarrel in the eaves, where the full moon sits in a milky sky, where I lift my glass to my mouth – I look at you and sigh.

Ireland – In your dreams.

zap

(A whispering wildlife presenter.)
The Dry Season is the time when The Elephant, the great ship of the Savannah must set out on her longest journey… a desperate search for water.

zap

(An advert. A man looks at a rose.)
(v.o.) A Rose is a rose is a rose is a rose.
(The man impulsively gives the rose to a woman.)
(v.o.) But eternity is in a stolen moment.

zap

(Whispering wildlife presenter.)
She has only one enemy, man. The poacher and his guns.

zap

(Stonethrowers in the intifada.)

zap

(The reporter on the cliff.)
This is the harsh north Atlantic ocean. Somewhere out there –

zap

(A trailer for shows later on.)
Coming up – *Seinfeld* Night – make yourself a cup of tea, put your feet up, and hang out with the guys. –

SEINFELD CHARACTER: I'm afloat, without an anchor my friend… and you are the rocks of
                meaningless death.

zap

(A teacher and pupils at MacDonalds university.)
McChicken Nuggets
McChicken Nuggets
McChicken Nuggets with Salty Fries
McChicken Nuggets with Salty Fries
And Smile.
(They smile.)
Will that be all?
Will that be all?
And smile.
(They smile.)

zap

(A science presenter.)
This the Panjshir Valley, high in the Caucasus Mountains…

zap

(A man vomiting. A voiceover speaks.)
How long will this drunk man vomit?
Twenty seconds: press one. Thirty seconds: press two. Forty seconds: press three.

zap

(The science presenter.)
The people here live on a diet of apricots and rice.
And scientists are asking – is that why they live so long?

zap

(A historian to camera.)
For the Palestinians, the Nakba or Catastrophe of 1948 is the defining national moment of loss.
And, inevitably it is to that trauma that they return … again and again in –

zap

(The science presenter.)
Is the secret – hidden in the apricots?

zap

(A shy couple who have chosen to live in a wilderness. An interviewer talks to them.)
There's really nothing here is there.
No.
It's just … wilderness.
Yes.
And you're going to live here.
Yes.
You're mad aren't you.
Yes.

zap

(A real person, speaking quietly to a camera.)
I will go home. I believe I will go home.

zap

(The reporter on the cliff.)
The storm's rising behind me. The air itself seems full of salt water. Night's falling and a bank of fog is sweeping in from the west. The stricken tanker seems, for now, beyond rescue. All the people here can do – is pray.

zap

(All pray.)
The shipping forecast.

The Apricots

[All except Callum, praying, kneeling, sitting up, bowing down.
Callum watches.
The praying continues, businesslike and quiet.

The praying ends and Paul and Graham stand apart, Kate and Lou are filling pots from the well. And then pouring the water back into the well. They work peacefully and calmly, ocassionally laughing with natural delight and joy.]

PAUL: How was your work this afternoon, brother?

GRAHAM: I worked in the orchard this morning, brother.
The harvest will be good if god wills it.

PAUL: If god wills it.
If you don't need to work now why not rest.
Come and play dice and drink water with me. Let's talk.

GRAHAM: I'd like that brother.
The sun's mild today.
Let's play here on the bare earth.

[They sit to play dice.]

PAUL: The clouds are low in the valley.

GRAHAM: The winter monsoon is coming soon … if god wills it.

PAUL: If god wills it.
You seem worried brother.
Your brow is knotted. This morning you didn't eat as many dried apricots as you normally do. Is everything well with you and your family?

GRAHAM: You're right, I am worried brother.

PAUL: Share your worries with me.

GRAHAM: I've had some news from outside the valley.
It's troubling.

PAUL: Tell me.

GRAHAM: Do you remember the woman from London who came here two monsoons ago and asked us about the food we ate and she asked us how it was that we people of the valley came to live until we are one hundred and thirty-six years old in many cases if god wills it.

PAUL: If god wills it.

GRAHAM: Do you remember that we told her that we drink only water, that we eat primarily the apricots we grow in our orchards, and also wholegrain barley which we use in our bread. We told her that the barley is also made into a porridge which we feed to our children.

PAUL: I remember brother.

GRAHAM: Yesterday, I received a letter from my cousin who went to seek his fortune in London. He said that all the women of the city are now buying Panjshir Valley Barley Bread, and they feed their babies Panjshir Valley Barley Porridge for a long long life. And everyone reads a diet book called *The Apricot Way*. The people of London they want to live as we do. They want to know our secrets.

PAUL:	Why worry, Brother. We can still live as we've always lived. If god wills it.
GRAHAM:	If god wills it. Brother, the young people are sailing to London and New York in rickety boats. Brother [ ].
PAUL:	Jeroboam.
GRAHAM:	Brother Jeroboam has bought a satellite television and every night people gather in his house and watch hardcore pornography. The apricot harvest gets smaller every year because of global warming probably and I don't know it just doesn't seem right. Something about it doesn't seem right.
PAUL:	A world of sadness is creeping into the valley like the first snowcloud of winter.

[Callum enters the scene.]

CALLUM:	Brothers.
PAUL:	Brother what brings you here?
CALLUM:	I have come to tell a story in the village this evening.
GRAHAM:	Welcome welcome.
KATE:	The storyteller has arrived.
LOU:	Welcome, brother storyteller.
PAUL:	It's always a great pleasure in the valley when you visit us, brother storyteller. What story do you bring us today?
CALLUM:	Today I bring a story of death and sadness.
GRAHAM:	That's a story we are ready to hear. We look forward to you telling it.
CALLUM:	If you will allow me to rest a moment and wash and eat a small repast.
PAUL:	Bring yoghurt and dried apricots for the storyteller.
GRAHAM:	Call the children together, clear a circle of bare earth, bring water in a … goatskin … light fires, do … things.

Seinfeld

[Lou is sitting out.

The main room in an American sitcom household. Kate is looking at a bag of apricots. Callum is doing yoga.]

KATE: What the! – Callum?

[Big cheer.]

          The refrigerator is full of apricots.

[Laugh]

          Where are all the Hersheys?

CALLUM: There's no space in my life for Hersheys, Kate. Not anymore.

[A look from Kate
A big Laugh.]

GRAHAM: Callum, you are Hershey bars. Hershey bars and checked shirts and sometimes a baseball cap. That's you.

[A big cheer.]

CALLUM: Not anymore. Apricots contain all the vitamins and minerals a person needs to live. Apparently there are guys in the Caucasus Mountains who live till they're two hundred years old because they only eat Apricots.

GRAHAM: Who wants to live till they're two hundred anway?
          …
          Oh yeah. I forgot. You do. You've got a thing about death.

[Laugh.]

CALLUM: I haven't got a 'thing' about death.

KATE: You do.

CALLUM: I don't. Death has a 'thing' about me.

[Laugh.]

CALLUM: Death won't leave me alone. It hangs around outside my apartment trying to get my autograph. Death follows me about staring at me with slavering retarded facial expressions. Death is my stalker.

[Laugh.]

KATE: I get it. Death is stalking you and apricots are your restraining order.

[Big laugh.]

CALLUM: When am I going to get some peace around here!
Look if you don't mind. I need to concentrate on my breathing.

[For a few moments, all are silent as Callum concentrates on his breathing.]

GRAHAM: Might as well be dead for all the fun he's having.

[Laugh.]

*[Paul enters.
A big cheer.]*

PAUL: Hi guys. Or should I say *(He whistles)*.

CALLUM: Quiet!

[Big laugh.]

GRAHAM: Callum's doing yoga. It's like the grave in here.

KATE: We have to be as quiet as sand. Callum's concentrating on his breathing.

[Laugh.]
[Graham steps out.]

PAUL: Why does he have to concentrate – breathing's not so hard is it?

KATE: It is for Callum.

*[Big laugh. Lou and Graham enter.
Big cheer.]*

GRAHAM: You've got to help us out, Louise. Callum's obsessing about death.

LOU: So what's new.

[Laugh.]

CALLUM: I am not obsessing about death. I'm doing yoga.

LOU: Guys, Guys. This is all my fault. Oh no.
I was reading *The Aprticot Way* and
I told Callum that it contains the secret of eternal life.
In the book it says the secret to long life is apricots and yoghurt. In the Caucasus Valley that's what they eat.
Not yoga – yoghurt – yoghurt. Yoga. Yoghurt. Yoga. I wish I had more mental stability.

[Big laugh.
Hugging.]

The Good Earth

[Lou is an elderly woman, showing Kate, her grandaughter, the land. Graham, Callum and Paul are out.]

KATE: Tell me what it was like, Gran, what was it like,
Before.
What was it like before the Catastroph?

LOU: I don't like to talk about the Catastroph love.

KATE: Please.

LOU: It makes me very sad.

KATE: Please talk about it.

LOU: Well.

KATE: Please.

LOU: Look at the earth girl. Get down on your hands and knees
and touch it. Grab it. Feel the texture of it. Smell it.

[Kate does so.]

Before the Catastroph the island was covered in things that grow. Everything you can see for miles around girl. That was ours. Ours to grow things on. Over there – that's where we grew carrots, not just ordinary carrots but the sweetest, purest, most delicious carrots in the whole of the celtic world. And there that's where we grew barley. And there … down the side of the hillock by the copse, that's where we grew random stuff. And the grass, girl, oh you should have tasted the grass, it was the sweetest [ ] our cows were fat and happy and every morning I would lead the cows out to the high pastures on Ben Somethingorother. We girls would play happily together as the cows ate the bracken and heather. I remember we would play flutes and guitars which we had whittled from wood during the summer months. We would play and sing.

KATE: What sort of things would you play and sing.

LOU: Oh nonsense. Just airs and hornpipes.

GRAHAM: Could you play one for us now?

LOU: No. It would be unseemly for an old woman of the type of myself to sing or play a frivolous tune of childhood. Women such as myself know very well when to stop.

GRAHAM: Of course.

KATE: Yes.

LOU: Old women of the type of myself, before, before the Catastroph would sing The Lament. I myself was taught it when I reached the age of twelve. I remember it very clearly. When I was a child, I and [ ]

[Lou drops out.]

CALLUM: and my brothers would sleep in that bed, that very bed there, and my mother and father would sleep on the peat by the fire. One night I woke up screaming. I felt terrible fear. And my mother came and stilled me. And she said. Did you have a nightmare Ruauauauariridgh. And I said Mother I dreamed of being chased by an evil darkness. And my mother hugged me close to her bosom and said to my father, 'Hector, it is time'. My father looked very serious. My mother said, 'Hector, the boy has had his first nightmare. It is time for him to be taught the lament.' Well, the next morning I was taken to the house of the bard. I was scared I can tell you. The bard was a man as old as I am now. My parents stood at the door of his cottage and I was sent in to see him. It was dark in the cottage. The bard asked me to sit. He asked me if I was ready to learn the song. I said I was ready. And then the bard began to sing. He stood in front of the fire and he sang the saddest song you could ever hear. A song of terrible terrible sorrow.

The song went like this: [ ]

Cowboys

[The cowboys have finished a long day's riding and are setting up camp under the stars. Paul is looking out at the trail ahead.]

PAUL: Rough country.

CALLUM: Another two days' ride I reckon. Then we can rest the horses.

PAUL: Two days. Maybe three.

CALLUM: Maybe three.

PAUL: I can see dust rising about a day's ride behind us.
They're coming.

CALLUM: What are we running from this time, partner.

PAUL: You know, in all the excitement. I clean forgot.
Maybe when they catch up, I'll remember.

CALLUM: Ruby Gonzales runs a cantina in town.
Nobody makes burritos and fried beans like Ruby does.
We can eat there.

PAUL: I guess a man could die happy with burritos in his belly
and Ruby Gonzales in his arms.

*[They busy themselves in the camp. They make the fire.
Callum whistles.]*

Kenya

[Lou is stalking a poacher.
Graham is out.]

LOU: Stay down.
Look.
Here. Tracks. They must be close by.
They're following the elephants.
Poachers.
Shhh.
Listen.

[She listens.]

CALLUM: What you looking at?

PAUL: Nothing.
It's a big country.
That's all.

CALLUM: Yuh.

PAUL: Big enough for a man to get lost in.
To lose himself completely.
To –

CALLUM: You want to eat?

[Callum goes to get food from the saddlebags.
Shots ring out.
Lou is shooting poachers.
Callum (as a Kenyan Poacher) falls dead.
Lou is injured.]

LOU: Cameron! Cameron! Where are you?
I think I shot one.
Cameron? Cameron?
Cameron are you all right.

GRAHAM: I'm all right. You got the bastard. Well done.

LOU: It had to be done.

[Graham hugs, kisses Lou.]

GRAHAM: You did a good job.
          …
          You're hurt.

LOU: It's nothing.
          It's just a nick.
          Got me on the arm. *(She winces.)*
          We have to find the elephants.
          We have to make sure they're OK.

GRAHAM: We have to get you cleaned up.
          The wound could be infected.

LOU: I have to find the elephants.

GRAHAM: Here, let me clean the wound for you.

[Graham tends to Lou.
Callum lies dead.]

PAUL: Sun's going down.
          I'll get the blankets from the saddlebags.
          Get some coffee in the pot.

[Callum and Paul around the campfire.
Paul whistles.]

          What is that tune.
          You got me whistling that damn tune now.

GRAHAM: I saw the elephants over by the waterhole,
          A family group two buck elephants and a hen elephant and a baby one.
          All dead.

LOU: He deserved what he got, the bastard.
          A family group.

GRAHAM: It's nearly dark, we'd better get back to the tents-cum-huts.
          There are visitors who'll want to be taken on safari tomorrow.

LOU: Sometimes life seems like such a fragile thing, Cameron.

GRAHAM: I know what you mean.

[Kate joins the boys sitting round the campfire.]

LOU: You know the tiny sparks of electricity that makes the skin move ever so slightly in
            our face, makes our eyes move, makes our bodies warm. All those tiny signals that
            tell us a person's alive. And then one day they just go. The electricity gets switched
            off. A dead body seems so solid, Cameron. It seems so like a stone.

GRAHAM: It's a natural process. We know that. We work with animals
            all the time. We know there's no pity in nature.

LOU: It's like we go through life losing everyone we care about
            and picking up stones instead. All those stones on our back.
            I hate it. It seems so insulting when you look at the stones.
            All that a person was, the whole space a person inhabited in
            the world, all the stuff that fills a person and in the end it's just
            Stones – sand.
            All those elephants, those lovely lovely elephants.

GRAHAM: C'mere.

[He hugs her.]

            C'mon now. Don't cry.
            Hey.
            You know what the kids in the village call you?

LOU: No.

GRAHAM: Dr Loulittle.
            You're doing a good job.
            Come back to the main reserve with me.
            We'll have a beer and watch the sun go down.

Tango

_____

[Kate is teaching the tango to Paul and Callum.]

KATE: Passion. Passion. Come on. Touch each other. You're in Buenos Aires, we touch.
             Here. Touch his bum. Here like this. Fire. You're full of fire. Feel the fire in your
             body feel the sparks. Every time your feet touch the ground sparks should fly. Your
             eyes. Look at each other. Honesty. Look directly into each other's eyes.

PAUL: Sorry about this.

CALLUM: It's OK.

KATE: Shut up. Shut your face.

[Kate gives them roses to put in their mouths.]

             Stop using words. Words are tricky little bastards. Sorry? What's sorry supposed
             to mean? Look. Touch. Do you like this man? Hold him. Pull him close to you.
             Look into his eyes. Laugh. Fight. Punch him. Punch him in the face. Then drink
             with him. Then kiss him. Then fuck him. Take him to a hotel, somewhere with a
             thin matress on a metal bed and a badly wired electric fan and wooden shutters
             and make love to him till the sheet is soaked in sweat and spunk and blood. C'mon.
             Feel some passion.

[Paul drops out.
Graham starts working on his guitar, touching the wood, tasting the wood.
Callum continues, Lou dances with him.]

KATE: That's not passion. That's Scottish country dancing. That's drizzle falling on a cold
             poke of chips. Touch her bum.
             You can't do it, can you?
             You want to but you can't.
             You want to kiss her but you can't.

CALLUM: I just don't think it's appropriate –

KATE: Shut up.
             You're using words again.
             How many times does this happen.
             You're sitting in the Vicky Bar or something, and she's sitting next to you and you
             want to grab her,
             and … and…
             to grab her and communicate to her with your whole body
             because god knows we'll all be dead and in the ground
             one day – and what do you do – you say some stupid words like 'serendipity' or 'by

jingo' or 'grand'.

That isn't passion.

Look this is how you do it.

[ ]

That. That's passion.

Guitar Making in Madrid

_____

[Graham is in his workshop, working on a guitar.
Paul is with him.]

PAUL: Which wood will you use?

GRAHAM: That depends on what you want to play Don Alfonso.
         If you want to play happy music, I'll probably use spruce or maple. Those are lively
         woods. They carry spring and bounce. If you want to play angry music then I'll use
         [ ] because that's a wood that's hard and aggressive.

PAUL: I want to play a lamenting song.

GRAHAM: Then I'll make the guitar out of ash.

PAUL: Why ash.

GRAHAM: The ash tree is [ ].
         What will your lamenting song be about?

PAUL: I don't know exactly. I have a feeling. I think it's important but
         I don't know how to communicate it in words.

GRAHAM: Try.

PAUL: Is it important?

GRAHAM: Of course it's important. This isn't China Don Alfonso. I don't run off a hundred
         crap guitars by machine and pay my workers nothing. I make musical instruments.
         For musicians to express their deepest feelings upon.
         If I'm going to make a guitar for you I have to talk to you. I have to understand
         what you want your music to say.

PAUL: I want to write a lament for socialism.

GRAHAM: That's a good theme for a lamenting song.

African Village

GRAHAM: God. Louise. You're here at last. Come in. Come in.
           I'm so glad you're here.

LOUISE: I couldn't not come.
           Not when I heard about [ ]

GRAHAM: Sit down. Sit. You must be tired.
           It's so good to see you.

LOUISE: It's good to see you to my friend.

GRAHAM: How long did it take you to get here?

LOUISE: Six days.

GRAHAM: Tell me about your journey.
           Wait.
           You'll have a beer.
           I've got a beer.

LOUISE: A beer.
           I couldn't. No. Really.

GRAHAM: You must. Please. I insist. I've been saving it for you.

LOUISE: Thank you.

GRAHAM: Now. Tell me about your journey.

LOUISE: Well I walked from [ ] to [ ]. It was a pleasant walk. Now that the rains have come
           I watched the farmers harvesting in the fields. Then I stopped at the clinic in
           Catacataca and I got some medicine for [ ]

GRAHAM: You brought medicine. Thank you sister.

LOUISE: And then I got a lift on a tractor as far as Kenya. Then I walked the rest of the way.

GRAHAM: It's good to see you.

LOUISE: How is [ ]?

GRAHAM: He's not well.
But he'll be happy to see you.
All in good time. Rest now. Rest.
Tonight we'll have a [ ] in your honour.

[Paul and Graham are in a Tapas Bar.]

PAUL: I just think there was a time when people believed that radical change was possible. When people really thought that we would take over the factories, you know. I know it seems naive, but that thing of just protesting … of badges and … you know – that all meant something. And you look around now and the trains don't fucking arrive and you stand on the platform like a fucking arse with all the other commuters and you think what am I doing here. I'm thirty-two and I dress like a fucking student. And I look at all the other poor bastards waiting in the rain for some decrepit piece of rolling stock and it used to belong to us. It used to be in the hands of the nation. And it was better then. Not because it actually was better but because you thought it would become better. Because it was up to us. We were working for each other. We were citizens not fucking customers. Not fucking clients. You know. I just wish I was engaged again. You know. Young again. Doing something like – I don't know those Wombles who protest against capitalism or something.

GRAHAM: I made the guitar for your lamenting song, Don Alfonso.
I made the sound board out of ash.
So that the instrument has a sad tone.
But I made the headboard out of pine.
Because there was a softness in what you were saying,
Like you weren't sure
And I made the body out of spruce because the timbre of
your voice when you spoke was bright and warm as though
you were remembering a summer day of the type we don't
get anymore.
Here.

[They play the guitar.]

The Photographer in Mexico City

[Kate is taking photographs. Callum is interviewing her.]

CALLUM: How long have you been a photographer, Kate?

KATE: Ever since I can remember. When I was a little girl, I used to run around in my pants taking photographs just of the garden, you know, my family, birds in the garden. That sort of thing.

CALLUM: One thing the critics have said is that there's an immense feeling of delight in your work. Your pictures convey a sort of essence of nature. They capture the city, the nuttiness of it. Would you agree with that?

KATE: Oh, I don't know. I don't like to think about that. I just take the photographs, you know, when it feels right.

CALLUM: You take the pictures and you never get them developed.

KATE: That's right.
I like to leave them in the camera.
You know.
Because I always think the best pictures are the ones you haven't taken to be developed yet. They're so full of possibility.
When you get them developed and people look at them. They lose something. They're not alive anymore. They're just stones.

[Kate's mobile rings.]

Hello.
…
OK.
Yeah…
I'll take the beetle. I'll be over in twenty minutes.
My lover.
I called him earlier on.
I said I wanted to see him.
I do that every few days.
I'd better go.
He's really nice.

Irish Wake

[All singing. Paul dead, wearing his scarf.]

ALL: I can't live, if living is without you.
                    I can't live, I can't live anymore.
                    (etc. to end.)

CALLUM: He loved that song.

GRAHAM: He loved it.

LOU: He could sing up a storm when he wanted to could old Paully O'Noley.

GRAHAM: And now he's dead.

KATE: Here's to him.

ALL: Here's to him.

LOU: He's dead all right. As dead as a stone in a bag of stones.

[All laugh.]

CALLUM: I remember a story. Do you know of a place called Ballynabally.
Well, one night Paully and I were up there doing a play that I'd written. *The Unfolding.* You might have seen it. Anyway it doesn't matter now. Paully was fantastic in it. He ripped the house apart every night and there was standing ovations and people throwing chairs at the ceiling and yelling and making their children dance for us and all kinds of things like that. Anyway that night after the show, Paully was in the mood for a drink – and you know Paully – God rest his soul he was a good man to his mother but he did love the ladies – anyway – that night he was wearing his best bib and tucker and dressed like a [ ]

[All laugh.]

              That was Paully O'Noley.
              That was Paully O'Noley.

[All weep.]

CALLUM: You're born and you live and you die he said to me.
              But for god sakes don't weep at my funeral.

Drink yourself into a stupor and kiss any girls for me and tell them I don't regret a minute of it.

KATE: That was Paully O'Noley.

LOU: He was a poet.

CALLUM: A poet and a gentleman.

KATE: And I loved him.

ALL: [ ]

Alyaska

KATE: We'll need to go to town soon for supplies.

PAUL: I heard there's a kid sick at the inuit settlement up at [ ]
          I'll need to take the plane.

KATE: I could take the other plane.

PAUL: I need to check the carburettors.
          When I flew into Anchorage it was making a funny noise.
          I just need to take a look at it.

KATE: What's wrong with the kid?

PAUL: Meningitis.
          I'd better get down there as soon as I can.
          They are neighbours.

KATE: You be careful. When you see Chief Muckaluck tell him I was asking for him.

PAUL: I will.
          Last time I went up there – remember – when Mary Sue was giving birth. They sent me back with a caribou. They'd been hunting. I had to sit the damn thing in the plane next to me. Strapped in and everything.

KATE: Still. It gave us meat for a whole winter. Even though I'm a vegetarian.

PAUL: Good meat.
Pure.
Wild meat.

[Kate goes out. Lou replaces her.]

LOU: They're great hunters. And they have great extended families.

PAUL: They do.
They care.
They live up here in this godforsaken place and they know it
the way my brother Clem knows Wall Street. They can read it
like a book. Those skills are dying out.
You know what's killing them?

LOU: Yeah.

PAUL: It's us. We're killing them.

LOU: Not you and me?

PAUL: No. Not us. We understand those ways. We have respect. We've learned – the hard
way. Remember those hunting trips they took us on. They were hard for us but we
learned. They look after each other. They don't have poor or rich people. They're
together. They work for each other and they respect the old and they share
everything. That's all dying.

LOU: What makes it so sad is they know how to live peacefully and calmly. They don't
go on rampages at the weekend. They don't have twenty-four hour Caribou shops.
They don't go oh – will I have this berry or that berry no I'll have them all
I'll just stuff a whole fat load of berries and caribou in my mouth and then go and
get fucking ratarsed. They know how to live calmly. And that's all dying.

PAUL: Sure as a stone drops in a lake.
How to skin a [ ] and how to pray to [ ] and how to heal a broken [ ] with herbs.
It's all gone.
I'll go and fire up the fucking plane.

Sherpas

[High on the mountain. Graham is preparing to leave to climb.]

GRAHAM: There's a storm coming.

CALLUM: The mountain's angry.

KATE: She's angry because the sahibs climb all over her and then just totally disrespect her. Talk about her like they've fucked her or something.

GRAHAM: Annapurna is a fickle mistress.

CALLUM: She's not a woman I would take for a wife.

GRAHAM: She'd always be asking you for money.

[All laugh.]

CALLUM: The mountain is hard like a mother and also when a mother is angry on behalf of her children she gets very violent but also gathers in her children to her skirts.

KATE: As we sherpas say:
The goddess welcomes to her breast
Those who dare to stop and rest
Her pointed peaks swell up high
Which makes the wolves howl to the sky
Her snowy hair and jagged teeth
Hide hidden beauty underneath.

PAUL: I'll come with you, Rongbu. Don't go alone.
There were avalanches near Camp three.

GRAHAM: Sahib Graham is sick. He has altitude sickness.

PAUL: He should never have climbed so high.

GRAHAM: He is my friend. I'm going to get him.

PAUL: He is very sick. He may be dead by now.

GRAHAM: I heard his voice on the radio.
He was breathing.
All things that breathe are sacred.

We have to bring him down.
The mountain hates death.

KATE: I think we should do a puja for the mountain.

PAUL: We've never performed the ritual this high on the mountain before.

CALLUM: She's right.

[They gather round the fire.]

ALL: [ ]

GRAHAM: Take this. Give it to the mountain.

KATE: But that's your lucky Carababa.

GRAHAM: I don't need luck.
The mountain is our mother. From now on I'm in her arms.
She'll take care of me.

[Graham leaves.]

People Working The Land

[Kate, Lou and Callum work the land, sowing seeds.
This continues for some moments peacefully.]

GRAHAM: What are you expecting from the crop this year.

PAUL: Twenty thousand single stems.

GRAHAM: What sort of quality.

PAUL: Kenya Grade A.

GRAHAM: That's a good harvest. I'll call my people in Amsterdam and have them send you a price. We'll air freight the roses to Schiphol and then market them on from there. What sort of price are you looking for?

PAUL: I'm looking for a bullshit price. Pennies. Kenyan pennies.

GRAHAM: Good. I'll make a good profit for both of us then.

PAUL: Excellent. Superb. Clap your hands over your fat belly.
Laugh. I get away with paying my workers twenty pence a day. Laugh. The profits
go to pension funds. Say –
'the profits go to pension funds.' Their fingers bleed.
They work fourteen hour days. Say 'Good'
No – not like that – like this – it's backbreaking.
It's in the hot sun and you're lucky to have this job at all. It used to be your
grandfather's land anyway and I took it so fuck you.
That's what I'm like. And you probably live huddled in dormitories dreaming of
your kids back home, no – I just make the kids work as well. And then a whole lot
of roses gets sent off to fucking Holland and sold to the Valentine's Day punter
at twenty quid a pop – Jesus you can't even buy a rose for the woman you love
without somebody being exploited like a fucking donkey. You might as well wield
the whip yourself – Darling, I love you, I want to marry you here's a rose and
here's a dead kid whose dad didn't have enough money to feed him and it's your
fault. Fuck.

[Paul continues over the next scene.]

The Glass-Bottomed Fishing Boat

[All are on a glass-bottomed fishing boat.]

KATE: All aboard the glass-bottomed fishing boat.
Come on board.
Careful of the step.
That's right.
Let me give you a hand.

[Kate gives everyone a tomato.]

Have a tomato.
Have a tomato.

PAUL: What do you do – make a paper rose. Grow your own rose. Put them out of the
only pathetic job they've got. Take their twenty pence a day away. Buy a fair trade

rose. Where am I going to get one of them at half-past six on Valentine's Day in Pollockfuckingshields I'll just pick a flower from some poor cunt's garden and give that to her and then she'll think I'm cheap. Which I'm not I'm just in love with a girl and don't want to kill people. I don't want people to die on my behalf in foreign fucking countries. Is that too much to ask.

[Paul exits.]

KATE: Welcome to my Glass-Bottomed Fishing Boat.
           My Name's Catherina Costacoffeebutic.
           And I'm going to be taking you round the island today.

LOU: It's just so beautiful.

KATE: Isn't it.
           Isn't it just brilliant.
           Shall we just – be happy
           Let's just – be happy
           Would anyone like a Cortado.
           Look at the fish for god's sake.
           Have you ever – been as content as this.

GRAHAM: What sort of things are we likely to see señora?

KATE: You'll see eels and dolphins and turtles and [ ]

The Poor Tent

[Callum, Kate and Lou welcome Graham in to their poor tent.]

CALLUM: Welcome, welcome Grahm.
           Sit.
           I'm sorry we don't have cushions.
           I would very much have liked to welcome you to our old
           house, not into this poor tent.
           But this poor tent is all we have so –
           Please make yourself comfortable.
           Girls, let Grahm have the cushion. Bring him some coffee.

GRAHAM: Thank you.
Please don't go to any trouble.
I brought a – small present.

CALLUM: You shouldn't have.

[Graham gives them a cassette recorder.]

GRAHAM: It's nothing, really, it's just – I thought you might like some
music and I had this – I brought it with me and I can buy
another one when I go home. I just remembered you saying
that you liked music and …

[Callum is in tears.]

KATE: We feel ashamed Grahm.

GRAHAM: Please don't feel ashamed.

KATE: No Grahm. It's just Dad used to love music so much.
In our old house, before the Catastroph we used to have music all the time. My
father's a very cultured man, Grahm –
He had a library of records of all the music of our country that used to take up a
whole room. A whole room in the house. And on Saturday evenings he would go
up there with his friends …

LOU: Dad knew all the poets and all the intellectuals of the city in those days. And
they'd go up to the room at the top of the house and listen to music and discuss
the future.

CALLUM: They're all gone now.
Some were killed in the Catastroph.
Some left.
Some are like us, refugees now.

KATE: And my mother, I remember one night when I was a girl I must only have been six,
and I heard music playing and I crept into the courtyard and I still remember the
scent of Jasmine …

LOU: In our old house we had a Jasmine tree in the courtyard Grahm and in summer
the scent filled every room.

KATE: And I crept up to the music room and I opened the door just a tiny bit and I
peeped in and I saw dad dancing with my mother to an old tune.

LOU:	Our mother was a beautiful woman.
KATE:	And from such a rich family. They were aristocrats. They sold horses and my grandfather had his own army but she was a wild spirit and she married my father even though he was only a doctor.
LOU:	And we peeped in to the room.
KATE:	And they were dancing.

[Kate hums the tune 'I can't live if living is without you'.]

CALLUM:	That's enough. Grahm, you don't know how much this means to me. I can't possibly thank you enough. All we have is this poor tent, and this poor food.
GRAHAM:	It's nothing. It's really nothing at all. It's just –
CALLUM:	Please, accept out hospitality. I'm afraid we can only offer you porridge and bread and coffee. The rations in the camp… you know…
GRAHAM:	I know. I… understand. I – please. Don't go to any trouble.
KATE:	Please have some apricots.
LOU:	I went to the market today because I knew you were coming and I managed to find some apricots.
GRAHAM:	I know how much that means. Believe me. Thank you.
CALLUM:	Please eat.
GRAHAM:	Let me share them with you.
CALLUM:	You're our guest Grahm. We still have our hospitality. Please, forget your surroundings. Let's all forget our surroundings. Eat.

[Graham eats.
They watch.]

GRAHAM:	Delicious.
KATE:	I'm ashamed to serve them to you.
LOU:	Those apricots have no flavour. In our old house, the market used to be just below our window. And you should have seen the apricots then.

KATE:	My mother would have sent a servant down. 'Rokaka' she would say, we have guests, go down to the market and get some apricots and only pick the very best mind you.
LOU:	Rokaka was killed in the bombing during the Catastroph.
KATE:	And she would bring back apricots so succulent and bittersweet you'd think they'd fallen from heaven.
LOU:	And we'd have sesame bread, and casseroles of lamb and carrots stuffed with rice and peas and
KATE:	And Dad would sit with you out on the roof of our house.
LOU:	On embroidered carpets and brocaded cushions and we'd serve coffee on low tables.
KATE:	And the sounds of the souk would drift up from below.
LOU:	And the stars would be rising.
CALLUM:	I wish you could have visited us then Grahm. We could have smoked the Nargila and talked about poetry. I know you like to talk about poetry.
GRAHAM:	I'm really not an expert.
CALLUM:	You're an educated young man. I don't meet many educated men any more I'm afraid. The men in the camps are good men but they're mainly farmers and artisans. I teach them a little but what can they really know about the sixteenth-century poets. But enough. Tell me about your life.
KATE:	Tell us about your house.
LOU:	If we visited your house, what would your wife serve?
GRAHAM:	If you came to my house in Glasgow we would ... we would [ ]
KATE:	In our old house we had a glass-bottomed fishing boat. And in the summer I would take the tourists out and we'd just look at the fish and then I would come home and eat tomatoes and then I'd come home and drink cortados and eat tomatoes I used to love tomatoes and then I'd just lie about in the sun, I used to love the sun, and that's what I'd do. Before the ctstrof. I probably haven't seen a tomato for five years. If I saw a tomato I'd probably cry.

GRAHAM: What do you want me to say?

CALLUM: How are your apricots.

GRAHAM: Lovely thank you.

KATE: We live in a fucking tent in some country that doesn't want us but that doesn't
            mean we're not human. I know what a tomato is.

CALLUM: You should have seen our old house.

GRAHAM: I'm sorry.

KATE: I know what tomatoes are supposed to taste like.
            You've got food mountains in big barns piled up to the fucking roof with rotting
            tomatoes and barns bloody great things somewhere near Belgium probably and
            you can eat until you're sick and puke fucking bloody marys for all I care –

GRAHAM: Right.
            I'm the editor of *The Guardian*.
            'Lets do a piece on refugee cookery.'

KATE: She has a life. Never mind olive oil, never mind recipes, never mind apricots. She
            has a fucking life. It doesn't take a lot of imagination. She has a life and a mother
            and now she's just sand.

GRAHAM: Prada did a season of menswear based on Intifada Chic, so they write about that.
            Let's fill the paper with pictures of old men with watery eyes. Let's write about
            London because that's all anybody in the whole world cares about because nobody
            else exists. Did you see what blah blah said about blah blah. It's a scandal. What's
            inside Elton John's cupboard. It's all so vacuous but I read the fucking paper. I
            read it. So what does that make me. I just want – to talk one to one on an honest
            level about what's happening. There's all this stuff in the world – suddenly we can
            go anywhere, talk to anyone anywhere in the world and all of a sudden we realise
            we've got nothing. Nothing worth saying.

CALLUM: You should have seen our old house.

LOU: I think I can hear planes.

CALLUM: The old house when it was full. Aunties and cousins and
            uncles and kids. The kids running up and down the stairs
            all over the place.

LOU: I can definitely hear planes.

[Bombs falling.
Lou is bombed.
Three times she flinches.]

CALLUM: Do you notice the light, Maria?
            I love the way the evening light makes the lagoon seem so soft, almost like Venice
            is hovering somewhere between being about to appear and about to disappear.
            Can you bring me a cigarette Maria. I'm going to smoke one. Only one. It's a
            celebration. I finished the novel. *The Unfolding* by Salvatore Salvatore. You know
            when I started writing it I thought it was a metaphysical story about faith but now
            that it's finished I look at it and I realise it's all about hope. The last word is hope.
            Are the family in the dining room. I love seeing them all there. All of them. Kids
            running about. Noise. I think I'll have a little grappa and a cigarette on the
            balcony and watch the sun set and then we'll eat. Together.

[The last bomb is very close.
Callum has a grappa and 'a cigarette?' He could just hold it.
Lou screams.
Then:]

LOU: Right, I'm George Bush right. Eating a pretzel. And it's like. Who'm I going to bomb?
            (Eats/chokes.)
            No because his daughter comes in. Not the pretty one the ugly one. There's a
            pretty one and an ugly one isn't there.
            So he's like.
            (Eats/chokes.)
            Fuck off.
            Cos she drinks the ugly one drinks and so he's…
            (Chokes.)
            Fuck off you ugly bitch. You've been drinking you fucking slag tart. What use are
            you? Get the other one. She's clever. She's better than you.
            No because he probably choked because he was drunk.
            He's like.
            (Drinks. Eats. Chokes.)
            Fuck off you ugly slag bitch. You're drunk. Fucking. Bring the clever one. Who
            should I bomb today? Get out of my sight you hideous whore. Bring your sister.
            Because he's probably fucking her sister. *(Chokes.)* Bring your sister I want to fuck

her. I don't want to fuck you. I want to fuck your sister up the arse until she bleeds all over the White House floor. I don't want you. Fuck off. I don't. *(Chokes.)* I don't.

[Callum alone.
A good moment of this.
Then:]

CALLUM: I don't know an enormous amount about it.
It just seems unfair.
When there's so much plenty in the world.
That some of that plenty can be denied to others.
I think it must be humiliating, I think the humiliation must weigh quite heavily on those people.
The people in those countries must be.

[ ]

And the bankers, the politicians,
I think they must think.
I don't know what they think.
The people who say – It's good for them to have fiscal discipline.
I think to say that – you must be,
You can't possibly believe that.
You can't possibly look at another person's life in that way.
So I can't believe the bankers think.
I'm doing a good thing.
They must be like.

[ ]

They must be.

[ ]

Surely, they must be.

[ ]

Surely they must hope.

The Shrine Ritual

The final section of the show is made up of a series of ritual actions of lament. These are performed to musical accompaniment played live on stage. The actions are unhurried and methodical.

This section begins with the lighting of a fire.

These actions include; burning photographs, laying flowers at a shrine, someone wrapping themselves in a football flag and scarf, someone quietly singing an old song to themselves, looking through a photograph album, arranging photographs on top of a piano, putting up photographs of missing people, lighting candles in small jars.

During this section the metal fence at the back of the stage is gradually transformed into a kind of shrine. Each of the actors finds an object from around the stage and attaches it in some way to the fence. Some of these objects have been used as props in some of the scenes, others have personal significance for the actors. They include flowers, scarves, photographs, wreaths, bouquets of flowers.

Also during this section each of the actors records a personal story of loss into an old-fashioned tape recorder. The audience can just make these out over the music. The tape is then played through the closing moments of the show.

The show culminates with all the actors singing quietly along with the music whilst performing ritualistic gestures around the fire, water and earth on stage.

They all take a handful of earth, turn towards the shrine and together throw the earth towards it as if scattering ashes.

THE END

Suspect Culture: Reaching Out

DAN REBELLATO

Over twenty years, the theatre company Suspect Culture created one of the most ambitious and complex bodies of work in British theatre. Based in Scotland, but with international reach and reputation, their work was widely acclaimed for its originality, range, and restless formal inventiveness that sought to capture, interrogate and transcend the contemporary world.

Characteristics of Suspect Culture's work were ambiguity and plurality. In *Mainstream* (1999), we follow the story of an encounter between a record company A&R person and someone from Personnel as they meet, argue, go for a drink, have a sexual encounter, and share an embarrassed hotel breakfast; but the story is splintered and scattered, showing us multiple different versions of every stage of the encounter, each possibility of the relationship, and the 'real' identities and actions of the two shift and shimmer and recede beyond reach.

The same might be said of Suspect Culture. They are known as an experimental theatre company, but they also made theatre for young people, literary adaptations, visual art installations, and a film. The company lived and worked in Scotland, but some critics found the work aggressively un-Scottish while others saw it as perhaps the most perfect representation of Scotland at the turn of the twenty-first century. The company's best-known member is the writer David Greig, but the shows were produced collaboratively by an ever-widening, global group of associate artists from Scotland, England, Spain, Italy and Brazil. For some critics their work was abstract and apolitical; for others it was fiercely and critically engaged in the contemporary world. For a few, the work was unemotional and ironically distant, but others echoed Greig's view that 'we're desperately, yearningly emotional [...] we're hopelessly naïve, we're romantic'.[1]

From *One Way Street* in 1994 – perhaps the first show that fully demonstrated their mature style – to *Stage Fright* in 2009, the company worked tirelessly in a range of forms eventually producing more than twenty theatre shows and several other works. Their prolific output, the shifting artistic team, the different styles and modes in which the company has worked make Suspect Culture difficult to pin down, but one can see a number of overlapping phases in their history. In addition, there are several recurring themes that cut across all of the work, regardless of the artistic mode or personnel. In this essay I will give a historical overview of the company, looking at the various phases in their development as a company, while also considering the way that artistic experiment and utopian politics are brought together in their productions.

EARLY YEARS (1991–1995)

Suspect Culture's early works took a great variety of forms and are clearly the work of a company feeling their way towards a style and a way of working. Nonetheless, these early apprentice works demonstrate a clear commitment to a new form of theatre-making and artistic work that would sustain the company right through its life.

Their first show, *A Savage Reminiscence*, a monologue imagining Caliban's reflections on life after the events of *The Tempest*, was performed at the Hen and Chicken pub theatre in Bristol, in a double bill with Sarah Kane's first play, *Comic Monologue*. The text was by David Greig and performed by Graham Eatough, who had met at Bristol University where the show was initially performed. Nick Powell, also studying at Bristol, wrote the music, beginning a collaboration that would span the whole of the company's history. Greig had directed a production of *The Tempest* in the Student Union at the end of his second year and the show suggested the loneliness of a character apparently discarded by the brutal narrative logic of Shakespeare's play. As such, it is a show about the cruelty of art. But it is also a piece of writing about writing, and a piece of theatre about theatre. At the beginning of the play, Caliban picks up a book from the pile left behind by the triumphant Prospero and reads the following line: 'So in the end…when one is doing philosophy…one gets to the point where one would like to emit an inarticulate sound'.[2] The book is Wittgenstein's *Philosophical Investigations* and captures two things about the fledgling company: first, its unabashed intellectualism. While it is easy to overstate this aspect of Suspect Culture's work – and some critics did duly overstate it – the company have always been happy to work at a high level of conceptuality, drawing on theory, research, and political thought. Unfashionably, at least when they started, they wanted to present themselves as artists and, Eatough in particular, found a particular conceptual and creative affinity between his work and that of visual artists such as Graham Fagen, with whom he would later collaborate on installation works. The name of the company itself, Suspect Culture, was a kind of Derridean pun between a description (of a culture that is suspect) and a prescription (that demanded that we be suspicious of culture).

Second, and perhaps in subtle contradiction to such austere theoretical allegiances, we can see in that quotation a dream of a kind of perfect, pre-conceptual form of communication. Wittgenstein is here discussing the impossibility of a purely private language, since, in his terms, all expression must exist within particular language games which are, by definition, public. What he expresses, uncharacteristically, is a moment of regret that the rules of a language game expose a communication and leave it prey to structures of syntax and interpretation that – one might feel – distance us from the original impulse of articulation. Wittgenstein's regret is reversed by Suspect Culture throughout their work, which, despite the complexity of culture, the inevitable forms of linguistic, social, political mediation that divide us, insists on the possibility of some pure communion between people that would overwhelm all possible barriers. It is a motif that runs right through Suspect Culture's work from *A Savage Reminiscence* in 1991 to *Static* in 2008.

What *A Savage Reminiscence* also anticipates is the collaborative nature of the company. Although Greig appears to be the writer and Eatough the performer, the roles were fluid and overlapping, the show created through collaborative discussion and co-direction. In addition, the surviving text does not give a full sense of the performance's physical inventiveness, its series of simple but striking images that clarified and focused the narrative ideas. Over the next few shows, this would evolve into a much more insistent gestural language, which drew on Brecht as well as DV8 and Pina Bausch, among others, demonstrating a company that refused to situate the text as the only or dominant source of meaning in performance. The idea of Suspect Culture was, from the start, to establish a collaborative form of theatrical creation and a multi-disciplinary system of theatrical semiosis.

David Greig who spent his teenage years growing up in Edinburgh watched the growing confidence of Scottish culture and the opportunities it afforded to emerging artists and persuaded Eatough to establish their new company in Scotland. For the Edinburgh Fringe Festival in 1992, Greig took over a venue, the Roman Eagle Lodge, redesignating it 'Theatre Zoo', and mounted a considerable programme of work including his own play *Stalinland*, a devised show *The Garden*, *An Audience with Satan* (based on Tony Parker's collection of interviews with murderers, *Life after Life*), and the second Suspect Culture show *And the Opera House Remained Unbuilt*, which, like *A Savage Reminiscence*, also went on a modest tour. *Opera House* concerned two theatre workers after the Second World War, haunted by the complicity of the masses, consumed with the dilemmas of the peace, and, above all, traumatised by the impossibility of art after unthinkable genocide.

These themes echo the mid-century preoccupations of German philosopher Theodor Adorno, whose collection of aphorisms *Minima Moralia* also provides the play's epigraph. Adorno's work offers a way into understanding how Suspect Culture's riddling, austere, and formally experimental shows were not an escape but an instance of deep political engagement. In their thematics and the experiences they provoke, Suspect Culture's work can be seen as an intense and profound theatrical exploration of his characteristic themes of totality, negation and utopia. Adorno's most famous pronouncement, and it is this spirit in which *Opera House* unfolds, is that 'to write poetry after Auschwitz is barbaric'.[3] It was a position that he would withdraw from later, but emerged from a sense of traumatised horror at the scale of the Holocaust, its unthinkable enormity, and the way in which a whole culture had been dominated, mobilised and organised in order to destroy a people. With such forces unleashed within a society, there could be no hiding place, no opposition, no escape: even poetry would ultimately be complicit with it, hence an act of writing poetry would necessarily be not just complicit in barbarism but inevitably barbaric in itself.

The shadows of the concentration camps are long, but one might wonder why Adorno's arguments might have seemed so keenly pertinent to a group of young British theatre-makers fifty years after these atrocities. The answer perhaps lies in the way Adorno developed his argument to encompass the entire functioning of contemporary capitalism. The argument that Adorno developed with increasing urgency in the quarter-century after 1945 was a philosophically bleak reinterpretation of Marx's theory of history. Marx described history as a series of forms of society, each succeeding the other culminating in a final form, communism. At this point the dialectical contradictions between the general (social organisation) and the particular (human needs and abilities) that have driven this restless historical development disappear, thus bringing 'the prehistory of human society to a close'.[4] Adorno, in common with many Western Marxists, did not share Marx's confidence that communism will follow capitalism so cleanly. In particular, Adorno argues that the motor of history, contradiction, is at risk because the system as a whole is transforming every level of that society in its image, effacing any contradiction between general and particular, subsuming the latter into the former.

In *Negative Dialectics*, Adorno calls this 'identity-thinking', taking as his model Marx's opening to *Capital* where he describes how money becomes a general measure through which all things must pass in order to join the system of exchange. In the process, the particularity of these things is stripped away so that their monetary terms become their dominant (or even sole) attribute; money transforms the world of things into a world of exchange values.[5] And if everything is identified only by its monetary value then everything enters into a single system where everything can be bought and sold until, on a fundamental level, everything is the same. Where once there was a multiplicity of differences, 'the spread of the principle imposes on the whole world an obligation to become identical, to become total'.[6] If the system of exchange were totally to conquer the social world, the dialectical movement that would drive society beyond capitalism (to what Adorno variously calls 'true society', 'utopia' or 'freedom') would grind to a halt, leaving us imprisoned in a world incapable of change.

One of the only glimmers of hope in this adialectical darkness is art and it is here that one can begin to see the instinctive appeal of Adorno's vision for young theatre-makers in the early Nineties. The value of art, for Adorno, is that it provides a source of profound opposition to the empirical reality that has been colonised by identity-thinking and exchange. In part this is because art is useless – or, to put it more formally, the aesthetic quality of art is not something that serves any utilitarian purpose; it is simply a quality that is to be enjoyed for its own sake. If this is true, then it will be peculiarly impervious to the system of exchange ('the prevailing realm of purposes'[7]), which involves extracting and commodifying the *utility* of an object. As Adorno puts it, 'artworks were purposeless because they had stepped out of the means-end relation of empirical reality'.[8] Or as David Greig once put it, 'its uselessness is its value'.[9] As globalisation spreads exchange extensively and intensively across the world at all levels, art is an increasingly oppositional voice speaking against totality. 'Art must be and wants to be utopia,' says Adorno, 'and the more utopia is blocked by the real functional order, the more this is true'.[10]

Suspect Culture's work, then, even at its inception shows signs of an artistic response to radically transforming political times. The collapse of Eastern European communism in 1989 and the dissolution of the Soviet Union two years later was the most significant moment in a twenty-year history that saw the ideological abandonment of restraints on capitalism – through exchange controls, import and export tariffs, welfare provision, border controls – in favour of a belief in the free market. In the 1970s the World Bank and International Monetary Fund had been captured by free-market fundamentalists who used a debt crisis in the early 1980s to impose neo-liberalism on the developing world. Meanwhile in Britain and the United States, Margaret Thatcher and Ronald Reagan tore up the post-war consensus (low unemployment, state support for industry, high welfare provision) in favour of an experiment, still ongoing, in free market solutions for everything. Although some have accused Adorno of pessimism and despair, in the early 1990s, with the triumphant resurgence of market capitalism, his ideas seemed more pertinent than ever. His own horrified vision of a historical process grinding to a halt was the flipside of Francis Fukuyama's notorious – and later rescinded – claim that the triumph of capitalism over communism meant 'the end of history'.[11]

Globalisation would be a major preoccupation of Suspect Culture's work and it came to the fore in a double bill of Petra's *Explanation* and *Stations on the Border*, under the title *Europe* (1994), which explored the dynamics of ethnicity and migration in Europe, against the catastrophic break-up of Yugoslavia.[12] The form of this production, the double bill, was a sign of strains within Greig and Eatough's creative partnership. Greig's playwriting career was beginning to take off, after the success of *Stalinland*, and this double bill yoked together a devised show and a text-based show somewhat awkwardly. The challenge of continuing to work with little or no money led to a year's hiatus in the work of the company before they came back together to make *One Way Street* (1995), a one-man show that took a wander through Walter Benjamin to produce an investigation of alienation, politics, and the experience of the city. It was a self-conscious attempt to return to the simplicity of *A Savage Reminiscence* but further exploring the gestural language, the fusion of movement and text and the intellectual precision now resting on a firm foundation of melancholy humour. The show was a considerable success, became the first Suspect Culture text to be published,[13] and would lead to the company's first successful application for funding. It is with the next show, *Airport*, that the professional life of the company really begins.

CHAMBER WORKS (1996–2002)

The second phase of Suspect Culture's work is characterised by intimate, intense productions, each wound around a set of decisive and insistent formal principles. *Airport* (1996), *Timeless* (1997), and *Mainstream* (1999) are the works that established Suspect Culture nationally and internationally, and saw them celebrated as one of the key companies in the new Scotland in a period of devolution and surging cultural confidence. The composer and musician Nick Powell and the designer Ian Scott were part of the creative team for *Airport* and established an artistic core of the company that lasted the life of the company. These phases are not precisely bounded, of course, and *Lament* (2002), somewhat separated from these others chronologically, nonetheless seems to be connected thematically and artistically, marking both a culmination of a certain style of Suspect Culture's work and, in its way, a lamenting farewell to those shows.

One thing that links these shows is their settings: an airport, an upmarket bar (*Timeless*), an hotel (*Mainstream*).[14] These are all instances of what French anthropologist Marc Augé has called 'non-places'; that is, places brought into being by the rapid expansion of communication and transport characteristic of globalisation.[15] These anonymous, functional places are to be contrasted with anthropological place, which is characterised by its historical rootedness, its firm relationship with particular identities. Without these precise co-ordinates we enter a world 'surrendered to solitary individuality, to the fleeting, the temporary and ephemeral'.[16]

The inhabitants of *Airport* reflect the emptiness of their setting. One character, Gordon Syme, appears to live at the airport, repeatedly failing to board his flight home, and instead creating fleeting acquaintances with the travellers passing through. Another continually invents personalities and histories for herself, admitting at one point that she's never before told anyone her name.[17] They recall Augé's comment that a person entering a non-place is relieved of the usual determinants of his or her identity and 'tastes for while [...] the passive joys of identity-loss, and the more active pleasure of role-playing'.[18] The sense of the setting as a non-place was emphasised by the design which enclosed the main playing space between two baggage conveyor belts, emphasising the transitional nature of the space – it is somewhere to pass through – while the sterility of these machines pointed up the functional neutrality of the place-as-machine. The transformation of people into things was enacted by wittily moving characters around the stage on trolleys and conveyor belts, turning people into baggage. (see p. 306).

In capturing both the frictionless joys of international travel and the numb commodification of national identity, *Airport* explores a central tension that runs through all of the work in this phase and beyond: between a desire for communication and contact and a recognition of the failures that erupt in all of these attempts. *Timeless* is exemplary in this respect. In the first of the play's three sections we see a group of university friends meeting for an informal reunion some years after graduating; their awkwardness is captured in a series of gestural character motifs. Ian's motif shows him raise his hand as if to wave to someone he's seen, not being seen and embarrassedly converting the gesture by rubbing the back of his neck. Each scene in the play is punctuated by awkward actions like these which give them an aestheticised quality, as we follow the development of the relationships through these gestures. In the middle section, we understand the cause of some of the present unease in a flashback to the last time they were together. The third and final section displays all the characters' most utopian fantasies of the perfect meeting they might have, where all that was unsaid is said without recrimination or misunderstanding. Hauntingly, although they are theatrically separated out by individual lighting, and each now have associated with them one instrument in the string quartet that underscored the performance, their unspoken desires are for perfect communion. Martin, a callous womaniser, admits that he would like to reach out:

If I could reach out my hand and say ...
If I just had that touch.
A touch that could transmit that thing you want.
That thing women want which is ...

Alan Wilkins, Graham Eatough and Silvia Carmona; *Airport*, Madrid.

Whatever it is.
I would. (p. 184)

But his desire is not simply strategic; he is not trying to find the perfect chat-up line. Elsewhere, his language is more clearly abstracted from his own interests, more utopian, when, picturing the scene, he states, 'I reach out my hand, with a kind of infinite slowness,/And say the perfect thing, which is: 'blah blah blah blah blah blah' (p. 174). The perfect thing cannot be spoken, of course, but these 'inarticulate sounds' stand in for it, holding it tantalisingly out of our view, marking the outlines of perfection. As such, *Timeless* is neither cynical about communication, nor naïve in its affirmation: it is utopian, accepting the communicative limitations of the present, but gesturing towards a time and space of purity and plenitude.

This desire to reach out across the barriers of atomisation and isolation is a motif that runs right across Suspect Culture's work. In *Airport*, there is a child-hood memory that, irrationally, seems to be shared by all of the characters. In *One Way Street*, the central character's misanthropic isolation is both emphasised and

Molly Innes, Paul Thomas Hickey, Kate Dickie and Keith Macpherson; *Timeless*.

counterpointed by the show's monologue form: the hated others that Flannery tries to evade are necessarily embodied by the same actor, creating a visual unity that defies his desire for escape.[19]

This is embodied even more insistently in *Mainstream*. The show concerns an encounter between a record company employee and a personnel consultant, who meet for an appraisal interview but end up having a one-night stand before parting, embarrassed, the next morning. The whole show takes place in a hotel, and we move between a conference room, the lounge bar, a bedroom, and the breakfast room. The play is suffused with the strange melancholy that inhabits non-places through which people only pass, something akin to that phrase for which there is no precise English equivalent, *l'angoisse des gares*. Throughout, the characters seem to be profoundly alienated from themselves, unable to identify their own feelings and looking outward to the vacuity of their surroundings for information about their identities. At one point the record company employee describes a recent purchase, a device that attaches to your car stereo:

it observes what you listen to and it builds up a profile of you ... then, when you're driving it automatically tunes to the station that's playing the type of stuff you like [...]

I used to think I was the sort of person who liked Radio 4
Until I had this gadget
It taught me who I really am (p. 208)

They find out about each other through a kind of commodity fetishism, asking for their favourite TV shows, sweets, songs, sports. They repeatedly assert and adjust their views of each other, of the 'type of person' they take each other to be. The CV, that universal passport of personal exchangeability, is constantly evoked, in debates about which personal attributes can be put down and which must remain excluded by it. These externally-derived definitions layer around the characters until it becomes difficult to say exactly who they might really be, though again, in extremis, the play affirms the idea of a self, lost in the postmodern chaos, but still seeking recognition; the framing image of the play describes someone trapped in a broken-down car on a motorway in a snowstorm, almost freezing to death:

I was only just alive. All the heat in my body had retreated inside me, away from my skin, away from my arms and legs. There was only the faintest detectable pulse being sent out from some deep core. So quiet it was hardly anything at all. Like one of those radio signals sent through space that just says, 'I'm here.' 'I'm here.' 'I'm here.' (p. 190)

Identity seems to have receded so distantly into these characters that it remains only as a kind of distress beacon, a residual black box appealing for someone's attention.

But character has not merely retreated into these characters; the production also poses character as a force over and above these individual characters. The particular staging device is that four actors play these two parts, and every combination of performers is seen several times across the length of the performance. The story is splintered into fifty-six short scenes, not structured in chronological order, with many of the scenes offering overlapping and alternative versions of particular conversations (e.g. scenes 3, 9, and 13). While two performers are playing a scene, the other two are often echoing it off-stage, sometimes glimpsed through the upstage screens, sometimes mirroring the action, sometimes multiplying the narrative still further. The linear story described above can thus not be described with any precision, since it is possible that we are watching one story or fifty separate stories. The stage is organised in four quarters, one item of furniture indicating each of the rooms the relationship passes through, but particular actions and lines of dialogue bleed across these zones, overflowing the spatial boundaries of the narrative, and the whole encounter seems to exceed the bodies of the particular actors, transcending its material representation, intensifying and sharpening the difference between what we see and what we feel to be happening.

What this creates is a shimmering, undecidable sense of character transcending the individual, experiences flowing non-naturalistically between bodies, asserting perhaps a broad sense of anti-individualistic commonality and continuity that counterpoints the painful and provisional moment of drunken intimacy that the personnel officer and the employee achieve – or may achieve – in that hotel room. Again, we are seeing a complex contradiction between contact and separation, communication and its failure, imperfection and perfection.

Lament (2002) is a transitional show in several ways but also, in my view, one of Suspect Culture's most perfectly imperfect pieces of work. In the three years between *Mainstream* and *Lament*, Suspect Culture had produced two rather larger-scale shows, *Candide 2000* (2000) and *Casanova* (2001), with complicated sets, longer running times, and bigger casts than the company were used to. While successful, both were demanding on the company's energies, and, like *One Way Street* seven years earlier, *Lament* was perhaps a deliberate attempt to make something more contained. To this end, the company gathered together a group of performers with whom they had already worked and therefore felt comfortable: Kate Dickie (*Timeless*, *Mainstream*), Louise Ludgate (*Mainstream*, *Casanova*), Callum Cuthbertson (*Mainstream*, *Casanova*), Paul Blair (*Candide 2000*, *Casanova*) while Graham Eatough returned to performing for the first time since *Airport*.

Although the theatrical scale may have been reduced, the show's ambitions were not. One aim was to produce something more manifestly political than previously attempted, but the ambivalence about communication and contact persisted as a key motif in the work. What was perhaps a personal anxiety in *Timeless* – how can we meaningfully communicate with each other? – is broadened into a directly political question – how can we meaningfully engage with politics? The same recognition of the barriers to making real contact, the elusiveness of direct communication, the impossibility of an objective view of the world degrade this project, as they degraded the relationships in *Timeless* or the encounter(s) in *Mainstream*. As such the performance becomes a commentary on politics, on the complex difficulties of what might constitute political theatre in an era of scepticism and doubt, and, as before, a utopian affirmation of the political impulse. The tone of the show was both

Gabriel Quigley on the set of *Mainstream*, Bulgaria.

politically angry and emotionally exhausted and yet, in the way the show expresses its sense of defeat, it avoids defeatism.

Lament's political affirmation lies in its attack on the means of representation themselves. In the opening sequence, the company members' comments about fantasy and loss were played on video while they themselves stood on stage, virtually motionless throughout, occasionally joining in with one of the recordings, sometimes anticipating, sometimes with a slight delay. It located the fragmented episodes of loss very much within their own experiences and beliefs, but also inserted a gap between expression and reception, underlining the sense of political frustration expressed by many members of the cast.

Lament's scenes take place across the world: Alaska, Nepal, Buenos Aires, Texas, Kenya, Madrid, Mexico, and elsewhere. But as if there were something rather too easy about the multiple global locations of *Candide 2000* or *Casanova*, *Lament*'s representations of the world bump up against their fictionality. The characters and locations of the fragmented scenes are all named with a kind of deliberate cursoriness, as if impatient with pretence: we meet, amongst others, Chief Muckaluck, Brother

Jeroboam, Ruauauauariridgh, and a tour guide called Catherina Costacoffeebutic. These names are not purely flippant; there was no smile as these names were used. It was as if the Other has become more and more difficult to grasp. As Nick Powell wrote during the development of the show 'I'm interested in how the digital, high-tech world both expands the scope of our world-view geographically but somehow reduces our sense of difference'.[20] Similarly, there are many evocations of an organic community life in the performance, but these too display awareness that these are now a fading memory (perhaps even a fantasy) for the West. In a small village in the developing world a storyteller arrives; this moment of magic and mystery calls for special preparations, but what they might be seems almost impossible to recover: 'Call the children together, clear a circle of bare earth, bring water in a … goatskin, light fires, do … things' (p. 265). Similarly, during the performance, gaps began to appear in speeches, as if suggesting the loss of all those things that totality has closed over and excluded. In one scene set in Alaska, two people lament the disappearance of the Inuit and the skills they carry with them, the text marking this disappearance: 'How to skin a [ ] and how to pray to [ ] and how to heal a broken [ ] with herbs' (p. 286).

Throughout the play, there are references to an unnamed and perhaps un-nameable catastrophe; the word itself appears in corrupted forms through the text – 'Catastroph' (p. 269), eventually as 'ctstrof' (p. 293). In 2002, this perhaps most immediately suggested the convulsion of global politics that followed the events of 9/11, but from this distance we can perhaps see it again in Adornoan terms as the closing off of utopia and the dominance of identity-thinking, or put another way, the unlimited extension of the market into every corner of our life. The only possible response to this catastrophe, says Adorno, is to think through these concepts and thereby negate them. *Lament* is a show that pushes at the very limits of representation, the limits of political engagement, and, by identifying these limits, allowed us to think beyond them.

EPIC SCALE (2000–2004)

At the turn of the century, Suspect Culture were well established in the landscape of Scottish theatre and the funding allowed them a certain security in which to build larger-scale projects that would fully embody the broad intellectual and global perspectives of their work. Several of the shows they made in the first decade of the new century were conceived for large theatre spaces, with an ambition and scale that outstripped anything they had attempted so far. *Candide 2000* was a loose contemporary adaptation of Voltaire's novella, set in a brand-new shopping mall

– 'Clearwater' – populated by a chorus of teenagers who regularly hymn the variety on offer:

> You can eat Chinese food
> Indian food
> Mexican food
> Italian food
> French food
> American food
> All different countries
> That's what it's like.[21]

The monotony of the syntax conveys the bland interchangeability of the foods on offer, the effect of identity-thinking on the particular culinary traditions of the world, bringing them under one system (or 'under one roof./Everything./That's what it's like').[22] That repeated phrase, which runs right through *Candide 2000*, is important too: 'that's what it's like' and takes us back to Adorno. Under identity-thinking the dialectic has ground to a halt and there is no difference between what is and what might be: hence the absurd tautology of saying of the world around us 'this is what it's like'. This was an echo, of course, of Dr Pangloss's repeated insistence that this is 'the best of all possible worlds' in Voltaire's novel and captures something of the contemporary political panglossianism that asserts that the way the world is is the only way it can be because, in the slogans of the age, capitalism is the only game in town and 'there is no alternative'.

Candide 2000 was a bold experiment, a huge production that filled the stage of the Royal Lyceum in Edinburgh. The larger audience required for such a show demanded a new kind of openness of production style and the show introduced a live band, led by Nick Powell, and the mall rats were played by local children, coached for a couple of days on each date of the tour.[23] Most of the episodes in Voltaire's book are given a precise contemporary equivalent and, despite its underlying desperation, the production emerged as a hugely enjoyable romp through the search for paradise. The scale of *Casanova* meanwhile harked back to the global perspective of *Airport*, following an international artist travelling the world both to gather works for a final exhibition documenting his own amorous adventures and to find the final woman who will complete his life. As this brief account suggests, it is a play about art, global travel, and sex. *Casanova's* own dissatisfied quest is for something that would end his desire for sexual conquest and his artistic journey. We are again in a world of globalisation and dissatisfaction.

It suggests, too, a restless dissatisfaction with the making of art itself: in the first production, empty display cabinets gradually filled the stage, an image of an empty creativity that suggested Suspect Culture asking hard questions about their own artistic journey. The production was itself a kind of obsessive collection, mixing cultural styles, from its opening speech in vaguely neo-classical rhyming couplets to a performance of The Who's 'I'm a Boy'.[24] Tellingly, a year later, Greig described the work of Suspect Culture in terms that recall Casanova's journey: 'Each new show,' he remarked, 'is a step along the road to a destination we will never reach'.[25]

These questions were further amplified in their epic piece *8000m*. While the show appears to be – and is – about mountain climbing, it is also rather profoundly a play about the limits of representation. There is nothing in *8000m* as textually peacockish as the rhyming couplets of *Casanova*: instead, the language of the play is deliberately flat; mountains are notoriously said to lure mountaineers to their deaths and it is as if the text of *8000m* is written in a way that wishes to confront the mountain but not be lured by it, to respect its it-ness but avoid trying to better it in language, to turn it into a metaphor, to scale it in poetry. Some of the more comic scenes of the play focus precisely on people trying to find a majesty of scale that can capture the mountain, whether that is a writer seeking out a telling detail that will capture the experience of the climb or a clichéd DJ interviewing the team's doctor ('That was, appropriately enough, "Ain't No Mountain High Enough"'[26]). Instead, Greig's text favours simple, unadorned language that seems determined to represent the mountain as simply and directly as possible. At times we are given purely factual information; one scene is largely a checklist of what the Climber has packed. There is a narrator's voice throughout who gives icily unsensational accounts of each stage of the climb:

> To navigate through the ice fall is like climbing through a city during an earthquake in slow motion. Blocks of ice the size of four-storey houses lean above you. At some point they will fall. Crevasses hundreds of feet deep open slowly beneath you. As you climb, you hear the ice creak and squeal as it shifts position.[27]

The simple recitation of information is sufficient to evoke an imaginative response to the material. Anything more highly coloured in the language would be hubristic. 'What can I write about it that hasn't been written?' asks the writer accompanying the climb.[28] The play's answer is to attempt to represent the mountain without metaphor or irony, to tread the narrow path and breathe the thin air of sincerity and directness.

Left: Colin McCredie (on the floor), Paul Blair and Jill Riddiford, and the mall rats, in *Candide 2000*; **right:** Paul Blair in *8000m*.

The choice of a mountain as the centrepiece of the show is not, perhaps, coincidental. Mountains have a special place in debates about art, where they are often cited for their capacity to evoke the particular aesthetic experience of the sublime. What characterises the sublime is a mixture of delight and terror, pleasure and despair. It is typically experienced at the sight of a vast and raging ocean, a huge chasm in the earth, or a vast and forbidding mountain. What is puzzling is why we might experience this terror – even when we are in absolutely no danger – and then why we might experience pleasure alongside it. For Immanuel Kant, the terror derives from our sudden experience of the incalculable gap between the physical size or power of the mountain and our capacity to encompass the image of the entire mountain in our minds; it's not the actual ability of the mountain to do us harm but the challenge that it offers to our powers of imagination. The mountain seems so much larger than us that it seems beyond calculation; it seems infinite. The mind, says Kant, cannot tolerate an 'infinite image' and hence we express a profound terror. But the pleasure of the mountain comes from the secondary realisation that while we cannot take an 'infinite image' into our minds, our human reason can contain the idea of infinity. Thus we experience the horror of discovering the limits of our ordinary perception and the pleasure of experiencing the capacities of our reason.

This may seem a circuitous route up *8000m* but it unlocks the ongoing aesthetic debates embodied in Suspect Culture's work. One might see any attempt to poeticise the mountain as an attempt to turn away from or deny its impassive scale, its dynamic challenge to the imagination. The steely simplicity of the text is a kind of sublime response to the mountain, a creative move that meets its immensity head-on and yet affirms the power of our rational creativity. This is, one might even say, a political gesture. Marx believed that the main driver of human history, which would eventually deliver us our freedom, was our creativity, tied to our reason that allows us to make things in better ways and learn from each other. The sublime and *8000m* are, in that sense, aesthetic experiences that put us in contact with those attributes which may make us free.

BROADENING AND DIVERSIFYING (2003–2009)

The idea of Suspect Culture as a company had always been to break out of the narrow confines of most British theatre practice. In one sense, this was geographical: 'we wanted to be a European company,' Greig recalled, 'by which I meant we wanted our work to cross borders and to collaborate with artists abroad. We wanted our work to be seen in a European context, not a British context.' [29] They wanted to break down the distinction between physical and text-based theatre.[30] Even more than that, the company was conceived as working across artistic forms, not exclusively a theatre company, but working across the arts. The later phases of Suspect Culture's work saw a return to that founding principle, with work that drew on a wider range of collaborators and often working in entirely new modes and media.

Suspect Culture's 'Scottishness' has sometimes seemed to require explanation. This determination to work beyond the confines of the nation, to cross over with other artforms, and, particularly, their utopianism, that seemed always to gesture at some non-located space where identity is loosened and fluid, worked against any simple connection with Scotland. The company were based in Glasgow, but of the creative core – Eatough, Greig, Powell and Scott – only Greig was Scottish and he, having lived for much of his early life in Nigeria, had little trace of Scotland in the voice and very little Scots in the writing. In the 2000s the broadening group of Artistic Associates made the personnel of the company even more overwhelmingly non-Scottish. Most Suspect Culture shows are either not set in Scotland or are not set anywhere in particular. In an early interview, Greig had insisted that playwriting and nationalism were incompatible: 'any playwright who tells you they're a nationalist is either a bad playwright or a bad nationalist'.[31] If Scotland appears in a Suspect Culture show, it's as likely to be the target of comic abuse as anything else; as Mrs Tennant remarks in *Casanova* defending an erotic exhibition: 'We need this exhibition now because this country is cold and mean and ashamed, and repressed, and violent and…straight […] This is a country that badly needs a fuck.'[32]

Despite all of this, it's important to understand how strong Suspect Culture's relationship to Scottishness is and showing how sheds light both on Suspect Culture and on Scotland itself. Scotland's most successful playwrights in the first half of the twentieth century, such as J.M. Barrie and James Bridie, had made their careers largely outside Scotland and largely in English. After the Second World War, there were many attempts to found a natively Scottish theatre and many agreed with Alexander Reid who wrote in 1958 that Scotland's contribution to world theatre will come from 'cherishing, not repressing our national peculiarities (including our language)'.[33] However, Scots as a language or dialect[34] seemed to be dying out, its demise hastened by the spread of television, dominated by the BBC's received pronunciation (ironically insisted upon by the Scottish Lord Reith). In 1968, Clive Perry, the director of the Royal Lyceum Theatre in Edinburgh, stated flatly: 'National drama with a tongue of its own is not for the future. Plays about contemporary Scotland will be in English with only a slight accent'.[35] And yet, defying augury through the late Sixties and Seventies, there was a flourishing of plays written, not quite in Scots but instead in what Liz Lochhead has called 'a totally invented […] theatrical Scots' and Donald Smith describes as 'a poetic form of non-naturalistic Scots'.[36] Through the 1970s, astonishing historical plays like Stewart Conn's *The Burning* (1971), Hector MacMillan's *The Rising* (1973), and Donald Campbell's *The Jesuit* (1976) were written, partly or wholly, in this lyrical, rhythmical stage-Scots and later plays like Roddy McMillan's *The Bevellers* (1973), or Stewart Conn's *Play Donkey* and Tom McGrath's *The Hardman* (both 1977) showed that the contemporary world could be captured in the same language. These plays and this revived attitude to Scots helped establish a distinctive identity away from the British English that had dominated Scottish new writing.

It is no accident that this revived theatrical interest in Scots coincided with a significant revival in Scottish Nationalism in the 1970s. The plays fostered and connected with a growing political dissatisfaction with Westminster's domination of Scottish cultural and political affairs. A key trigger was the discovery of North Sea Oil in 1970 and the conspicuous failure of Scotland itself to benefit from the riches it produced. This was most famously anatomised in 7:84's *The Cheviot, the Stag and the Black, Black Oil* (1973) which drew on Scottish folk performance traditions to tell its story of colonial and neo-colonial exploitation and brilliantly stoked the fires of nationalism. MacMillan's *The Rising* took as its subject an historical uprising against English tyranny which placed contemporary events in a clear context. In 1979 a referendum on devolution for Scotland fell foul of a controversial rule which, unusually, required not simply a majority of those voting but the support of at least 40% of the total electorate. In the event a narrow majority voted in favour of devolution but the proposal failed to meet this additional requirement.

This led to a period of uncertainty and retreat for Scottish nationalists through the 1980s and, in some ways, it was not in the political but the cultural – specifically theatrical – realm that Scottish confidence continued to grow. The decade was a period of great infrastructural growth in Scottish theatre: local government spending on theatre in Scotland increased in real terms by 128% between 1982 and 1993 and the grant for the Scottish Arts Council by 23%. Between 1980 and 1992, the Tron, the Dundee Rep, the Arches, the Tramway and the new Traverse Theatre all opened and the King's Theatre, Edinburgh, had a huge refurbishment.[37] Glasgow's Mayfest was founded in 1983 and 1990 saw the city take on the mantle of European City of Culture. High-profile large-scale shows Bill Bryden's *The Ship* and Communicado's *Jock Tamson's Bairns* both in 1990 exemplified this theatrical daring and confidence. A new generation of writers like Liz Lochhead, Chris Hannan, and, above all, John Byrne created a new idiomatic Scottish language which moved on from the Scots language of the 1970s without returning to British English. As David Greig remarked, these writers seemed to be saying 'to create Scottish theatre you don't have to write in Scots, nor do you have to write in English'.[38]

This change in the attitude towards theatrical language in Scottish theatre again reflected a significant shift in the politics of the era. The campaign for Scottish devolution in the 1970s had concentrated on a traditional enmity with England. In common with other British left-wing parties, this had gone along with hostility to the Common Market. But in 1988, Jim Sillars, the leader of the Scottish National Party, persuaded his party to abandon its hostility to Europe and instead embrace a policy captured in the enduring slogan 'independence in Europe'.[39] The policy also entailed changing focus from an exclusive – and ancient – hostility to England; by appealing to Europe, the SNP was appealing over the heads of the English to the European Community, and, at the same time, resituating itself as a modern party, in tune with the latest developments in Europe at the very moment that the British government under Margaret Thatcher was drifting in an ever more Eurosceptic direction. As Sillars wrote a year later, embracing the European project would mean activating intellectual and cultural powers 'long buried in our provincial soil' to the lasting benefit of the country: 'Scotland's people, politicians and media would be compelled to cast our intellectual net much wider than hitherto [...] we would be involved as never before in the big issues, the formulation and testing of big ideas in the future of Europe'.[40] As we have seen, the theatre was ahead of politics here; the Edinburgh Festival, Mayfest, and the City of Culture suggested a performance culture already attuned to international influences. Glasgow Citizens Theatre had already established a tradition of adapting European classics for the Scottish stage and a series of hugely successful adaptations of the works of Québécois playwright Michel Tremblay into idiomatic Scots through the 1980s echoed the SNP's interest in forging connections between smaller nations battling for self-determination.

It is in this context that Suspect Culture's Europeanism should be seen. Greig recalls the feeling in Scotland when the company was founded:

By the time I'm coming back to Scotland in 1990 the civic identity of Scotland is largely settled and so is the theatrical identity of the country [...] When Suspect Culture was founded, Europeanness was the big, interesting question to both Graham and I. What's being European like? [... we] were clear that we could miss out London and there was nothing to stop us making a direct connection between Glasgow and Madrid or Glasgow and Milan.[41]

Without making a claim for a particular party allegiance, one can see in the three parts of this recollection a kind of theatrical reconstitution of Jim Sillars's SNP policy. *Airport* did indeed make the connection between Glasgow and Madrid, as well as between the minority nations of Scotland and the Basque Country. In this context the company, too, have picked up the new-found appetite for looking outward, a positive interest in Europe (Greig contributed to *two* shows called *Europe* in 1993), and an enthusiasm for European intellectual traditions. In Tom McGrath's *The Hardman*, one character acidly reports of a particular transaction: 'Everything is very cordial. Everything is very English', implying that English itself has a repressed emotional quality.[42] The company's avoidance of Scots perhaps contributed in some quarters to their reputation for intellectual coolness. Others, perhaps more attuned to shifts in Scotland's cultural self-image, found in their work 'a brand of cool, stylish Scottish international modernism'.[43] For all of these reasons, what is precisely Scottish about Suspect Culture's work is its refusal to be narrowly Scottish.

An early example of the company's renewed commitment to working in new modes came with 2003's *One, Two*, led by longtime Suspect Culture artist Nick Powell. Several shows had featured onstage musicians – *Timeless*, *Candide 2000*,

Lament – but this show took that a step further. Rather than music being an accompaniment to the show, this time the music was central, Powell's band OSKAR occupying centre stage figuratively and literally, the story, such as it was, emerging around and through the music. In typical Suspect Culture style, it told the story of a relationship, in a splintered and layered style, the text telling of loss and longing. Rather than the music scoring the behaviour of the characters, it seemed as though the music was propelling the characters or, driving and developing their relationship. OSKAR's music was both melodic and degraded, dramatic chord changes alternating with repeated violin figures, scrubbed over with agitated washes of electronica. The textual fragments emerged from devising and, for the first time, Graham Eatough took the writer's role on the production; David Greig was occupied with co-directing his own play *San Diego* for the Edinburgh International Festival. *One, Two* opened at the Traverse Theatre at the same time and it was a fascinating sign of the shared creative language of the core artistic team that David Greig's production of *San Diego* in many ways resembled a Graham Eatough production for Suspect Culture and Eatough's text for *One, Two* bore many of the hallmarks of a play by David Greig.[44]

After the demanding devising process that led to *8000m* – which included the company climbing a mountain together – the company reorganised, with Eatough remaining the artistic director of the company and the other members redesignated artistic associates, on the understanding that they would not need to be involved in every show. It was an opportunity for the company to draw in artists and theatre-makers with whom they had formed positive relationships. These included the writer Renato Gabrielli and actor Sergio Romano from Italy, Mauricio Paroni De Castro from Brazil, Andrés Lima from Spain, and, from London, me.[45]

In 2005, the first fruits of this broadening of the artistic team came in *A Different Language* written by Gabrielli and performed by Romano and British actor Selina Boyack. As Mark Fisher's *Guardian* review noted, the show recalled aspects of previous shows, notably the mixture of languages in *Airport* and the alienated vision of identity seen in *Mainstream*.[46] The story followed an Italian man ('Uomo') and a British woman ('Woman') as they both sign up to a dating site. We see their fumbling and comic attempts to squeeze their identities through the website's questionnaires and then their slow discovery of each other through the site. The play is entirely bilingual underscoring the sense of two people divided by language, technology, and geography. Mistranslations tumble over misunderstandings as the two actors performed a largely virtual relationship face to face on an ingenious ribbon stage that suggested both the competition of a racing track and the paradoxes of a Möbius strip.

Bilingualism was pushed further in my own script for the company, *Static* (2008). The show was a co-production with Graeae, a theatre company that places disabled artists and audiences at the heart of their work. The two languages at work in the play were English and British Sign Language which together told the story of a woman suddenly and shockingly widowed. Finding a compilation tape made by her dead husband, she begins to believe messages are being sent through the air to her. Eventually she uncovers the meaning of the tape and is able, at last, to grieve. Some of the scenes took place in BSL, others in English. Much of the time, scenes were rhymed (reminiscent of *Mainstream*) elsewhere on the stage in the other language. But unlike *A Different Language*, the intention of the bilingualism here was to offer slightly different experiences for audiences fluent in BSL and those in English. The dead man and his sister communicated largely in BSL, while the widow, Sarah, and her friend spoke mostly in English. At times the BSL and the English supported and translated for each other, but at others they communicated entirely different things. The effect was to offer a kind of theatrical support to Sarah's belief that there are messages in the air around her if only she could tune into them. In addition, having Steven Webb (who played the husband) echoing the English scenes in BSL created a theatrical ambiguity: was he there as a character or there as a signer? It generated a ghosting undecidability across the stage.[47]

Static was in the tradition of Suspect Culture's desire for perfect communication across any barrier, in this instance the most decisive barrier of all: death. Sarah's wish to hear messages from her husband in tapes recorded in empty rooms may be irrational but it was not presented as preposterous, the play affirming the desire if not the practicality. There was a kind of cheeky bravado in making a show about music and deafness, which one might think are incompatible, though the signed songs and the general fetishism about music expressed through characters like Martin ('Music isn't just music,' he often insists, 'Music is also everything else.'[48]). A motif that runs through the play is a series of reviews of gigs that didn't happen, wouldn't happen, or couldn't happen (the Beatles' Sgt Pepper gigs, the Smiths reunion tour, Elvis at Live Aid), again, music as utopian impulse, transcending the limits of the real. In the penultimate sequence of the play, Sarah discovers that her husband had sent her a message in the titles of the songs on the tape; suddenly unlocking her imprisoned grief, she experiences a flood of feeling and we moved into a sequence where the cast sign to Rufus Wainwright's 'Agnus Dei'. The move is into an entirely private mental space, but it may also be into an imagined metaphysical space too. The production did not legislate between them.

A somewhat similar connection between the mental and the metaphysical structured *The Escapologist*, written by Simon Bent, and inspired by Adam Phillips's

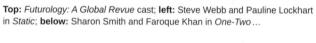

Top: *Futurology: A Global Revue* cast; **left:** Steve Webb and Pauline Lockhart in *Static*; **below:** Sharon Smith and Faroque Khan in *One-Two…*

Houdini's Box. The play weaves together a series of consultations between a therapist and his clients. Almost dreamlike, the scenes fade into one another, a trigger word taking us from the present into a memory, a submerged trauma surfacing suddenly. One of the therapist's clients is a roofer who is faced with the opportunity to do an undetectably bad job, another's father hoarded stuff in his attic. These images were picked up in Laura Hopkins' elegant design, the stage floor became a grid of ceiling joists. The actors trod carefully, avoiding the spaces between, the design forcing a physical language of tension and fear. In toto, this became an image of the mind itself, the consciousness walking a narrow path to avoid plunging into darkness and danger. Throughout there was a ferocious sense of people's repressed anger and fear and distress and loss. Here the barriers of communication are psychological, and not just between people but within people too. To open up these bruised, repressed channels of connection these patients turn to the therapist, Paul, as a kind of miracle-worker, a mystical figure who can turn pain into clarity. But throughout the show we are shown the complex layers of self-preservation, repression built on repression, captured in Paul's attempt to analyse a young girl:

PAUL: Where do you go when you hide.

SHANNON: That's a secret.

PAUL: What's a secret.

SHANNON: I'm not telling.[49]

Theatrically, this was given sharp focus by a scene in which Doctor and patient play a strange therapeutic game where Shannon 'hides' in plain sight and Paul tries to find her. When he fails to find her – indeed, perhaps fails to understand the rules of the game – Shannon insists 'I can't escape, I can't escape … I must be here somewhere'.[50] The horror of selfhood in *The Escapologist* is embodied in a young girl who wants to escape and wants to be found.

The remaining theatre show from this period was, in some ways, the most jubilantly uncharacteristic piece Suspect Culture ever made. *Futurology* (2007) was a co-production with the then-new National Theatre of Scotland. Several different elements converged on this production: as with *Lament*, Greig and Eatough wanted to make a more explicitly political show, 'particularly the sense of apocalypse that is hanging once more over our everyday discourses,' said Greig at the time, 'peak oil, global warming, eco-catastrophe – that sort of thing.';[51] they also wanted to work in a somewhat more 'popular theatre' mode than they had tried before; connected with both of these ambitions, it seemed appropriate to work with a wider group of the

Artistic Associates.[52] The form that emerged was a kind of revue, bringing together a number of popular-theatre acts, the cast included a clown, a dancer, a contortionist, a band, and a ventriloquist act. The story told was of an international climate change conference, presided over by the sinister Mayor of an unknown world city. The cast were delegates to the conference, and the central figure was the hapless representative of the Sandwich Islands, whose homeland was at imminent risk of being submerged by rising sea levels. The conference proceedings were presented through songs and dances, sketches and performances. A negotiation between two delegates is presented as a tango; climate catastrophe was offered through a graceful contortionist act; and the conference's final anodyne memorandum of agreement ('We aspire to face the future together') was presented as an all-cast comedy number. The show toured to conference centres across Scotland.

The show was on the whole received well by critics, though the site-specific aspects worked against it. Conference centres with their open halls and breeze-block walls do not have the focus needed for a theatre show, which created a chilly atmosphere that worked against the popular-theatre feel that we were striving for. It was striking that when the show eventually played at the Brighton Festival in a proper performance venue, it came more fully alive. Greig feels that if the show had a fault it was that it 'wears its heart too much on its sleeve. It's too naked a statement of its authors' vulnerabilities and weaknesses.'[53] Certainly, the topic of climate change is not one for which many people have yet found a fully satisfying theatrical form.[54] Eatough is more positive, seeing the show as 'a really mature realisation of what Suspect Culture does well'.[55] One can see *Futurology* as a classic Suspect Culture show: the politics were utopian, persisting despite the cynicism and game-playing of international climate politics. Anyone who followed the devastating compromises and failures of the Copenhagen Climate Change Conference may remember *Futurology* as prescient and realistic, rather than a comic cartoon.

But the show was unusual for Suspect Culture at that phase in their work, which, in the late 2000s, was focused beyond theatre itself. In 2008, Eatough wrote and directed his first short film, *Missing*, based on Andrew O'Hagan's book of the same name. The piece explored the experience of those whose loved ones suddenly vanish, the unhealing emotional wound, the fantasised images of return. The film had some affinities with the thematics of *Static* and was, indeed, shown before some performances of that show at the Tron. Two years earlier, Eatough collaborated with the visual artist Graham Fagen on the installation piece *Killing Time*. It was a visual art exploration of some iconic images of twentieth-century theatre, different rooms in Dundee Contemporary Arts turned into environments recalling *Waiting for Godot*, *Look Back in Anger*, *The Dumb Waiter* and *The Cherry Orchard*. The gallery

Theatremorphosis by Dan Rebellato, *Stage Fright*, CCA, Glasgow.

visitor walked between these spaces, and a video installation suggested that a harlequin figure had moved between these spaces too, creating strange affinities between them, undoing chronology – or, killing time – by weaving these strange abandoned settings together into a single narrative haunted by genocide, nuclear catastrophe, and alienation.

That interface between theatre and the visual arts was the focus of Suspect Culture's final show, *Stage Fright*. The show was a gallery show at the Centre for Contemporary Arts in Glasgow and brought together artists and theatre-makers – Luke Collins, Graham Eatough, David Greig, Patrick Macklin, Sharon Smith & Felicity Croydon, Nick Powell & Jonny Dawe and Dan Rebellato – to make pieces that excavated the ground between theatre and visual art. This is an area that had been explored through live and performance art but, with a sense that some of that work had already solidified into an orthodoxy, the show attempted to find new areas of overlap or productive contradiction. Powell and Dawe's piece was a wittily austere apparatus that consisted of a door in a wall, with two cloth drops that were automated to appear to fly in an image of the same door. The

Stage Door by Graham Eatough, *Stage Fright*, CCA, Glasgow.

permutations of the various doors created their own musical rhythms, while the eye tried to make sense of and organize the different doors in order of fakeness (of course, all the doors were equally fake and all were equally real). Graham Eatough's installation was in two parts; the entrance to the CCA was an immersive recreation of a backstage area, complete with make-up mirrors, showers, discarded scripts, and a props table; the café area was transformed into a stage-in-waiting, pine trees suspended above the audiences heads, as if awaiting a cue to be flown in and effect a scenic transformation. The installation turned the CCA space inside out; first, the gallery became a kind of theatre; second, the audience seemed to be entering through the stage door, the environment constituting them as performers, seeing the backstage first and then entering a realm of performative potentiality, where undetermined change might take place. It was a statement of intent, insisting on the theatre's ability to interrogate a gallery space and using the resources of a gallery space to interrogate the theatre. It was an open piece; one felt drawn to try piecing the show together from the contents of the props table, the image of the trees; it all hinted to a kind of Athenian forest of transformation, but whether this would be political or metaphysical, sexual or historical, was left tantalizingly out of grasp.

Other pieces explored the mechanics of ordinary theatrical production. For his piece, David Greig filmed himself in real time writing a short performance piece. He then had the actor Callum Cuthbertson filmed, in the same space, wearing the same clothes, performing the piece over precisely the same time. The two images were shown on screens either side of a desk, asking questions about the gaps between intention and expression, creativity and interpretation, page and voice, all imagined in the evocative space of an empty desk. In my own piece, a performer stood in a large metal cage in the middle of a gallery. They had a short (45") text – a different text each day – to perform as soon as the gallery opened. Once they had finished they were required immediately to perform it again exactly as they had done it the last time. This would continue through the day and as small changes, accidents, and slips of the tongue took place they would become incorporated into the performance with the result that the text virally degraded through the day. The texts collectively told a multi-stranded story about a series of transformations: a brutal husband turns into a bear, a child in a crashed car is reborn repeatedly as a girl, then a boy, then a girl, and on. The piece was an attempt to capture some of the central, yet often ignored dynamics, of theatrical production: the gap between writer and performer, the mixture of liveness and repetition, the voyeurism of the audience, the power of the performer, the creativity of the actor over the course of a long run.[56]

The last night of *Stage Fright* was the last night of Suspect Culture. Its funding had been withdrawn the previous year and present and former cast members gathered in the CCA to see images from past shows, hear extracts from performances, and remember a company that had for a few years embodied a new kind of Scotland of artful, cultural hybridity, utopian leftishness, and restless artistic experiment, and represented that Scotland to the world. Its influence can be felt across Scottish theatre, from companies like Vanishing Point right up to the National Theatre of Scotland, with its international outlook and reputation, and its commitment to formal innovation. Responding to news of the company's demise, Scottish academic Trish Reid wrote: 'considering its track record in collaborative and interdisciplinary work, its international status, and its reputation for innovative practice [...] Suspect Culture has been and remains one of our most innovative arts companies and as such it is among our most precious'.[57]

1. Mark Fisher and David Greig. 'Suspect Cultures and Home Truths.' *Cosmotopia: Transnational Identities in David Greig's Theatre*. Eds. Anja Müller and Clare Wallace. Prague: Litteraria Pragensia, 2011, p. 27.

2. *A Savage Reminiscence: or, How to Snare the Nimble Marmoset*, Typescript, 1991, p. 3; the quotation is from Ludwig Wittgenstein, *Philosophical Investigations*, Revised Edition, Translated by G. E. M. Anscombe. Oxford: Blackwell, 1968, p. 93.

3. Theodor W. Adorno. *Prisms*. Trans. Samuel Weber and Shierry Weber. Cambridge, Mass: MIT Press, 1981, p. 34.

4. Karl Marx, *Selected Writings*, Second edition. Edited by David McLellan. Oxford University Press, 2000, p. 426.

5. Ibid., pp. 481–488.

6. Theodor W. Adorno, *Negative Dialectics*, Translated by E. B. Ashton. London: Routledge, 1973, p. 146.

7. Adorno, *Prisms*, p. 23.

8. Theodor W. Adorno, *Aesthetic Theory*, Edited by Gretel Adorno and Rolf Tiedemann, Translated by Robert Hullot-Kentor. London: Athlone, 1997, p. 139.

9. David Greig, 'Paying the Piper', a talk given at the Edinburgh Festival, 13 August 1999, quoted in Mark Fisher, 'Folding stuff gets into the act,' *The Herald*. 17 August 1999.

10. Adorno, *Aesthetic Theory*, p. 32.

11. Francis Fukuyama, 'The End of History?' *The National Interest* (Summer 1989), pp. 3–18.

12. This double bill should not be confused with David Greig's contemporaneous play for the Traverse Theatre, *Europe*, with which it shares a title and some thematic concerns, but little else.

13. In Philip Howard. *Scotland Plays: New Scottish Drama*. London: Nick Hern, 1998.

14. We might also mention *Candide 2000*'s shopping mall, and *Futurology*'s conference hall.

15. Marc Augé, *Non-Places: Introduction to an Anthropology of Supermodernity*. Translated by John Howe. London: Verso, 1995, p. 34. Note that Augé does not use the word 'globalisation' in his book.

16. Ibid., p. 78.

17. David Greig, *Airport*, Performance Script (Spanish Tour), Typescript, October 1996, pp. 23–26, 36.

18. Augé, *Non-Places*, p. 103.

19. David Pattie makes this point in '"Mapping the Territory": Modern Scottish Drama', *Cool Britannia? British Political Drama in the 1990s*. Eds. Rebecca D'Monté and Graham Saunders. Basingstoke: Palgrave, 2007, p. 149.

20. Nick Powell, e-mail 11 December 2001, printed in the programme for *Lament*.

21. David Greig, *Candide 2000*, Rehearsal Draft 2, Typescript, January 2000, p. 2.

22. Ibid., p. 56.

23. This built on two previous shows created with young people, *Local* (1998) and *The Golden Ass* (2000).

24. David Greig. *Suspect Culture: Casanova*. London: Faber and Faber, 2001, pp. 9–11, 117.

25. Isabel Wright. 'Working in Partnership: David Greig in Conversation with Isabel Wright.' *Trans-Global Readings: Crossing Theatrical Boundaries*. Ed. Caridad Svich. Theory/Practice/Performance. Manchester: Manchester University Press, 2003, p. 158.

26. David Greig. *8000m*. Typescript. n. pag. [p.22].

27. Ibid., [p.49].

28. Ibid., [p.43].

29. Isabel Wright, pp.157–8.

30. See the interview with Eatough in this volume, pp.12–13.

31. David Greig. 'Internal Exile.', *Theatre Scotland* iii.11 (1994): p.8.

32. Greig, *Casanova*, p.87.

33. Quoted in Randall Stevenson and Gavin Wallace. *Scottish Theatre since the Seventies*. Edinburgh: Edinburgh University Press, 1996, p.8.

34. Whether Scots is a language or a dialect is widely and passionately debated but for the purposes of this chapter I hope I can remain agnostic.

35. Quoted in Randall Stevenson, 'Drama, Language and Revival', *The Edinburgh Companion to Scottish Drama*. Ed. Ian Brown. Edinburgh: Edinburgh University Press, 2011, p.76.

36. Quoted in Stevenson and Wallace, p.5; Donald Smith, '1950 to 1995, A History of Scottish Theatre. Ed. Bill Findlay. Edinburgh: Polygon, 1998, p.270.

37. Donald Smith, '1950 to 1995', pp.293–4.

38. Mark Fisher and David Greig, 'Suspect Cultures and Home Truths,' p.17.

39. James Mitchell, Lynn Bennie, and Rob Johns. *The Scottish National Party: Transition to Power*. Oxford: Oxford University Press, 2012, p.32.

40. Lindsay Paterson, ed. *A Diverse Assembly: Debate on a Scottish Parliament*. Edinburgh: Edinburgh University Press, 1998, pp.200–201.

41. Mark Fisher and David Greig, 'Suspect Cultures and Home Truths', pp.18–19.

42. Tom McGrath and Jimmy Boyle. *The Hardman: Scots Plays of the Seventies*. Ed. Bill Findlay. Dalkeith: Scottish Cultural Press, 2001, p.341. Yet the play also reveals Scotland's divided instincts: the play is about a real Glasgow gangster and in the scenes from his life, he speaks Scots but when he speaks to the audience and we are to see the richness of his thoughts, he speaks in English.

43. Joyce McMillan, *The Scotsman*, 22 February 1999.

44. Note that *San Diego* was initially written for (and presented to) Suspect Culture, though Eatough and Greig agreed that this ambitious play would be better supported by the resources of the International Festival.

45. My own connection with the company goes back to Bristol, where David Greig and I were near-contemporaries. Apart from handling lighting for touring dates on two early shows, I mainly followed Suspect Culture's work as an audience member for a decade. In 1998, the company set up their *Strange Behaviour* series of day-conferences to which I contributed academic papers and creative pieces and in 2003 published the first substantial academic essay on the company, '"And I Will Reach Out My Hand With A Kind of Infinite Slowness And Say The Perfect Thing": The Utopian Theatre of Suspect Culture.' *Contemporary Theatre Review* xiii.1 (2003): 61–80, on which this chapter draws. In the late 2000s, I joined the company as an Artistic Associate, and contributed to three shows, co-writing *Futurology* with Greig, writing *Static*, and contributing *Theatremorphosis* to *Stage Fright*.

46. Mark Fisher. Review: *A Different Language. Guardian*. 1 March 2005. http://www.guardian.co.uk/stage/2005/mar/01/theatre1

47. The play could be regarded as the creative analogue of my essay 'When We Talk of Horses: Or, what do we see when we see a play?' *Performance Research* 14.1 (2009): 17–28, which draws attention to some complexities in the 'ordinary' way we watch stage fictions. *Static* exploits some of the ambiguities in the structures of theatrical representation.

48. Dan Rebellato. *Static*. London: Oberon, 2008, pp. 25, 70, 82. Aleks Sierz in *Rewriting the Nation: British Theatre Today*, London: Methuen Drama, 2011, captures this expanded sense of music, remarking that in the play 'music is a metaphor for life's glory' (p. 217).

49. Simon Bent. *The Escapologist*. London: Oberon, 2006, p. 45.

50. Ibid., p. 76.

51. Quoted in Peter Billingham. *At the Sharp End*. London: Methuen Drama, 2007, p. 91.

52. The show was devised and developed by a large group – Mauricio Paroni De Castro, Graham Eatough, David Greig, Renato Gabrielli, Nick Powell, Dan Rebellato, Sergio Romano – though eventually the text was written by David Greig with contributions from me and music from Nick Powell. The show continued to be rewritten and reworked through rehearsal.

53. Mark Fisher and David Greig, 'Suspect Cultures and Home Truths', pp. 27–8.

54. It was striking that four years later the National Theatre's collaboratively written *Greenland* (2011) demonstrated the same ambition, the same earnestness, the same chaotic globalized structure, the same focus on a climate conference and created the same ambivalence among audiences.

55. See p. 31.

56. The texts, images and further discussion are available at my website: http://www.danrebellato.co.uk/theatremorphosis/

57. Trish Reid. 'Scottish Arts Council Wields the Axe.' *Contemporary Theatre Review* 18.3 (2008): 398–401.

Index

Numbers in **bold** indicate images; numbers in *italics* indicate works by the author concerned or playtexts.